DATE DUE

HISTORY OF
THE AMERICAN PEACE MOVEMENT
1890-2000

HISTORY OF
THE AMERICAN PEACE MOVEMENT
1890-2000

The Emergence of a New Scholarly Discipline

Edited by

Charles F. Howlett

Studies in World Peace
Volume 18

The Edwin Mellen Press
Lewiston•Queenston•Lampeter

Library of Congress Cataloging-in-Publication Data

History of the American peace movement, 1890-2000 : the emergence of a new scholarly
discipline / edited by Charles F. Howlett.
   p. cm. -- (Studies in world peace ; v. 18)
   Includes bibliographical references and index.
   ISBN 0-7734-6017-9
   1. Peace movements--United States--History. I. Howlett, Charles F. II. Series.

JZ5584.U6H57 2005
303.6'6--dc22

2005053876

This is volume 18 in the continuing series
Studies in World Peace
Volume 18 ISBN 0-7734-6017-9
SWP Series ISBN 0-88946-586-X

A CIP catalog record for this book is available from the British Library.

Front cover: Peace and Disarmament Parade in New York City, 1916
     Courtesy of the Swarthmore College Peace Collection

The Edwin Mellen Press
Box 450
Lewiston, New York
USA 14092-0450

The Edwin Mellen Press
Box 67
Queenston, Ontario
CANADA L0S 1L0

The Edwin Mellen Press, Ltd.
Lampeter, Ceredigion, Wales
UNITED KINGDOM SA48 8LT

Printed in the United States of America

In Memory of

Arthur A. Ekirch, Jr. and Kendall A. Birr

TABLE OF CONTENTS

LIST OF ORGANIZATIONS AND GROUPS

American Civil Liberties Union (ACLU)

American Friends Service Committee (AFSC)

American Peace Mobilization (APM)

American Peace Society (APS)

American Society of International Law (ASIL)

American Union Against Militarism (AUAM)

Carnegie Endowment for International Peace (CEIP)

Church Peace Union (CPU)

Civilian Public Service Camps (CPS)

Clams for Direct Action at Seabrook (CDAS)

Committee for Non-violent Action (CNVA)

Committee for a SANE Nuclear Policy (SANE)

Congress on Racial Equality (CORE)

Fellowship of Reconciliation (FOR)

International Association of Machinists (IAM)

League for Industrial Democracy (LID)

Massachusetts Peace Society (MPS)

Movement for a New Society (MNS)

National Association for the Advancement of Colored People (NAACP)

National Council for Prevention of War (NCPW)

National Peace Federation (NPF)

National Organization of Women (NOW)

New York Peace Society (NYPS)

Non-Governmental Organizations (NGO)

Peace History Society (PHS)

Socialist Party (SP)

Southern Christian Leadership Conference (SCLC)

Student Nonviolent Coordinating Committee (SNCC)

Student Peace Union (SPU)

Students for a Democratic Society (SDS)

Universal Peace Union (UPU)

Voice of Women (VOW)

War Resisters League (WRL)

Women for Racial and Economic Equality (WREE)

Women's International League for Peace and Freedom (WILPF)

Woman's Peace Party (WPP)

Women's Peace Union (WPU)

Women Strike for Peace (WISP)

World Peace Foundation (WPF)

Young Communist League (YCL)

FOREWORD

This is a fine book about *what historians do* that also helps readers to explore the question, "What did historians do *when they opened up and established a new field of history?*" This combination is what makes the book so worthwhile. It is what made peace history so exciting for a number of historians in the past nearly half century.

Those of us who first entered the field together, if I may write personally to the reader, were products of the fifties. Our era gave us an awareness of war as a brutal and brutalizing social system, and also a belief that peace was a realistic goal. That sense derived from progressive and international visions that had been expressed in World War II but were already threatened by Cold War, Korean War, and anticommunist extremism. We became engaged in research that took seriously both warfare and efforts to prevent it. Organized peace advocacy was not quite a new subject of historical enquiry at that time, but it was the subject of only isolated histories, like Merle Curti's.

In the sixties a few historians organized. Mostly younger scholars, we held small conferences to compare our work and to explore the dynamics of social conflict, international affairs, and peace activism: how could we follow up on Curti's "Retrospect"? We worked the sources at the Swarthmore College Peace Collection and brought new collections to it. Indeed, the SCPC became a connecting point for many of us. Peace history was an exciting endeavor because it was and remains collective.

Since then the field has become an institutionalized, replete with its own Peace History Society and a recognized journal, *Peace and Change*. It is recognized by major historical bodies, has links to other social sciences and humanities and to historians abroad. It has generated its own reference works, notably biographical dictionaries of internationalists and peace leaders and a 328-title series of classic works in the field. It encompasses a bibliography numbering in the thousands of books and articles. Appropriately, the editor of this volume, Charles Howlett, has monitored the field (and contributed to it) since his 1986 AHA pamphlet with Glen Zeitzer and his 1991 book, *The American Peace Movement: References and Resources.*

Here, in *History of the American Peace Movement, 1890-2000,* is access to what that coterie of historians did. The book's structure helps. It begins with Howlett's brief introduction to the U.S. peace movement itself. It concludes with his extended essay on the field of peace history as it has evolved in the United States. In between the editor has placed a judicious selection of essays on several facets of the historic movement, arranged chronologically. The same quality and range of writings could have been achieved with a different section, but Howlett's choices are representative and significant studies.

The result is a guided tour of the American peace movement that is also a sample of how various historians have dealt with it. If historical writing it is to be appreciated, it must be read and not only read about. In order to understand what any historians did, the reader must ask what they were trying to do. What values engaged them? What problems did they address?

Historians encounter some challenges simply as a part of their trade. If they build narrative stories out of primary sources, for example, they have to establish accurate chronological sequences and reasonable suggestions about cause and consequence. In turn, they have to research primary sources and, if their field is new, they may even have to locate those sources and put them in order. Ideally, they imbue their narratives with significant patterns, with meaning beyond sequence, beyond even cause and effect: they interpret. A sensitive reader who is willing to ask questions can find evidence of a historian wrestling with these tasks in each chapter of this anthology.

Peace historians are disciplined by the criteria of professional history. They are subject to the demand for accuracy and thorough documentation. They are subject to the rule of transparency, whereby the author's point of view, line of reasoning, and sources are all disclosed. Perhaps most important, the subject of study—individual or group, event or line of development—must be put into a broad context in order to attain historical meaning. This criterion is what lifts historical interpretation beyond propaganda or proselytizing. Can you, as reader, identify the changing historical contexts of peace activism in the various chapters of this book? What difference does each respective context make for the respective activists—and for the historian writing about them?

Peace historians face some challenges in common with others who study social reform movements in related fields like labor and women's history, the story of civil rights movement, and environmental history. The most common unit of analysis is a reform group, a nongovernmental organization bent on change. For this reason, peace historians more or less consciously employ what sociologists call a social mobilization approach. There are some exceptions, historians for whom the individual reform is most basic. Irwin Abrams, authority on Nobel Peace Prize laureates, is a good example, as is Joanne Robinson, biographer of pacifist A.J. Muste.

In any case, by far most peace historians are *engaged* by their subject, as Howlett puts it, in the sense that they share the driving values and goals of those they study. Or historians may share the activists' sense of being torn between values in tension: as the great Czech pacifist Premysl Pitter once said to me: "well, life is dilemma." Often we write of individuals we admire. But not always and not altogether: part of the drama of peace history is the internal conflict over goals and strategies of the movement: in this respect persons and organizations are more or less admirable. And, like them or not, their relative effectiveness is worth studying. Can you, as reader, discern the interplay of values between the historians in this volume and those of whom they write?

Like activists, historians differ about the role of values, strategies, and contexts for peace movements and their constituent organizations (as illustrated in my study, "At the Hands of Historians: The Antiwar Movement of the Vietnam Era"

(*Peace and Change*, July 2004, 483-526). A dramatic example of debate over history was Michael Cromartie's 1989 collection of "Essays on Pacifism and Politics," *Peace Betrayed.* More subtle differences of interpretation show up in treatments of related subjects over a wide range of time, however. Can you, as reader, find variations in approach and judgment among the chapters in this volume? If so, how can you account for them?

Distinctly among studies of reform movements, peace history is about public efforts to influence government foreign policy. There is a transnational bias in the field because war and peace know no boundaries, because peace advocates long have organized across national lines, and because the propelling vision of many peace activists has been humanitarian and global. Indeed, peace historians have met in international association since the 1986 conference at Stadtschlaining, Austria. Their transnational orientation is compromised, however, by the ways the study and teaching of history in the United States (as in other nations) remains largely divided between this nation and other regions. The bibliography of the field is organized along a national bias, which is reflected even in this volume.

There are a few exceptions such as *The Garland Library of War and Peace,* the Kuehl and Josephson biographical dictionaries, the Russian-American project, *Peace/Mir,* and such studies of transnational networks as Sandi Cooper's excellent history of the 19th century European movement, *Patriotic Pacifism,* and Lawrence Wittner's epochal *The Struggle Against the Bomb* (1993-2003). Indeed, each chapter in this volume reflects that transnational context and orientation in one way or another, even if only by nuance. As a searching reader, can you identify it and suggest how it affects what the author did?

It is all here in this rich collection--everything a reader needs to survey the American peace movement and to explore what a representative group of historians did in collaboration with others to create the field now recognized as peace history.

Charles Chatfield, July 2005

H. Orth Hirt Professor of History Emeritus

Wittenberg University

PREFACE

This anthology is a scholarly analysis of the twentieth century evolution of a movement whose significance has increased in importance over the last eighty years. Its focus is interpretative and offers fresh perspectives by a growing number of historians explaining how the peace movement has transformed itself from one opposing war to one proclaiming the need for social, political, and economic justice. Equally important, these essays point out the growing contribution historians have made to the study of peace history. The field, itself, and publications, demonstrate its vibrancy and expansive interest. The study of peace history has, indeed, captured the attention of those studying various aspects of American military, diplomatic, and social history. Peace movement activism in the last half of the twentieth century, and the current record, may very well represent the greatest social movement of our times.

The volume is arranged chronologically, emphasizing how the movement shed pre-World War I elitism and adopted a more critical examination of the capitalistic system and its failings to prevent war. The initial contribution by the late, noted historian, Merle Curti, provides a brief synopsis of the historical undercurrents of the peace movement prior to World War II. It sheds important light on who the pioneers of the peace crusade were and what mitigated their effectiveness. The tragedies of World War I represent a major turning point in the movement's history. These essays detail the changes, which took place within the movement from that point forward. Thus, the influence of liberal pacifism, the evolution from nonviolent passive nonresistance to direct action, and efforts to build a safer world through crusades against racism, gender inequality, and environmental awareness have all become part of the peace movement's objectives. The collection concludes with a historiographical essay by the editor detailing the large body of literature that now exists on peace history in American society.

vi

Although these essays point out the variety of groups, individuals, and factions that were organized in favor of peace and justice, not simply opposition to war, it is fair to question whether or not there has been a consistent, single peace movement. History will point out otherwise. Yet, what is clear is that the movement, despite its varying responses to different global conflicts and the numerous coalitions formed, has set its sights on eradicating all forms of societal injustice. The articles taken together suggest very clearly that the peace movement has become more socially and politically conscious as the risks of a global annihilation have increased. What does need further examination, however, are the cultural and nationalistic factors making for war. Just as important, how do peace advocates address those perpetual dilemmas of what to do when the values of peace collide with decency, humanity, and justice. Much more work remains to be done.

Over the years, I have been most fortunate to have been part of a committed professional organization dedicated to exploring the rich historical tradition of peace and social justice activism: the Peace History Society. Two members, in particular, have been most supportive of my endeavors. The late Arthur A. Ekirch, Jr., and Charles Chatfield, H. Orth Hirt Professor of History Emeritus at Wittenberg University, deserve most the credit for my research interests in peace history. An eminent scholar, himself, Chatfield's generosity knows no bounds. Were it not for the late Kendall A. Birr, I may have found another calling. He encouraged me to continue my research pursuits and dare to ask those questions most in need of answers. My colleagues in the education department at Molloy College have been supportive and gracious in their comments. I wish to thank especially Dr. Bernadette Donovan, OP, Dr. Audrey Cohen, and Eileen Szablinski. This work would not have been possible without the steadfast devotion of Chris Collora. His journalistic skills paid enormous dividends.

Charles F. Howlett

INTRODUCTION

Charles F. Howlett

What is peace history? It is defined as the historical study of nonviolent efforts for peace and social justice. Peace history has become widely recognized and accepted as a subfield of the discipline of history, and as part of a larger multidisciplinary approach known as Peace Studies. Peace historians generally see themselves as engaged scholars, involved in the study of peace and war and in efforts to eliminate or at least restrict armaments, conscription, nuclear proliferation, colonialism, racism, sexism, and, of course, war. The work of peace historians presents alternatives to the policies they oppose.

The discipline of peace history can be classified into three categories. First, conflict management, which involves achieving peace through negotiation, mediation, arbitration, international law, and arms control and disarmament. Second, social reform, which involves changing political and economic structures and traditional ways of thinking. And third, a world order transformation, which incorporates world federation, better economic and environmental relationships, and a common feeling of security.

In terms of the American experience, the peace movement has its own history, leadership, organizational base, and social reform tradition. Throughout its history the movement for world peace has been a purposive and collective attempt by numerous and well-intentioned people to change the thinking of individuals and reform societal institutions. In this context, the vicissitudes of peace history writing have followed the general currents of American historiography. Just as the early participants in the American experience lived the history they chronicled, so pacifists themselves did most of the early peace writing. Using an array of literary forms -- biographies, narratives, autobiographies, and pamphlets -- these early peace activists described their hopes for a warless world.

The experience of two world wars destroyed illusions about the prospect of abolishing war through treaties, appeasement, or even isolation. Peace history lost its momentum. The realities of power politics, the cold war, atomic weapons, superpower mentalities, and wars of national liberation detracted from the post World War II international spirit. The ideology of the 1960s, however, breathed new life into the subject of peace history. It was greatly influenced by the social movement favoring a more representative history that included women, minorities, the poor, and the less articulate members of society.

In the wake of the Vietnam War, a major effort was launched to make peace history a permanent feature of American historiography. Peace activists were joined by the general public in an effort to understand the roots of pacifism. The result of this dual desire to consider both the philosophical foundations of pacifism and its practical political applications was an outpouring of scholarly work and curriculum development. Thus, as with all social movements, the peace movement in American history has been blessed with a clearly defined ideology and a specific strategy: to preserve peace, war must be stopped.[1]

The attempt to prevent war as an organized effort began in the early nineteenth century. The peace movement that emerged resulted from a century of European wars culminating in the Continental struggles of the Napoleonic era and extending to the New World in the War of 1812.[2] This movement was one of organized nonsectarian war resistance. It stimulated the first period of significant growth in the history of the movement. The spreading of evangelical Christianity and romantic faith in human perfectibility caused the initial major peace groups -- New York Peace Society, Massachusetts Peace Society, American Peace Society -- to publicize the benefits of peace. Largely through the establishment of private volunteer societies, the peace movement gained force as an elemental humanitarian calling. As part of a wider social movement in antebellum America, peace leaders of this era expressed a humanitarian concern for people as Christian individuals. Typically, these peace seekers were romantic reformers. They were inspired by a religious conviction that war was un-Christian and by a wave of humanitarianism that expressed itself in a variety of reform movements like women's suffrage, abolitionism, and penology.

Merle Curti's "Retrospect," his conclusion to his classic study of the peace movement, *Peace or War: The American Struggle, 1636-1936*, describes most effectively the leadership's makeup during the formative years. According to Curti's analysis, they were mostly community leaders and respectable citizens. Many were preachers, lawyers, merchants, and public servants. Most were "Congregationalists and Unitarian gentlemen accustomed to social deference and committed to moral improvement through gradual enlightenment." They based their appeals on persuasion and reason. As well-educated members of a northeastern urban middle class, these reformers insisted that peace promoted trade and prosperity; that wholesale bloodshed was ruinous to property; and that war involved financial deficits such as inflation, public debt, and excessive taxes. Yet, if there was one major shortcoming in their analysis, Curti insists, it was that these arguments were premised on a set of conservative politics cemented in blueblood status. The "middle-class prejudices and practicality," he notes, ". . . blinded them to many of the economic causes of war, which they seldom appreciated even in broad outline."[3] In contrast to the "modern" movement that emerged at the start of the twentieth century, one advocating protest and action based upon nonviolent civil disobedience, the fledgling peace movement was largely defined by its cerebral and biblical existence. The momentum it had gathered, however, was quickly halted by the onset of the Civil War.

The peace movement as a social reform endeavor gradually became subordinated to the Union's struggle for survival and the abolition of slavery. With the reunification of the states the postwar peace movement began touting the basic goals of establishing a world court and international arbitration. It now began moving in three distinct directions: "Geographically, it was gaining a broader base of cooperation. Organizationally, it was achieving continuity. Politically, it was becoming fixed upon a special Anglo-American relationship."[4] The new cosmopolitan, or worldly-minded, peace advocates began arguing for the necessity of Great Power cooperation and control of the underdeveloped world. The advent of a new century saw the peace movement direct its attention on educating the masses, Christianizing "backward" peoples in other parts of the globe, and endowing organizations for the scientific study of international disputes. A preference for institutional and professional association -- instead of personal and voluntary ones -- characterized the composition of the movement.

The turn-of-the-century peace movement would be most notably characterized by its attraction to men of wealth, social standing, academic prestige, and organizing ability. According to David S. Patterson's research, membership in the peace movement was "drawn overwhelmingly from well-educated, Anglo-Saxon, and Protestant elites" who "perceived militarism and interstate conflict . . . as an anachronistic survivals of an earlier, unenlightened era rather than endemic or growing evils of modern life."[5] Many of the cosmopolitan methods for achieving peace like arbitration and institutional settlement of disputes, attracted more practical-minded peace seekers to the cause. The American peace movement as it entered the twentieth century became a pragmatic enterprise. Following this new direction, the movement became a prestigious calling, devoted to the legal settlement of disputes, the maintenance of governmental contracts, the development of internationalism, and the encouragement of the "scientific" study of war and its alternatives. Strategically, reflecting the Progressive movement's response to the growing complexities of American society -- a result of the urban-industrial transformation then taking place -- peace efforts shifted from "moral absolutes to specialized utilitarian knowledge" and "bureaucratic forms" emphasizing efficiency.[6] Most tellingly, the conservative standing of its leadership tempered any radical sympathies within the movement's corpus.

Many of the movement's new recruits were not absolute pacifists as they had been in the past. Instead, they were "practical" men: academicians, men of mugwump (liberal Republican) backgrounds, leaders in the business world, bureaucratic experts befitting progressive reforms, members of the emerging profession of international law. They were not interested in peace because they felt war to be an unmitigated evil. Rather, in their opinion, peace represented a secondary reform to be trumpeted and abandoned according to circumstance. Equally important, was their distinctly elitist approach to peace. In their view only the literate gentlemen of the middle and upper classes could better understand and identify with the "civilized" quality of their movement than could the "unenlightened" masses. Not surprisingly, the elitist leaders relied on contacts in government circles for their influence and shunned involvement with immigrant, moderate socialist and labor groups. Despite the widespread domestic reform efforts of progressives, the prewar conservative nature of the peace movement had not proved particularly appealing to those possessing a liberal persuasion. "The liberals disinterest is understandable," Patterson observes. "The overwhelming majority of them were preoccupied with domestic issues; international reform seemed very remote by comparison. . . . Many liberals who were to become peace leaders and internationalists during and after the First World War showed no interest in foreign affairs, let alone the peace movement before 1914."[7]

That would change, however, by the second decade of the new century. As noted in Charles Chatfield's and Charles DeBenedetti's works, the Great War shook the foundation of the American peace movement from top to bottom. The movement would find itself undergoing a major transformation. It was dramatically restructured between those who supported the war and those steadfastly opposed to it.[8] With the advent of American military intervention in 1917, the movement's course and direction was forever changed. More and more opponents of war now proved receptive to a socialist analysis of the nature of capitalism's failings and more radical, though nonviolent, in their prescriptions for its overhaul and displacement.[9] In particular, female, and liberal pacifist and nonpacifist organizations were established such as the Women's International League for Peace and Freedom (WILPF), the American branch of the Fellowship of Reconciliation (FOR), and the War Resisters League (WRL). "These groups," one peace historian writes, "attracted not only peace seekers disenchanted with the timidity of the peace societies and endowed organizations but impelled many more pacifistic liberals and socialists into the cause for the first time. Many of these antiwar newcomers. . . boldly linked peace advocacy with social justice causes."[10]

World War I became the impetus behind the establishment of the "modern" American peace movement. Unlike the vestiges from the older movement, this one understood that peace required social reform as well as social order. Biblical and legalistic interpretations were now supplanted by a more rigorous examination of the socio-economic forces within the politics of choice making for war. The "modern" movement, revolutionary in both outlook and undertaking, sought to "advance peace as a process in human social relationships." Leaders of this movement understood justice as the amelioration of social wrongs and not simply the adjudication of courts; they viewed nationalism in terms of cultural diversity rather than some form of Anglo-Saxon exclusivity; they saw war as a by-product of militarism, nationalism, and imperialism and not merely as an irrational outburst of mass ignorance; they sought a reformed and democraticized international system by which responsible policymakers would manage peace through applied social justice and world agencies. Peace became much more than simply the absence of war. The advocates of the "modern" movement believed "that, for peace to advance in the world, reform must advance at home through the nonviolent extension of justice under order. . . . It literally thrived on the success of other reform endeavors, like racial justice and women's rights, that aimed to grant each person his or her due."[11]

The birth of the "modern" American peace movement ultimately established "what proved to be the mainstay constituencies of twentieth-century peace activism: church people, organized women, college students, and undifferentiated social reformers."[12] Organizationally, since World War I, the "modern" American peace movement has continuously evolved from the experiences of pacifist opposition to the war and internationalist agreement on the social processes of peace. Tellingly, the postwar peace movement viewed peace as a social process based on individual and group cooperation sustained through common values and institutional and cultural mores. Collectively, it was agreed that opposition to all forms of organized violence was tantamount to the achievement of social justice at home and abroad.[13]

The creation of the "modern" movement, however, came with its own price tag. It became a reflection of the "larger value-tensions" characterizing "the modern tradition of citizen peace activism." World War I tested the peace seekers' commitment to peace and their support for an allied victory in the name of national self-determination. There were those who sacrificed their peace principles and condoned the use of weaponry to free subject peoples from the heavy hand of militaristic autocracy. "This clash in core values," one historian has pointed out, "typified the persisting value-tensions and sometimes contradictions -- between peace and justice, peace and security, peace and freedom -- that came to characterize modern American peace tradition."[14]

The fragile nature of the "modern" movement was quickly tested by the 1930s. The euphoria greeting the signing of the Kellogg-Briand Pact (1928), outlawing war as an instrument of national policy, and intense efforts with labor groups to promote economic justice, despite the onslaught of the Great Depression in 1929, gave way to the growth of fascism in Europe and Japanese militarism in the Far East. Lawrence Wittner's scholarship shows that by 1935 the peace movement underwent a disastrous split. The most obvious sign was the collapse of the League of Nations Association when confronted by heightened European militarism. Staunchly pacifist groups suddenly realized their inability to prevent war in Europe and began directing their attention to isolating America from that war. Internationalist elements, on the other hand, gradually shifted to doctrines of collective security. By the end of the decade pacifists, in particular, divided their attention between cooperative political activity with neutralist groups and turning inward to prepare for the coming war.[15]

Interestingly, with the start of World War II and the eventual military participation of the United States, pacifist organizations like the Fellowship of Reconciliation and War Resisters League grew in membership and income. Perhaps the century's most recognized pacifist in the United States, A.J. Muste, exemplified the "modern" movement's emphasis on social and political justice. Faced with increasingly hostile pressure to conform to the dictates of war, Muste and his followers "sought out [their] pacifist brethren for encouragement in maintaining an otherwise exceptionally lonely stance."[16] During the war Muste and others defined their peace activism in terms of opposition to conscription. Counseling conscientious objectors and working to ensure their protection in the form of Civilian Public Service Camps were manifestations of the liberal and pacifist persuasion during the Second World War.

East-West tensions in the postwar period and the growing threat of atomic and, later, hydrogen destruction led the "modern" movement to more overt acts against militarism and war. In James Tracy's research he illustrates the more aggressive nature peace activists undertook in the name of peace and justice. Nonviolent direct action, popularly referred to as civil disobedience, represented the most significant development within the peace movement. As cold war tensions multiplied, numerous war resisters demonstrated "their opposition to the U.S. Cold War policies and domestic racial injustice by publicly burning their draft cards and committing nonviolent civil disobedience. . . ."[17] Marked by confrontational tactics such as sit-downs and protest marches, instead of just literary forms of propaganda, the movement would no longer consider its mission one of passivity and reticence. Thus the evolution from seventeenth century Quaker nonresistance to legal nonviolent resistance after the Great War and, finally, to civil disobedience (direct action) in the 1950s captures the spirit and progression of the "modern" movement.

But just as important, the use of civil disobedience would also move beyond the traditional and more personalized commitment of nonresistance. Nonviolent force was now considered relative to the demands of time and place. By the early 1960s the concern for domestic change, widely symbolized by the civil rights movement, "demonstrated more vividly than other developments in recent American history the political possibilities of active pacifism and loving nonviolence."[18] In their commitment to social change peace activists found an expanding base of political activity contingent upon the exploration of nonviolent action and the need for social redemption.

Certainly, the magnitude and scope of the anti-Vietnam War demonstrations bear ample testimony to the influence of such tactical strategies. Prior to American military involvement in Vietnam in the mid-1960s, women's groups were already "providing both animating force and mass audiences to the necessary peace reform."[19] A recognizable feminist peace activism that had been born during the First World War was now calling for a redress of grievances to the injustices of modern society. Harriet Hyman Alonso describes for us the growing "militant" feminism that had expanded in force as a result of the publication of Betty Friedan's *The Feminine Mystique* and the prolonged war in Southeast Asia. More and more women were now stepping out of their assigned role of motherhood. As early as 1961, Washington-area housewives organized Women Strike for Peace. "End the Arms Race -- Not the Human Race" was a favorite slogan of the newly-created organization.[20] Moreover, as opposition to the conflict in Vietnam expanded, feminists equated the war to their own struggle for social and economic justice. Mothers of those sons fighting in the war also caused them to highlight their own biological gift of nurturing and protecting the human species.

The "modern" peace movement's commitment to peace and justice remained in force after the Vietnam War had ended. The long and continuous struggle to build a better global society persisted throughout the remainder of the twentieth century. Barbara Epstein's observations reinforce the expansive nature of the movement and its allied causes. Peace reformers have aggressively focused their attention on ecological matters such as toxic herbicides and environmental hazards posed by the construction of nuclear power plants. They have mobilized in the form of mass demonstrations to protest the proliferation of nuclear weapons and have consistently worked to expose and eliminate the institutionalized sexism and racism in American society. Equally important, the "modern" movement has come to embody a more "personalist" approach to politics -- one emphasizing the responsibility of the individual, the closer relationship between personal and political life, and the significance of local community action.

Certainly, these developments and trends have not been lost despite the current war in Iraq. In fact, when the war was launched in 2003, veteran peace activist, David Cortright, correctly observed: "We have created the largest, most broadly based peace movement in history -- a movement that has engaged millions of people here and around the globe. . . . In practically every sector of society -- business executives, women's groups, environmentalists, artists, musicians, African-Americans, Latinos -- a strong antiwar voice has emerged."[21] Although the massive antiwar rallies and vigils that took place in thousands of communities and urban centers did not stop the war, they were by no means a reflection of the weaknesses of the peace movement. Rather, the war represented more the failures of democracy and the entrenched cultural power of American nationalism than it did the commitment of those dedicated to a safer world.

Clearly, assessing the full impact of the historic contributions of the peace movement remains a matter of conjecture. Quite naturally, it has both supporters and detractors. But if one were to examine the evolution of the peace movement from the First World War to the present, it becomes quite apparent that it has successfully developed more sophisticated forms of political and moral relevance. In large measure, the movement was radically transformed during World War I. That cataclysmic event represented the turning point in the history of the peace movement. The emphasis from passive nonresistance and opposition to war to one of demonstrable nonviolent civil disobedience in the name of peace and justice accounts for the movement's contributions to American social and political action. Since World War I the peace movement has "successfully analyzed global conflicts, worked effectively in lobbying for legislation and waging election campaigns, and mobilized large numbers of Americans for efforts that ranged from militant civil disobedience to unprecedented mass demonstrations." In its efforts to build a safer world the "modern" movement has continued to grapple with two of humanity's most troubling issues: "how to secure a larger measure of justice without betraying human values; and how to avoid the mass slaughter that advances in science and technology portended." Throughout the movement's long history, peace scholars have pointed out that the true objective is to make peace "a more 'realistic' option than war."[22]

Clearly, as a disciplinary view of war, peace history attempts to expand and refine the traditional roles of diplomatic history, political science and international relations, and the sociological and cultural aspects of armed conflict. In the realm of diplomacy, the "modern" American peace historians are not just concerned about what diplomats did or what happened when countries exchanged a declaration of war or negotiated treaties. Basically, unlike peace history, diplomatic historians have been covering events until the moment when the belligerents broke diplomatic relations and then continued the story once the peace process got underway. Diplomatic historians have been good at telling how wars began and ended, but have not offered much in the way of explaining the economic, social, political, and cultural aspects of war itself. Peace historians, however, are much more interested in ways to prevent wars and how mobilized groups have attempted to counter the powerful symbols of patriotism and power politics among nation states.

The same might be said for the study of political science and international relations. The disciplinary perspective in this field has constantly emphasized the shifts in power and the struggle for power among various national states. Since World War II the field has been dominated by the "realist" school of international relations. Disavowing the idealism generated by World War I Wilsonians, these scholars consider war endemic and part of a natural confluence involving shifts in power associated with the beginning of armed conflict. The study of alliances, international tensions, and military buildups suggested that power politics itself represented a series of steps to war, and that each aspect increased the chances of conflict between equally competing states. While scholars of the "realist" school maintain that wars occur when a rising state challenges the dominant power of the system, none have been able to provide a precise explanation of war.

Where the discipline of peace history offers exciting challenges to the study of war is found in its concern with the social effects caused by armed conflicts. Along these lines, peace historians have been addressing issues such as the changes in the status of women and minorities through participation in war, propaganda, media and culture, environmental impact of living due to technological changes, and the growing economies of warfare. Peace history research tends not only to look at war as an abnormal intrusion into the routines of everyday life, but also as a major social institution itself. The discipline has argued that the abolition of war does not necessarily require a profound change in human behavior. Rather, peace historians have been recounting the importance of an informed citizenry desirous of changing the more sinister aspects of the nation-state system and its social components.

The essays included in this anthology are excellent examples of historians at work because, as Charles Chatfield, himself, notes, "it is a field of history with a definable origin, evolution, recognition, and absorption into related fields such as diplomatic, military and social change."[23] These historians have done an excellent job of tracing the evolution of the peace movement from small, elitist societies to a far broader social movement that now consists of transnational connections. Their sophisticated analyses, moreover, lends credence to Larry Wittner's observation that "the peace movement is probably the largest social movement of modern times."[24] These scholarly essays thus represent a valuable resource book for all interested researchers seeking a fuller appreciation of the "modern" American peace movement as a social justice endeavor.

NOTES

1. For historiographical assessments consult, Charles DeBenedetti, "Peace History in the American Manner," *The History Teacher* 18 (November 1984): 75-110; Gerloff Homan, "Peace History: A Bibliographical Overview," *Choice* (May 1995): 1408-1419.

2. Consult Samuel Eliot Morison, "Dissent of the War of 1812," in Samuel Eliot Morison, et al., *Dissent in Three American Wars*. Cambridge, MA.: Harvard University Press, 1970, pp. 3-20.

3. Merle Curti, *Peace or War: the American Struggle, 1636-1936*. New York: W.W. Norton & Co., 1936, pp. 34-37.

4. Charles DeBenedetti, *The Peace Reform in American History*. Bloomington: Indiana University Press, 1980, p. 67.

5. David S. Patterson, "Citizen Peace Initiatives and American Political Culture, 1865-1920." Charles Chatfield & Peter van den Dungen, eds., *Peace Movements and Political Cultures*. Knoxville: University of Tennessee Press, 1988, p. 195.

6. *Ibid.*, p. 195.

7. David S. Patterson, "An Interpretation of the American Peace Movement, 1898-1914." Charles Chatfield, ed., *Peace Movements in America*. New York: Schocken Books, 1973, p. 20; Patterson, "Citizen Peace Initiatives," p. 195.

8. Blanche Wiesen Cook, "Democracy in Wartime: Antimilitarism in England and the United States, 1914-1918," in *Peace Movements in America*, pp. 39-56.

9. Charles DeBenedetti, "Alternative Strategies in the American Peace Movement in the 1920s," in *Peace Movements in America*, pp. 57-58.

14

10. Patterson, "Citizen Peace Initiatives," p. 200.

11. Charles DeBenedetti, ed., *Peace Heroes in Twentieth Century America*. Bloomington: Indiana University Press, 1986, pp. 5-6.

12. *Ibid.*, p. 9.

13. Robert H. Ferrell, "The American Peace Movement" in Alexander DeConde, ed., *Isolation and Security*. Durham, N.C.: Duke University Press, 1957, pp. 82-106.

14. DeBenedetti, ed. *Peace Heroes*, p. 8.

15. Lawrence S. Wittner, *Rebels Against War: The American Peace Movement, 1933-1984*. Philadelphia: Temple University Press, 1984, Chapter 1, *passim*.

16. *Ibid.*, pp. 54-55.

17. DeBenedetti, ed. *Peace Heroes*, p. 11.

18. *Ibid.*, p. 13.

19. DeBenedetti, *The Peace Reform*, pp. 14-15; Harriet Hyman Alonso, "Suffragists for Peace During the Interwar Years, 1919-1941," *Peace and Change* 14 (July 1989), pp. 243-62.

20. Wittner, *Rebels Against War*, p. 277.

21. David Cortright, "What We Do Now: An Agenda for Peace," *The Nation* (April 21, 2003), reprinted in Randy Scherer, ed., *The Antiwar Movement*. Farmington, MI.: Greenhaven Press, 2004, pp. 147-48; "As Peace Core Evacuates, Peace Movement Activates," *The Wall Street Journal* (October 21, 2001), p. B 1. Peace activists are still continuing to mobilize. US Labor Against the War issued a Mission Statement in Chicago on October 25, 2003, reminiscent of the Vietnam years, which stated: "We are living in an era in which the government has manipulated our nation's fear of terrorism to launch wars, destroy our economic security, undermine government services, erode our democratic rights and intensify racism, sexism, religious discrimination and divisions among working people." On March 5, 2005, moreover, the organization sponsored a major conference in New York City, "Students and Educators to Stop the War," aimed at organizing teacher unions, schools and campuses, and sponsoring workshops analyzing the roots of war and critiquing ideologies supporting the war in Iraq. Consult, www.uslaboragainstwar.org and www.campusactivism.org.

22. Wittner, *Rebels Against War*, pp. 302-306.

23. Charles Chatfield to author, January 16, 2005.

24. Lawrence Wittner to author, January 19, 2005

CHAPTER ONE
RETROSPECT
Merle Curti

In his classic history of the American peace movement, the late Pultizer-Prize winning historian, Merle Curti, reflects on three general assumptions about pacifist ideals and peace movements that eventually shaped the parameters of the field: an instrumentalist view that the history of pacifist ideals could help change the world; a subjective belief that the story of peace movements can be just as exciting and rewarding as accounts of battles and wars; and a rational belief in the public value of assessing the true meaning of patriotism and nationalism. This brief conclusion to *Peace or War* captures Curti's feelings that the study of history must not dwell on the glories of war, which is only temporary and terribly destructive, but on the efforts of "rational," "intelligent," and "concerned" human beings who recognize the true value of human relationships and their enduring importance to society. Yet, Curti also cautions his readers to consider the perpetual dilemma of what to do when the values of peace are in apparent conflict with decency, humanity, and justice. When reading this essay consider the following: What are the historical attributes of peace crusaders and peace movements?; What did Curti see as the major shortcomings in the struggle against war?; What internal conflicts and rivalries have de-energized its effectiveness?; Why have peacemakers failed to address adequately the economic forces making for war?; and, lastly, How did the religious, middle class nature of the movement originally inhibit its broader appeal?

THREE hundred years have passed since Roger Williams protested against the most patent brutalities of war. These three centuries have witnessed the slow, faltering development of what finally became the American struggle against war. At first only a few unheeded men, such as John Woolman, denounced war as both unchristian and opposed to reason and justice. Immediately after our first great national war for independence, however, public men enjoying great prestige spoke out in condemnation of the war method and according to their lights sought policies that promised peace. But in spite of the faith fairly widely cherished even at that period that America was destined by fate to lead the world in peace, the new republic followed the example of older states in conquering territory and consolidating national unity through wars.

Yet each war was followed by a revulsion of feeling against the appeal to battle and by a renewed resolution to prevent similar catastrophes in the future. This resolution was first expressed in a systematic way after the second great national war did come to an end in 1815. In that year small groups of religious and humane men banded themselves together in forming societies to spread the word that war was unjustifiable from every point of view and to work for its ultimate abolition. At first these organizations were inconspicuous without means, resources or a rank and-file membership of any consequence, they were all but outcast' groups. As the second quarter of the nineteenth century ran its course, however, they won a recognized place among the philanthropic reform movements of the time. More important than this, they developed a program, tactics, and literature of war and peace which in broad outlines anticipated all that was to follow in subsequent periods.

When civil war stalked up and down the land the peace movement all but declared its bankruptcy, for only a few stood the test of that ordeal. Peace men themselves were unable to resist the emotional contagion of the time and the argument that the Civil War was an exceptional war, a war in the interest of freedom and justice and of ultimate peace itself, a war, therefore, which peace men might in conscience support. Another reason for the failure of peace men to stand by their colors in this crisis was that they had not thought out an alternate, nonviolent method by which the economic values of the North could replace those of the South, by which freedom and justice could be promoted. Finally it was clear that the crusade for peace had failed because it had not attacked the basic causes of war.

Although a few critics within the peace movement made some such analysis of its collapse, the greater section which renewed the struggle against war in the years after Appomattox did not take these lessons to heart. The respected leaders continued to rely on moral suasion and on appeals to the government in favor of treaties of arbitration, an international court, and a congress of nations--the program of the pioneers. The ever-increasing activity on the part of pacifists was undoubtedly an important factor in the development of a wider public interest in the negotiation of permanent treaties of arbitration. In rejecting these treaties the Senate was responsive to the pull of nationalism and to the fear of many important economic groups that compulsory arbitration might jeopardize their interests. Against such forces the labor of the peace men was impotent, for all the sentiment in their favor.

A minority of staunch men of peace, bent on attacking the causes of war, were dissatisfied with the emphasis which their colleagues put on the program of general propaganda against war and on arbitration treaties as a substitute. This relatively small number of pacifists were vaguely aware of some of the seeds of conflict scattered over the land. They made a mild but honest effort to neutralize some of the economic forces that seemed to them to invite war: these lovers of peace tried to solve the conflict between capital and labor through arbitration and through popularizing the profit-sharing idea. But they made no realistic effort to win the masses of labor to their support nor did they detect in the internal development of our economic life the forces, which presently led to the Spanish-American War and to imperialism. Thus their efforts to check the navalism, which accompanied the national expansion beyond the seas were for the most part futile. Those that ruled American economic and political life were not converted by the argument that increased expenditures for the army and navy were wasteful, unnecessary, and provocative of. war.

Nevertheless the rapid growth of navalism and of a jingoistic spirit in the early years of the twentieth century aroused much opposition on the part of liberal Americans who detested imperialism and who were at heart devoted to the ideal of peace. The organized foes of war enlisted many new recruits from this group of their fellow citizens. Men of wealth devoted millions to the cause. Leaders of the church, the school, the press, of business and of labor, expressed approval of the efforts the peace movement was making to curtail military expenditures, to secure the negotiation of permanent treaties of arbitration, and to further the development of the international organization which the conferences at The Hague had initiated. Political leaders likewise paid tribute to the peace cause, and officially moved in the direction indicated by the protagonists of peace. In the years immediately before the outbreak of the World War the peace movement became so active and so respected that it seemed to some of its leaders as if at last a nation-wide struggle against war was under way, and that war itself must presently be conquered.

With our entrance into the World War, however, the peace movement again collapsed. A few, to be sure, resisted public opinion and the government, and paid a heavy price. This remnant and an ever larger number of Americans who, after the Armistice, denounced the brutality and futility of the war, guided a new peace movement which in the twenties and early thirties gained a wider hearing than any earlier protest against war had won.

The majority in the new peace movement put great trust in the importance of winning the government over to the support of an international organization designed to check future aggression and to preserve peace. When the United States rejected the League of Nations, the peace movement by and large continued to exert an ever greater amount of pressure to compel the authorities in Washington to resume the lead which we had held for a moment in Wilson's time in the official, world-wide movement to limit war.

The government responded. The Washington Disarmament Conference, the Kellogg-Briand Pact, the increasing amount of cooperation with the League of Nations, all bore witness to the fact that the government was no longer indifferent to the claims of pacifists. Renewed hope surged in the hearts of lovers of peace with each official victory for the cause.

But as expenditures for the army, the navy, and for aviation increased, and as war clouds darkened, it became clear that peace was still a long way off. Discouraged with the efforts made at Geneva, to curb war, an important section of the peace movement determined to try to safeguard American neutrality in case of another general conflict. As the Senate Munitions committee disclosed, the relation between the sale of materials of war, loans, and propaganda to our entrance into the world conflict in 1917, the conviction deepened that the struggle against war could best be pursued, at least for the time, in this direction. The response of the government to this sentiment and pressure seemed to many the greatest achievement the peace movement had ever won.

And yet as the year 1936 began its course the danger of war in the world--the fear that America might become involved--was more widely and openly expressed than ever before. Had the peace movement indeed failed? If it had what were the reasons for its failure?

In spite of the widespread feeling that the antiwar movement was fundamentally weak and ineffective it had not altogether failed. It had certainly contributed to the development of peace consciousness--to genuine and widespread opposition to war and the clamor for peace. It had certainly been one of the factors in the gradual acceptance by the government of one plank after another in the program of the pacifists. It could also record other victories, such as occasional checks on the growth of navalism and militarism, and contributions to the peaceable solution of international tension, as in the crisis with Mexico in 1927.

A more intangible but very significant advance was the achievement of the increasing realism, which characterized the philosophy and tactics of the peace movement in the years that had just passed. Intelligent leaders more and more recognized the necessity, of utilizing on a mass sale all the new propaganda devices and the technique of pressure politics that their more successful antagonists had developed. At least some leaders recognized the necessity of probing more, deeply into the economic causes of war and of directing against them a frontal attack.

Keeping in mind all these achievements, the positive and important character of which is clear, we may now well ask why the peace movement failed in its larger objective--why the abolition of war now seems more remote than it did in 1920 or even in 1913.

Some of the weaknesses of the peace movement, weaknesses certainly contributing to its relative ineffectiveness, are apparent to anyone who reads its history. In the first place, foes of war have dissipated some of their strength by internal conflicts and rivalries, by duplication of effort, and by ineffective marshaling of their all-too-meager resources. These internal conflicts were to some extent inevitable; they represented essentially different philosophies and assumptions. Moreover, probably all the emphases that were made served a purpose, for many different constituencies were to be won, and no single program would have appealed to all potential supporters. Yet a movement so divided could hardly expect to have great practical influence.

Another weakness in the peace movement has been the tendency of its leaders to over simplify certain forces, which draw men to war. In general they have failed to understand the glamour and the hare of war for great masses of people. They have underestimated the attractiveness of the very horrors of war. They have frequently failed to see that it provides great numbers of plain folk with opportunities for adventure, for heroic deeds, for escape from the drab existence of everyday life on farms and in towns and cities; that in short it may give people new direction, a new purpose, a larger life.

Perhaps the forces of war would not be as dominant as they now are had the advice of William James been taken with more seriousness; had the peace movement spared no effort to provide outlet for the sense of adventure and the love of heroism in everyday pursuits. But this would have been a big order, things being as they were; and possibly not much could have been done to build effective "moral equivalents for war."

It is not probable that weaknesses such as these have been major hindrances in the long struggle for peace And only those with is strong leaning toward individualism, or great faith in the power of well-disciplined minority groups, could feel that greater headway would have been made had the small band of friends of peace unanimously resisted the wars to which in the past they have so largely succumbed. Again, this is an imponderable. But it is reasonable to suppose that the movement of complete and unequivocal opposition to all war, in wartime as in peacetime, must become far larger than it has shown signs of becoming before it can be expected to deter the government from embarking on war or from effecting an early cessation of a war once launched. The spiritual strength which the absolute pacifists in past wars won and in some measure imparted to their more pragmatic or less courageous fellows has been an important factor in the maintenance of the virtues so necessary for the successful waging of peace. But the war-resisters have underestimated the strength of the enemy.

One reason for the slow advance of peace does stand out as of major importance: peacemakers have not adequately fought the economic forces that make for war. It is quite true that racial and nationalistic as well as other psychological factors have been important cases for the wars America has made and for the complex situation, which today threatens war. Some aspects of the capitalistic order have undoubtedly promoted peace. But by its very structure this system, based on a profit making economy, has also favored the forces of war. The desire for profits has played an important part in the willingness to float war loans and to sell munitions and contraband to belligerents, regardless of the dangers to peace, which such policies involved. The desire for profits on the part of munitions venders has helped to neutralize the efforts of peacemakers and of governments themselves to curb the growth of militarism and navalism. The desire of newspaper owners to enhance their profits by enlarging the circulation of their journals has played a part in crusades made by influential newspapers for stimulating a martial spirit; and the close relationship through advertising of most great newspapers with the more conservative business enterprises has naturally tended to make them follow warlike leads taken by the latter. Moreover, the competition for markets and for raw materials has stimulated international tension and the desire for ever greater navies to protect trade interests.

In still other ways a profit-making society has no doubt promoted the willingness to rely on war as a method of solving unpleasant and stubborn problems. The recognition on the part of astute men that a war in 1897 might bring an end to the hard times of that period, and the fear in the early part of 1917 that war was necessary to prevent an economic collapse were not of course major causes of the decisions to fight, but it is not unreasonable to assume that such hopes and fears, at least unconsciously, influenced the decisions. The desire of workers for jobs and for higher wages must have made many toilers advocate preparedness and welcome war. In short, while individual capitalists have sincerely desired peace, war has been functional to the capitalistic system itself.

Most friends of peace, coming from the middle classes, have naturally accepted the existing economic order and have not seen the threats to peace inherent in it. The pioneers failed to respond to the pleas of early labor leaders; and most of their successors were deaf to the argument of socialists that peace could not be won as long as our whole society was built on the desire for profits. No one can say whether war would be less likely today had earlier friends of peace made frontal attacks on the profit-making system. The great majority of American workers would certainly have been rendered as hostile or as indifferent as they have been to the pleas of Socialists and Communists. Moreover, if friends of peace had attacked the profit-making order in their general attack on war, the government might have shown itself less willing to cooperate with other nations in promoting peace than it has; might have shown more favor to imperialists and militarists than it has. Too many imponderables are involved to answer this question with any certainty.

Nevertheless it seems clear that a continuation of the policies and tactics of the past will bring diminishing returns. It is true that a large section of the population now acclaims and desires peace, to judge by polls of opinion recently taken. The government itself claims to be working against war and for peace. But it is reasonable to infer, from past experience that if further and more substantial progress is to be made, friends of peace must probe more deeply into the causes of modem war than they have ever done before, and that in particular they must attack hidden, hitherto resistless economic forces with more effective instruments than any used thus far in the struggle.

If the American struggle against war is ever to result in a final victory, still more will surely have to be done. The historian is not a prophet, and he cannot say with any finality what must be done. But certain inferences may be made from our knowledge of the peace movement in America. Unless pacific means are found for securing a greater degree of justice, in all categories of human relationships--racial, national, and economic; unless new and more effective ways are found for curbing the forces that make war seem of value or of profit in one or another way to powerful groups--unless these things are done the struggle against war in America in the world probably; will not end. Pacifists have sincerely and ardently desired peace; but they have in general desired the benefits of the existing order to an even greater degree. Revolutionary critics of war have also sincerely and ardently desired peace; but many of them have desired a new and a more just economic order to an even greater degree. In the light of the long sweep of history it seems probable that the present economic and social order, with its many invitations to war, will be modified, or even replaced by one more definitely collectivistic and democratic.

The problem of true peacemakers is to determine how this can be achieved peacefully and without sowing new seeds of conflict. The challenge is a greater challenge than the peace movement in its long history has ever faced.

CHAPTER TWO

INTERPRETATION OF THE AMERICAN PEACE MOVEMENT, 1898-1914

David S. Patterson

In this essay and his subsequent book, *Toward a Warless World: The Travail of the American Peace Movement, 1887-1914* (1976), State Department historian, David Patterson, offers an exacting critique of the keepers of judicial arbitration within the pre-world War One peace movement. In this analysis, Patterson dissects the four types of prewar peace advocates: pacifists, federalists, legalists, and generalists. He is highly critical of their failure to stand behind any one program for international reform. He discusses the shift from non-institutional pacifism to institutional pacifism. He also examines how the political culture in prewar America created elite peacemaking tendencies and how the First World War transformed and radicalized the movement. When discussing this article consider the following: How did the timidity of traditional peace societies and the endowed organizations, such as the Carnegie Endowment for International Peace, respectability arouse the ire of pacifistic liberals and socialists?; How did absolute pacifists boldly link peace advocacy with social justice causes?; What tensions existed between devout pacifists and non-pacifists opposed to war in general?; In what ways did the elitism of pre-World War One peace supporters and the idealism embodied in their efforts blunt attempts for meaningful peace and place a conservative veneer over the entire movement?; How did American military intervention in the Great War assist in transforming the peace movement from one of respectability to nonviolent engagement in the name of social justice?

I

The American peace movement in the two decades before the First World War grew rapidly in terms of the proliferation of peace societies, active membership and financial backing. From a tiny nucleus consisting of the American *Peace* Society and Universal Peace Union, both of which began long before 1898, peace work became a popular avocation in the first years of the twentieth century. Annual meetings on international arbitration at Albert Smiley's hotel resort on Lake Mohonk, New York, begun in 1895, were consistently attended by almost all the leading friends of international peace, after about 1900; and beginning in 1907 many peace leaders organized biennial peace conferences in various American cities. In the decade before the outbreak of the European war advocates of peace also created many new peace and internationalist societies, most notably the American Society of International Law, the New York Peace Society, the American School Peace League, the Chicago Peace Society, the American Society for Judicial Settlement of International Disputes and three endowed institutions, the World Peace Foundation, the Carnegie Endowment for International Peace and the Church Peace Union. In this decade alone American friends of world peace established more than forty-five peace societies, and after 1911 the Carnegie Endowment provided the American Peace Society with an annual subvention from which it supported its affiliated peace organizations.

Yet when the European w a r erupted in 1914, almost all peace groups either remained aloof from the immediate issues of American neutrality or were too divided to influence the foreign policies of the Wilson Administration. As a result, some of the more active peace workers, dissatisfied with the existing peace groups, cooperated with like-minded newcomers to the movement in forming still other peace organizations to deal with the pressing problems arising out of the World War.[1]

Beneath the usual descriptions of the peace movement lie some important unanswered questions. Only a few historians have attempted more than a partial survey of the leadership of the peace movement for the years 1898 to 1914; even less have they analyzed its common and distinctive features. To what degree is it possible to generalize about these peace workers as a group? And since the growing popularity of the peace cause inevitably added to the variety of temperaments and programs in the movement, exactly what were their differences? Finally, what were the internal weaknesses of the movement, which accounted for its impotence and eventual reorganization after 1914?

The answers require analysis of the backgrounds and assumptions of the thirty-six leaders who set the tone of the American peace movement between 1898 and 1914.[2] Such analysis will show that although the leaders of the peace movement were remarkably similar in social backgrounds and shared certain fundamental values, the movement failed to sustain its growing influence after the outbreak of the European war for two major reasons. First, the many divergent approaches to peace questions which existed in subdued fashion during peacetime surfaced under the pressures of a war-torn world and greatly accentuated the internal divisions in the movement. Second, despite the growing public interest in the peace movement, the strong elitism of the pre-war leadership which frustrated efforts to cultivate a mass following before the war facilitated the dissolution of the superficial support of the peace leaders after 1914.

II

It is not surprising to find considerable diversity in such a large group of peace leaders. Consider their ages. In 1909 when the movement was maturing, the age span ranged from the eighty-seven-year-old Boston minister, Edward Everett Hale, to the youthful student enthusiast at the University of Wisconsin,

Louis Lochner, only twenty-two; and there were representatives of all age groups between these extremes. Nor can it be said that the age of a peace worker had any direct relationship to his position on peace questions. About the most that can be said is that in 1909 the average and median age of the peace leadership, both between fifty-four and fifty-five, was older than the leadership of the domestic reform movements of that day.

More revealing than their ages was their length of service in the peace movement. Almost all of the peace leaders who had shown interest in the peace and imperialist movements before 1900 were distinctly pacific-minded in their abhorrence of international violence. They a l s o were more sympathetic to domestic reform movements than the later participants, most of whom tended to be conservative on domestic matters, more cautious or "practical" in their promotion of international reform, and more deferential toward political authority.[3] Of the pre-1900 recruits, few besides the Quakers--Alfred Love, head of the Universal Peace Union; Benjamin Trueblood, secretary of the American Peace Society and editor of its journal, *Advocate of Peace;* and William I. Hull, history professor at Swarthmore College--can be considered absolute pacifists in the sense that they refused to sanction any given war. But America's war with Spain and the imperialistic aftermath deeply disturbed almost all of them. If they had not been full-fledged members of the American peace movement before 1898, they actively cooperated with peace workers in the anti-imperialist movement and moved effortlessly into the peace movement once the anti-imperialist agitation subsided. For them the peace movement became in part the proper instrument for organizing American opinion against possible future imperialist ventures and against navalism, which dominated American thinking on foreign affairs at the turn of the century. They opposed the use of American military force in other lands but, unlike many isolationists who shunned America's participation in world affairs, these peace workers actively urged their government's participation in movements for permanent peace. Responding to the reality of America's emergence as a major world power, they advocated treaties of international arbitration, mediation and conciliation procedures and a broad educational campaign as rational alternatives to international conflict. A few even developed general proposals for world organization. Because they all espoused pacifism or inclined in that direction and worked for international cooperation, they might best be called pacific-minded internationalists.[4]

By contrast, of the post-1900 recruits only four of the youngest-Congregationalist minister and editor of *Christian Work*, Frederick Lynch; editor of the *Independent*, Hamilton Holt; and the two college student leaders of the Cosmopolitan Club, an international friendship society, George Nasmyth and Louis Lochner--flirted with absolute pacifism, and they affirmed their love of peace more on emotional than on philosophical or religious grounds. Unlike those who had earlier entered the peace movement, nearly all these latecomers had fewer regrets concerning their nation's navalism and imperialism. They accepted America's rise to world power as largely inevitable and essentially beneficent, and they viewed the peace movement as the most useful vehicle for convincing American governmental leaders to promote a harmonious international order.

In terms of their peace ideas, these post-1900 additions to the peace movement fall roughly into three groups: generalists, world federationists and legalists. Fannie Fern Andrews, organizer of the American School Peace League, the Chicago clergyman, Charles Beals; Arthur Deerin Call, officer of the Connecticut Peace Society and American Peace Society; Samuel Train Dutton, head of Teacher's College at Columbia University; the Reverend William Short, secretary of the New York Peace Society; Lynch, Nasmyth, and Lochner most often advanced extremely broad and general proposals for the promotion of world peace. These generalists shared the positive goals of the earlier recruits in urging their government to promote international good will in its foreign policies. While they occasionally talked about the need for international organization, they rarely detailed its functions.[5]

The world federationists were more dearly internationalists. These internationalists shared the peaceful aspirations of the pacific-minded and generalists, but were unwilling to wait for the conversion of the masses to the goal of world peace or of the nations' widespread acceptance of arbitration and conciliation procedures for the resolution of international disputes. They wanted the major world powers to establish permanent international institutions which would formalize and regularize the conciliation process. They talked most often of the creation of some kind of world federation. Their proposals ranged from Andrew Carnegie's general program for a league of peace composed of the leaders of the major powers of Europe and the United States, who would agree to use economic sanctions and as a last resort an international police force against aggressor states, to more specific arrangements for the creation of an international legislature which would develop procedures for preserving the peace. Hamilton Holt, Richard Bartholdt, a Republican congressman from St. Louis, Missouri, and Raymond Bridgman, journalist and author, also urged the establishment of an international executive to apply the legislature's decisions to specific controversies.[6]

The third group composed of Nicholas Murray Butler, president of Columbia University; George Kirchwey, professor of international law at Columbia; James Brown Scott, international lawyer and frequent adviser to the State Department; and Elihu Root, Roosevelt's second Secretary of State and later Senator from New York, emphasized international law. Its members also were internationalists but they promoted only the creation of a world court. They were primarily legalists, who argued that international congresses, like the two Hague Peace Conferences, could gradually formulate a code of international law, which justices of a world court could apply and further develop in their decisions between disputants.

With so many individuals involved in the peace movement, it is not surprising that there were numerous approaches to the peace question. Indeed, the differences among the peace workers were in some respects fundamental. Those individuals who inclined toward pacifism challenged reliance on armaments; but the other leaders soft-pedalled the armament question and in a few instances readily tolerated the large navy boosters in the Navy League.[7]

In addition, the legalists questioned other peace workers' faith in arbitration treaties. In their view the arbitral process might settle many controversies, but it was no panacea and contained inherent weaknesses. They pointed out that men trained in politics and diplomacy rather than well-known jurists almost always decided arbitration cases. The art of negotiation and the spirit of compromise rather than any higher concept of abstract justice were the guiding principles in these arbitrations. Compromise was also common in arbitration because of the need to harmonize different or fragmentary concepts of international law. The legalists wanted to purge the procedures of international conciliation, of their haphazard, arbitral features by creating a judicial court composed of renowned judges, appointed for life and sitting in continuous session, who would rule on the "rights" of countries in accordance with the "facts" and the established law. In their view, only the correct application of accepted international law could bring true international justice, a prerequisite for any stable world order.[8]

Tensions also existed between the legalists and the world federationists. Less confident in the wisdom of nation-states to decide the rules of right conduct, the former branded schemes for an international legislature and executive as too radical. Such authoritative institutions, they pointed out, involved the surrender of national sovereignty, which nations were not yet prepared to accept. They also claimed that even if a world federation became a political reality, its use of force to preserve the peace would probably result in oppressive and unjust actions. For the legalists only renowned judges were impartial and the only acceptable sanction for their decisions was the very gradual development of "a world-wide public opinion" properly educated in the rights and duties of nations in the international community.[9]

Differences even developed within each group. Among the world federationists, for example, Hamilton Holt at times favored the establishment of some kind of international police force, but Raymond Bridgman was much more skeptical of any kind of sanctions.[10] So, too, although most of the pacific-minded members feared the possible harmful consequences of an international police force, three of the strongest opponents of national armaments--Lucia Ames Mead, Boston intellectual; Edwin Ginn, a text-book publisher; and William I. Hull-- cautiously endorsed the creation of a small international police agency with limited powers to enforce the peace.[11] Furthermore, Jane Addams was developing a peculiar brand of pacifism which had little in common with that of other pacifists. Much as she wrote about peace, moreover, she often seemed more interested in domestic than international reform. This was suggested when in the presidential election of 1912 she supported Theodore Roosevelt, certainly no friend of the peace movement.[12]

Temperamental and tactical differences also threatened the fragile unity of the movement. William Jennings Bryan's erratic opposition to imperialism, his alleged radicalism and political partisanship, his flamboyant rhetoric and his deliberate avoidance of membership in peace organizations embarrassed or annoyed some peace advocates.[13] Moreover, Andrew Carnegie and Edwin Ginn were jealous of their reputations as leading philanthropists of peace and refused to cooperate in establishing their peace funds. In addition, Ginn, believing the peace movement could strive toward business efficiency, often disagreed with the directors of his own World Peace Foundation who through speeches and writings were more interested in uplifting their audiences to their high-minded aims.[14]

But all these differences paled in comparison with the fundamentally divergent views between the pacific-minded and the leaders of the Carnegie Endowment. The latter strongly disapproved of the emotional and "radical" tendencies of the peace societies. Unlike the peace societies and the World Peace Foundation, which actively disseminated their message of pacific internationalism to literate Americans, the Carnegie trustees promoted almost entirely the extremely cautious goal of international understanding among a small group of scholars and international lawyers. Compared with the Endowment's financial support of international law and other non-pacifist groups, its subsidy to the peace societies amounted to a mere pittance, and by 1913 several Carnegie trustees began to suggest the curtailment of the Endowment's subvention unless the societies abandoned their pacifistic emphasis.[15]

III

The many views and temperaments in the peace movement foreshadowed the divergent responses to the world crisis after 1914, but before that date a tenuous consensus existed among the peace forces. Indeed, a dominant note of the American peace movement before 1914 was the relative absence of overt controversy. The advocates of peace frequently appeared on the same platform at peace congresses and rarely engaged in extensive debate over their different viewpoints. When they recognized their differences, they usually assumed that they were more complementary than conflicting. Especially absent was severe public criticism of their colleagues. Edwin Mead, a vigorous anti-preparedness advocate, even convinced himself that it was "ridiculous" to believe that the Carnegie trustees did not advocate the reduction of armaments although some of them were prominent supporters of the Navy

Navy League, and the leaders of the New York Peace Society deliberately attempted to minimize differences of opinion in the movement.[16]

There are a few obvious explanations for this failure to emphasize their real differences. Perhaps most important, during these years of relative peace and isolation, the pressures for defining and defending one's position on the peace question were minimal. Moreover, there existed a few areas of general agreement which helped to maintain an uneasy unity in the movement. First, all endorsed periodic international congresses for the discussion of questions of common interest. Second, they all assumed that the United States as a satiated and relatively secure power should take the lead in advancing specific proposals leading to a more harmonious international order. Third, although only the legalists were very precise in their definitions of international law, all conceded the importance of the development of "law" in establishing nations' rights and duties in the world community. Finally, none opposed the establishment of a court of arbitral justice as the next, most practical step toward instituting a new world order following the Second Hague Peace Conference's endorsement in principle of this institution.[17]

But there were also other, often deeper reasons for their cooperative behavior. One was their similar backgrounds. The social origins of almost all the thirty-six peace leaders were so remarkably alike that it was easier for them to tolerate different approaches to world peace than if their backgrounds had been more diverse. Despite their wide age-span and different lengths of service in the movement, from every other sociological perspective their social origins were virtually identical.[18] All but six--Bartholdt, Carnegie, Love, Lucia Ames Mead, Hannah Bailey (head of the peace department of the W.C.T.U.), and James Slayden (Democratic congressman from Texas)--had received college degrees, and nearly two-thirds also had earned professional certification in their chosen fields of law, education or religion. Since only relatively affluent families could usually afford to send their children to college in that day, these figures, together with other information on their parents' social standing, indicate that almost all the peace workers came from the middle or upper classes and, upon reaching maturity, formed an educated elite among the professional classes.[19]

These similarities went beyond their social class, however. Only the Chicago Unitarian minister, Jenkin Lloyd Jones, Fannie Fern Andrews, Carnegie, Scott and Bartholdt were foreign-born, and of these only Bartholdt came from a non-English-speaking nation or migrated to the United States after early childhood. Of the native Americans all but Hull, Slayden, Short and Theodore Marburg were born east of the Mississippi and north of the Mason-Dixon line. Moreover, although many were reared in small towns, they early moved to large cities whose cultural and intellectual advantages seemed inevitably to attract men and women of education and intellect; and by 1909 nearly three-fourths of the peace workers lived in six metropolitan areas -Boston, New York, Philadelphia, Baltimore, Washington, D.C., and Chicago.[20] In addition, all were Protestants and about one-half came from strongly religious households, thought seriously of the ministry as a career or were ordained clergymen.[21]

In sum, the social characteristics of the thirty-six peace leaders were overwhelmingly urban, professional, Anglo-Saxon and Protestant. In many instances, in fact, the sociological ties were more than casual. Among the New York peace workers Frederick Lynch had been a classmate of Hamilton Holt at Yale and of William Short at Yale Theological School. Lynch married one of Samuel Dutton's daughters and introduced Short to his future wife.[22] George Kirchwey and Dutton also had received degrees from Yale and, together with James Brown Scott and Nicholas Murray Butler, became professors or administrators at Columbia University. All of these peace workers figured prominently in the formation and programs of the New York Peace Society or the Carnegie Endowment. The same close ties existed among Boston peace workers. Before moving to New York,

Dutton was a school administrator in the Boston area and frequently discussed educational problems in a Boston reform organization, the Twentieth Century Club. His exposure to many Boston friends of peace in this group first introduced him to the peace movement. Furthermore, Lynch's and Call's early contacts with other Boston advocates of peace helped to foster their growing interest in the cause.[23]

IV

But of more far-reaching importance than their social backgrounds, though in large measure derived from them, were the common attitudes and values the peace workers expressed in the movement. Most important, their approach to the peace movement was distinctly elitist. The political conservatives in the movement deliberately discouraged participation by the lower classes, but even more progressive elements gave little emphasis to them. With a few exceptions, most notably Jane Addams and William Jennings Bryan, they assumed that literate gentlemen of the middle and upper classes could more easily understand and identify with the civilized quality of their movement than the unenlightened masses. Not surprisingly, they relied upon their contacts with friends in governmental circles for their influence and shunned involvement in politics and contacts with immigrant, moderate socialist or labor groups. The high-priced dinners and formal receptions of the New York Peace Society and the Carnegie Endowment, Albert Smiley's handpicked conferences at Lake Mohonk, and the leadership of peace societies limited to educators, ministers and philanthropists exemplified this same elitism.[24]

In most instances, theirs was not deliberate snobbery. Rather, reflecting the Mugwump traditions and teachings which were common among many reformers of that era, they assumed that the man in the street was an important factor in public opinion only to the extent of his ability to absorb their own ideas. Until education could enlighten the general public, these leaders assumed that they alone were the proper custodians of the peace movement. Even progressive reformers like Lynch, Lochner and David Starr Jordan, while expressing greater faith in the populace, upheld the Mugwump emphasis on enlightened l e a d e r ship and agreed that international reform would have to come from above rather than from below. Lynch, for example, assumed that "It is the prophets and leaders who make the changes of the world. The talk of *vox populi* is often more of a delusion than a reality." While they regularly expounded their views on the peace question to formal gatherings, they rarely engaged their audiences in public discussion or attempted to include them in the daily operations of the peace movement. Indeed, fascinated by great leaders of the past and present, they easily tolerated the growing involvement in the movement of influential conservatives whose participation seemed to confirm the dignity of their own peace work.[25] In consequence, the peace movement increasingly acquired an aura of gentility and respectability but at the expense of widening the gap between the peace leaders and the masses.

The peace leaders managed to maintain an uneasy consensus on other values. Above all, they shared an unquestioning belief in the reality of moral values. The acceptance of moral values as the mainspring of human behavior was deeply ingrained in the American character, as the Puritans, transcendentalists and anti-slavery reformers had earlier demonstrated; and the most pacifistic internationalists frequently referred to the humanistic values of their forebears. They also derived added inspiration for their ethical values from Christian humanists and Enlightenment philosophers throughout the Western world. Unlike American ultra nationalists, who had little faith in the pervasiveness of ethical principles beyond the water's edge, these pacific-minded individuals optimistically believed that these values existed universally and already exerted a far-reaching influence on the foreign policies of nation states.[26] Other international reformers were less sanguine. They agreed that the acceptance of moral values was widespread, but they assumed that they were most obviously present in their own land and to a lesser degree in other so-called civilized or Christian nations.[27]

In the long run, the distinction between the pacifists' humanism and the other peace workers' more limited emphasis on civilized nations was crucial. The latter, more readily believing in the essential virtue of American conduct in foreign affairs, could more easily justify their nation's forceful intervention in the affairs of other states for the sake of reforming their policies along American or "civilized" lines than those inclining toward pacifism, who were profoundly skeptical about the use of force in foreign affairs. During peacetime, however, this distinction caused no difficulties.

If the peace leaders had believed only in the reality of moral values in international life, they would have had difficulty in explaining why nations had resorted to wars throughout history. But they were not Pollyannas. Admitting that man was not inherently good and might even be instinctively pugnacious, many peace workers tempered their optimism with warnings about his combative instincts. James Slayden lamented that "the spirit of the people is inclined toward war," and Holt agreed that "the great mass of men and women almost prefer war to peace."[28] Yet they stopped far short of the conclusion that mankind was therefore inevitably doomed to recurrent wars. Rather, international cooperation was still possible and worth the quest. In general, they advanced four explanations for resolving the apparent contradiction between their awareness of the persistence of international tensions and their continuing hopes for a peaceful world order.

First, the pacific-minded and a few other internationalists often blamed wars on a tiny minority of munitions makers and military men who, motivated by greed and glory, cleverly fabricated war scares and promoted wars.[29] Second, peace workers emphasized moral education. Assuming the individual had a moral sense and a capacity for reason, they stressed education as vitally important in developing these qualities. Proper education, they believed, could overcome man's ignorance, the major reason for his deviation from moral rectitude. Despite different emphases in educational philosophy, all asserted the primacy of the educator's moral function.[30] Third, they all believed that permanent international machinery would restrain man's passions and thereby reduce the chances for war. Once nations established arbitral tribunals, commissions of inquiry and especially a world court, then international controversies could be removed from the potentially wrathful populace and placed in the hands of cool-headed, impartial administrators. While promoting international agreements requiring submission of almost all kinds of controversies to the appropriate agency, in practice they accepted almost any agreement as a positive step in the long-range goal of world organization.[31]

An imposing obstacle to the implementation of permanent international institutions, however, was the reluctance of governments to relinquish their freedom of action to international agencies. Many peace advocates, especially the legalists, seemed to understand the practical difficulties, but on the whole the peace workers minimized t h e m . R e f l ecting their faith in enlightened leadership, they believed that a few statesmen understood the advantages of such agencies and could establish them without waiting for the education and conversion of world public opinion. The negotiation of many arbitration and conciliation treaties as well as the nations' acceptance in principle of a court of arbitral justice seemed to suggest that many statesmen were already interested in. developing peacekeeping machinery.

They further argued that there was no need to invent institutional arrangements, for the American Constitution provided the perfect model for world organization. Accepting unquestioningly the superiority of the American federal system, many peace advocates naively assumed it could function effectively on an international scale. Minimizing the differences between the cultural and political harmony of the American experience and the anarchistic condition of world politics, these advocates of peace extended the analogy of the American judiciary, legislature and executive to the international sphere.[32] The international reformers' confidence in American political institutions further underscored the limits of their internationalism. While thinking they were internationalists, their faith in the unique blessings of the American experience indicated a distinct though often unconscious nationalist loyalty as well. Instead of advancing a reasoned and full-scale critique of the excessive nationalism of their day, almost all peace workers assumed that national rivalries would be a reality until foreign leaders came to adopt American values and institutions. In this way peace workers held out vague hopes for world peace in the future without risking much, if any, of their present prestige or respectability.

The peace workers foresaw no difficulties in looking to the future for vindication of their movement because, fourth and most commonly, they always linked morality to progress. They assumed that progress was a natural force operating automatically in human affairs. While they differed in the emphasis they gave to the desirability and direction of progressive currents, they all shared this faith in moral progress. Those inclining toward pacifism believed that moral progress was at work throughout the world. As evidence of this advance, they often cited the decline of major wars among Western nations in the modern era.[33] Others, more restrained and less humanistic, stressed the slow, steady enlightenment of the great powers. Marburg, for instance, believed that only the Western nations were agents of progress. Butler was more vague but emphasized that the movement toward the organization of the world was as "sure as that of an Alpine glacier."[34]

The peace workers also explained progress in material terms. As the movement acquired a "practical" outlook, the pacifists' attacks on war as murderous and therefore immoral declined, while they increasingly joined with their friends in the peace movement in opposing war because it was destructive of material comforts and generally wasteful. They also agreed with them in deploring the high costs of war preparations, which burdened the populace with taxes and restricted the funds available for programs of human betterment. Yet they refused to accept militarism as a growing evil of modern life. Rather, they regarded it as an anachronistic survival of an earlier, unenlightened era and as incompatible with modern industrialism.[35] Citing the enormous productivity unleashed by the industrial revolution and the resulting expansion of international trade, they viewed these developments as essentially beneficent. Commercial intercourse brought the business interests closer together, hastened the development of international amity and facilitated the movement toward the federation of the world.[36] It was no accident that businessmen began to flock to peace meetings in these years, for they fully shared both the peace leaders' elitism and their faith in material progress. They warmly praised arbitration treaties as tangible manifestations of the rational, businesslike approach to international relations, and they characterized war as harmful to the material prosperity of all nations.[37]

With such a sturdy faith in moral and material progress it was inevitable that the longer world peace prevailed the stronger were the peace workers' convictions that the day of permanent peace was within their grasp. Superficial signs of progress toward their goal, especially the proliferation of international conferences and arbitration treaties, the conversion of Presidents Taft and Wilson to their high-minded aims, the reaction against the large-navy forces in Congress and the growing acceptance of the peace movement among the educated classes nourished their confidence in the future of the movement. The desire for "peace" became so infectious that even the leading boosters of the Navy League felt it advisable to proclaim their strong opposition to war.[38] Susceptible to words and gestures which provided more than a glimmer of hope for the future, a few peace leaders looked forward to the day when their movement would achieve victory.[39]

Actually, most peace workers did not think in terms of the imminent millennium, for they had frequently traveled in Europe and regularly corresponded with their trans-Atlantic counterparts on the European situation, and realized that the recurrent European crises had increased the existing tensions between the rival alliance systems to the point where a future clash between them might quickly precipitate a general war. They also recognized that the Balkan wars had led to a resurgence of the military spirit and war propaganda throughout Europe.[40] But if these peace leaders understood the immediate dangers to the European peace, only Trueblood predicted the likelihood of a major war. All the other advocates of peace, perhaps unconsciously unwilling to question their faith in inevitable progress, repressed their deeper fears about the European situation.[41]

The aftermath of Sarajevo seriously tested the superficial unity of the entire movement. For some of those most emotionally committed to the cause, the shock of war was traumatic. Carnegie, Trueblood and Edwin Mead fell seriously ill in 1915 and there is evidence that their illnesses were as much psychosomatic as physical in origin.[42] Not all the peace workers suffered so unhappily, although the World War undermined their most optimistic assumptions about world politics and forced a painful reassessment of their approaches to peace questions.

V

The American peace movement did not entirely collapse after 1914, but the pressures of the war brought to the surface its internal weaknesses. The failure of the peace workers was not their inability to prevent the European bloodbath which was beyond their control. They failed in the first place because of their optimistic and rather shallow assumptions about world politics. Surely they placed too much faith in the rationality of man, were too confident in their reliance on moral education, overestimated the applicability of American values and institutions and underestimated the importance of national self-interest and power in international relations. Moreover, in emphasizing inevitable progress, the peace workers tolerated the *status quo* in international life while still holding out hope for a gradual evolution toward a peaceful world order. Such talk tended to gloss over the real and menacing international problems of their day. In particular, while disliking excessive nationalism, they advanced neither trenchant nor persistent critiques of it. Even the few criticisms of the military and armament interests failed to probe deeply into the virulent imperial and national rivalries which fostered the armament race. Moreover, if all the peace advocates disagreed with the ultranationalists' emphasis on national power and prestige as the legitimate ends of foreign policy, they expressed a sense of mission which they could invoke to justify the forceful application of American ideals of peace, freedom and justice on an aberrant Europe. As the pressures for American involvement in the European conflict increased, only the most pacific-minded consistently resisted the temptation to approve military intervention as a prerequisite for obtaining an American version of international order.

It is important, however, to place the failure of the peace advocates in proper historical perspective. One should remember that they lived in an age far removed from the intense ideological conflicts and cataclysmic wars of post-1914 generations. Theirs was a confident era when all kinds of reform really seemed possible. Given this hopeful atmosphere in American domestic life and Americans' inexperience in world affairs, it is understandable why the peace leaders often made strained analogies between American values and institutions and international reform. Moreover, the peace advocates were not dismissed as eccentrics by the American public but represented part of a larger cultural elite which assumed moral progress and which thought in abstract, if not idealistic terms. If one insists upon the validity of moral judgments in history, then it is better to view the peace movement within the broader context of the inadequacies of that entire culture.[43]

The elitist assumptions which the peace leaders shared with other leaders in America also account for the weaknesses of the pre-war peace movement. Although most of the earliest leaders consistently expressed a concern for human values, they reflected to a lesser extent the conscious elitism of many of the later recruits. In consequence, despite its growth the prewar peace movement never developed meaningful contacts with movements for social and political change. Its rhetoric reflected this elitism. While it was always lofty in tone, it became less warmly humanistic and more coldly intellectual. Its idealistic message could arouse the interest of high-minded individuals in the peace movement, but because it expressed no urgent social message it could not sustain the active involvement of a reform-minded generation in the cause.

Even if the peace workers had surmounted their class biases, it is doubtful whether they would have aroused much more public commitment to the cause before 1914. During a time of peace and isolation as well as of a predominant interest in domestic reform, it would have been difficult to win over large numbers of people to the peace movement. Given the paucity of public commitment to their programs, perhaps they were wise in accepting the reality of the nation-state and in cultivating the educated elite and political leaders to their long-range goal of a peaceful world order. A unified and concerted effort among peace leaders might have converted American and perhaps European statesmen to a workable formula for world order.

But they could not agree on a formula. Beyond a tenuous agreement on general values and a common desire for world peace, they differed fundamentally on the specific details for the realization of their goal. The pacific-minded, federationists and legalists disagreed on the proper means to the idealistic end. As long as relative peace lasted, they were able to minimize their differences. But the World War intensified interest in international institutions and soon compelled the peace leaders to define more explicitly their peace proposals for the postwar world. The war especially necessitated a thorough discussion of the thorny question of sanctions in any authoritative international body. The world federationists endorsed the use of force against nations which refused to submit their international disputes to arbitration or conciliation; but the legalists insisted upon adequate rules of law, a world court and a general agreement among nations on the specific powers of the court as pre-requisites to any forceful sanctions; and some inclining toward pacifism opposed all sanctions.[44]

When the peace advocates began to realize their divergent views after 1914, they gradually reorganized their movement into several autonomous organizations, each of which more clearly defined its priorities and programs. While these new groups helped to encourage President Wilson's growing interest in the principles for a new international order after the war, none had sufficient influence to convert him to a specific formula. Perhaps aware of the lack of harmony on the details of world organization, Wilson felt little compulsion to adopt any one of their plans. At the same time it is not surprising that Wilson's proposals for an international organization should fail to receive the undivided support of peace workers once they began to consider the specific features of the proposed League of Nations.[45]

NOTES

1. General accounts of the movement for these years *are* A. C. F. Beales, *The History of Peace: A Short Account of the Organized Movements for International Peace* (New York, 1931), ch. 10; Merle Curti, *Peace or War: The American Struggle, 1636-1936* (New York, 1936), chs. 6, 7; Ruhl J. Bartlett, *The League to Enforce Peace* (Chapel Hill, 1944), ch. 1; Robert Endicott Osgood, *Ideals and Self-Interest in America's Foreign Relations; The Great Transformation of the Twentieth Century* (Chicago, 1953), ch. 5; and Barbara S. Kraft, "Peacemaking in the Progressive Era: A Prestigious and Proper Calling," *Maryland Historian*, I (Fall, 1970), 121-144. A study focusing on religious pacifists is Peter Brock, *Pacifism in the United States: From the Colonial Era to the First World War* (Princeton, 1968), chs. 21-28. Important biographical studies which also cover the World War years include Merle E. Curti, *Bryan* and *World Peace*, in Smith *College Studies in History*, XVI (April-July, 1931); John C. Farrell, *Beloved Lady: A History of Jane Addams Ideas on Reform and Peace* (Baltimore, 1967); Philip C. Jessup, Elihu Root (2 vols. New York, 1988); and Warren F. Kuehl, *Hamilton Holt: Journalist, Internationalist, Educator* (Gainesville, Fla., 1960). Two recent studies of internationalists are Sondra R. Herman, *Eleven Against War: Studies in American Internationalist Thought, 1898-1921* (Stanford, 1969); and Warren F. Kuehl, *Seeking World Order: The United States and International Organization to 1920* (Nashville, Tenn., 1969).

46

2. This paper will focus almost exclusively on thirty-six leaders of the American peace movement. Admittedly, any list in such a large movement is somewhat arbitrary, and scholars' interpretations of the movement will differ considerably as long as they fail to agree on a definition of a peace worker. For instance, Michael Arnold Lutzker, "The 'Practical' Peace Advocates: An Interpretation of the American Peace Movement, 1898-1917" (unpublished Ph.D. dissertation, Rutgers University, 1969), 235-268, lists fifty-three individuals, only sixteen of whom appear in my list. Lutzker's sample differs from my own primarily because he focuses almost exclusively on the so-called practical peace workers, most of whom were tardy recruits and who managed the wealthier peace organizations, especially the Carnegie Endowment for International Peace. As Lutzker admits (p. 229), in 1910 at least "twelve trustees of the Carnegie Endowment had no prior institutional connection with the peace movement," yet he includes some of them in his sample. My main standard in selecting the thirty-six was active participation in the peace movement for most if not all of these years. Indexes for determining regularity of involvement were long-term membership in peace or internationalist organizations and/or fairly consistent participation at peace congresses in the United States. Those who participated in the peace movement only marginally or for brief periods have not been included. By these standards the thirty-six, listed alphabetically, were: Jane Addams, Fannie Fern Andrews, Hannah J. Bailey, Samuel J. Barrows, Richard Bartholdt, Charles E. Beals, Raymond L. Bridgman, William Jennings Bryan, Nicholas Murray Butler, Arthur Deerin Call, Andrew Carnegie. Samuel Train Dutton, Edwin Ginn, Edward Everett Hale, Hamilton Holt, William L. Hail, Charles E. Jefferson, Jenkin Lloyd Jones, David Starr Jordan, George W. Kirchwey, Louis P. Lochner, Reim Ann Lockwood, Alfred H. Love, Frederick Lynch, Theodore Marburg, Edwin D. Stead, Lucia Ames Mead, George W. Nasmyth, Robert That Paine, Elihu Root, James Brown Scott, May Wright Sewall, William H. Short, James L. Slavden, Albert K. Smiley and Benjamin F. Trueblood.

3. Twenty-one were involved in the peace and/or anti-imperialist movement before 1900: Addams, Bailey, Barrows, Bridgman, Bryan, Carnegie, Ginn, Hale, Hull, Jefferson, Jones, Jordan, Lockwood, Love, Edwin and Lucia Mead, Paine, Sewall, Slayden, Smiley and Trueblood. Only Smiley failed to question McKinley's foreign policies between 1898 and 1900.

4. For evidence of peace workers' statements opposing the Spanish-American War, imperialism and navalism see Trueblood, "Present Dangers of Territorial Acquisition," *American Friend,* V (July 7, 1898), 632-633; Love's account in *Peacemaker,* XVI (May, 1898), 206-215; Mrs. Lockwood in *ibid.,* XVII (December, 1898), 111.114; Jordan, *Imperial Democracy: A Study of the Relation of Government by the People, Equality before the Law, and Other Tenets of Democracy to the Demands of a Vigorous Foreign Policy and Other Demands of Imperial Dominion* (New York, 1899); [Edwin Mead] "Editor's Table," *New England Magazine,* XVIII, new series (May, 1898), 385-392; Bridgman, *"Brute or Man—The Annexation Problem," ibid.,* XIX, new series (September, 1898), 82.93; Isabel C. Barrows, *A Sunny Life: The Biography of Samuel June Barrows* (Boston, 1913), 151-154; Addams, "Democracy or Militarism," in Central Anti-imperialist League, *The Chicago Liberty Meeting Held at Central Music Noll, April 30, 1899. Liberty Tract, No. I* (Chicago, 1899), 35-39. Robert L. Beisner, *Twelve Against Empire: The Anti-Imperialists, 1898-1900* (New York, 1968), ch. 8, interprets Carnegie's opposition. Also see *Washington Wife: Journal of Ellen Maury Slayden from 1897-1919* (New York, 1963), 16; Slayden's statements, Congressional *Record,* 56th Cong., lst sess., XXXIII (May 7, 1900), 5233-5284, and (May 15, 1900), 5549-5552; the petitions of Ginn, Bailey, and other friends, of peace in ibid., 55th Cong., 3rd sess., XXXII (December 12, 1898), 90.

5. Nasmyth, address, *Report of the Fifteenth Annual Meeting of the Lake Mohonk Conference on International Arbitration, May 19th, 20th, and 21st, 1909* (Albany, N.Y., 1909), 150-152. (Hereafter cited as *Lake Mohonk Conference,* with the year of the conference added.) Lochner, address, *Lake Mohonk Conference, 1910,* 185-188; Call, address, *Lake Mohonk Conference, 1919, 34-38.*

6. Carnegie, *A League of Peace: A Rectorial Address Delivered to the Students in the University of St. Andrews, 17th October, 1905* (Boston, 1906), 32-37; [Holt] "A World Legislature," *Independent*, LVII (July 7, 1904), 46-47; Bartholdt, "The Parliament of Nations," *ibid.*, LVIII (May 11, 1906), 1025-1026; Bridgman, *World Organization* (Boston, 1906), esp. 41-70.

7. For the fullest evidence of differences on military preparedness see the discussions in *Lake Mohonk Conference, 1906,* 21-38; *Lake Mohonk Conference, 1907,* 128.142; *Lake Mohonk Conference, 1908,* 150. Root was simultaneously an officer of the Navy League and president of the Carnegie Endowment, and several members of the New York Peace Society also were members of the Navy League.

8. Butler, address, *Lake Mohonk Conference, 1907,* 16-17; Kirchwey, address, *ibid.,* 181-182; Root's speeches, "The Hague Peace Conferences," April 15, 1907, and *"The* Importance of Judicial Settlement," December 15, 1910, *Addresses on International Subjects,* ed. Robert Bacon and James Brown Scott (Freeport, N.Y., 1969 edition), 140-142, 148-150; Scott, address, *Proceedings of International Conference, Under the Auspices of American Society for Judicial Settlement of International Disputes, December 15-17, 1910, Washington, D.C.* (Baltimore, 1911?), 3-4; Marburg, address, *Proceedings of Second National Conference, American Society for Judicial Settlement of International Disputes, Cincinnati, Ohio, November 7-8, 1911* ed. Theodore Marburg (Baltimore, 1912?), 84-85. Cf. Lockwood, *Discussion, American Society for Judicial Settlement of International Deputes,* 1910, 99-100; "Is Arbitration a Failure" *Advocate of Peace,* LXXIII (January, 1911), 3-4; Call, "The Friendly Composition of International Disputes," *ibid.,* LXXVI (March, 1914), 61-62.

9. Kirchway, address, Lake *Mohonk Conference,* 1910, 95-96; *Marburg, address, American Society for Judicial Settlement of International Disputes,* 1911, 81-82; Scott, "The Constructive Peace Movement," *World ToDay,* XXI (February, 1912), 1789-1792; Root, "Nobel Peace Prize Address" [1914], and "The Sanction of International Law," April 24, 1908, *Addresses on International Subjects*, 157, 25-32.

10. Bridgman, *The First Book of World Law: A Compilation of the International Conventions to Which the Principal Nations Are Signatory, With a Survey of Their Significance* (Boston, 1911), 283-284.

11. Kuehl, *Seeking World Order,* 118, 152, 166.

12. Addams, *Newer Ideals of Peace* (New York, 1907); Jones to Addams, Oct. 12, 1912, and Jordan to Addams, Nov. 25, 1912, both in the Jane Addams Papers, Swarthmore College Peace Collection, Box 4.

13. Root and Butler, both conservative Republicans, were barely able to tolerate Bryan. Also see *Autobiography of Andrew Carnegie* (New York, 1920), 364. Other peace leaders either disliked his erratic behavior on the issue of imperialism or his "radical" domestic proposals but later praised his conciliation treaties as Secretary of State. Jordan to Bryan, Feb. 7, 1900, William Jennings Bryan Papers, Manuscript Division, Library of Congress, Box 24; and Jordan to Jessie Jordan, Apr. 29, 30, 1913, David Starr Jordan Peace Correspondence, Hoover Institution on War, Revolution, and Peace, Stanford University, Box 1. Also, *Peacemaker*, XIX (November, 1900), 105; Dutton to Bryan, July 24, 1913, United States Department of State Papers, National Archives, Record Group 43, 500.A3/15; Curti, *Bryan and World Peace*, 150-152.

48

14. Peter Filene, "The World Peace Foundation and Progressivism, 1910-1918," *New England Quarterly*, XXXVI (December, 1963), 484-491.

15. David S. Patterson, "Andrew Carnegie's Quest for World Peace," *Proceedings of* the *American Philosophical Society*, CXIV (October 20, 1970), esp. 379-382.

16. For an extremely inclusive definition of the peace movement see Lynch, "The Leaders of the New Peace Movement in America," *Independent*, LXXIX (September 28, 1910), *629-638.* Mead, "Peace Trustees and the Armament Crass," *Unity*, LXX (October 3, 1912), 72-74; New York Peace Society, *Year Book, 1910-1911 (n.p., n.d.)*, 22.

17. For periodic international congresses see the memorial of the American Peace Society presented to the Massachusetts House of Representatives, reproduced in *Lake Mohonk Conference, 1903*, 137-140; an this and other areas of agreement, see the platforms of the Lake Mohonk Conferences for the years 1901, 1904, and 1906 to 1914. Also, Kuehl, *Seeking World Order*, 104-106, 112, 214-116, 171.

18. The findings of the social backgrounds of the peace workers in the following three notes come from Allen Johnson, Dumas Malone and Richard Livingston Schuyler, eds., *Dictionary of American Biography* (22 vols., New York, 1928-1938); *Who Was Who in* America *(3 vols.,* Chicago, 1943-1960); *The National Cyclopedia of American Biography (62 vols.,* New York, 1898 1967); and biographies, memoirs and autobiographies of individual peace workers.

19. Of the twenty-three in professions, Barrows, Beals, Hale, Jefferson, Jones, Lynch and Short were ministers; Bryan, Gino, Kirchwey; Lockwood, Marburg, Paine, Root and Scott were lawyers; and Butler, Call, Dutton, Jordan, Mead, Nasmyth, Smiley and Trueblood had obtained higher degrees in the liberal arts or education. Bridgman and Holt also attended graduate school for two years but received no degrees; both became journalists.

20. Between 1909 and 1914, the following peace workers had died: Barrows (1909), Hale (1909), Paine (1910), Smiley (1913), Love (1918) and Ginn (1914). Of the surviving thirty in 1914, only Bailey, Jordan, Sewall, Bryan, Bartholdt and Slayden did not live in one of these six cities, although the latter two as congressmen and Bryan as Secretary of State technically resided in Washington, D.C.

21. Bailey's father was a minister, Smiley, Trueblood, Hull and Nasmyth had Quaker parents; Ginn, Mead, Dutton, Addams and Bryan bad thought seriously of the ministry or church service as a career; and Barrows, Beals, Hale, Jefferson, Jones, Lynch and Short became clergymen. In addition, Mrs. Lockwood's second husband was a minister.

22. Charles Herbert Levermore, *Samuel Train Dutton: A Biography* (New York, 1932), 80-83, 91, *97.* Author's interview with Short's son, Frederick W. Short, February 13, 1969.

23. The Twentieth Century Club of Boston, 1894-1904 (n.p,, n.d.), 3-4, 13-16, *21;* Levermore, *Dutton*, 51, 81; Lynch, *The One Great Society: A Book of Recollections* (New York, 1918), 3-5, 11-15; Edson L. Whitney, *The American Peace* Society: A Centennial *History* (Washington, D.C., 1928), 271.

24. Butler to Dutton, Jan. 21, 1908, New York Peace Society Papers, Swarthmore College Peace Collection, Box 2; Levermore, Dutton, 90-91; and Ellen Slayden, *Washington Wife*, 189-190. A few critics occasionally pointed out the elitism of the movement. Bartholdt, remarks, *Proceedings of the Second National Peace Congress, Chicago, May 2 to 5, 1909*, ed. Charles E. Beals (Chicago, 1909), 327; Lucia Mead, address, *Book of the Fourth Americans Peace Congress, St. Louis, May 1,*

2, 3, 1913, ed. Walter B. Stevens (St. Louis, 1913), 376.377; and John Haynes Holmes to Short, Jan. 27, 1914, New York Peace Society Papers, Box 4. Far attacks by immigrants, laborers and Socialists on the peace leadership see A. M. Simon's ointments, *Survey,* XXII (May 22, 1909), 279; New York *Times,* December 13, 1911, p. 1, mi. 8, p. 2, col. 1; and Vincent St. John, "The Working Class and War," *International Socialist Review,* XV (August, 1914), 117.

25. Dutton, address, *Proceedings of* the *Third American Peace Congress* held in Baltimore, Maryland, May 3 to *6, 1911,* ed., Eugene A. Noble (Baltimore, 1911), 335; Lynch, *The Peace Problem: The Task of the Twentieth Century* (New York, 1911), III; Mead, "The Literature of the Peace Movement," *World Peace Foundation, Pamphlet Series,* No. 7, Part IV (October, 1912), 1-14; Jordan to Ginn, Feb. 3, 1912, David Starr Jordan Papers, Supplementary Correspondence, Hoover Institution on War, Revolution, and Peace, Stanford University; Lochner, address, *Lake Mohonk Conference, 1910,* 188. The perceptive analysis of Carnegie's shameless hero worship of political leaders in Joseph Frazier Wall, *Andrew Carnegie* (New York, 1970), 914ff, can be applied to a lesser degree to all peace workers.

26. Bridgman, *The Master Idea* (Boston, 1899), 212-228; Trueblood, "The Historic Development of the Peace Idea," June, 1900, *The Development of the Peace Idea and Other Essays,* ed. Edwin D. Mead (Boston, 1992), 1-35; Mead, address, *Official Report of the Thirteenth Universal Peace Congress, Held at Boston, Massachusetts, U.S.A., October Third to Eighth, 1904,* ed., Benjamin F. Trueblood (Boston, 1904), 31-33; Holt, typescript, The Federation of the World [1907-1914], 3-4, 7, 26-27, Hamilton Halt Papers, Mills Memorial Library, Rollins College Box 91; Hull, "The New Peace Movement: A Series of Addresses delivered in 1908-1909," *Swarthmore College Bulletin,* VII (September, 1909), 25.32; Beal., *The Higher Soldiership* (Chicago, 1912), 20, 23ˉ29; Lucia Mead, *Swords and Ploughshares, or The Supplanting of the System of War by the System of Law* (New York, 1912), 1-12.

27. Marburg, "The Backward Nation," *Independent,* LXXII (June 20, 1912) 1365-1370; Smiley, address, *Lake Mohonk Conference, 1909,* 9ˉ10; Butler, address, 24-25; Dutton, address, *Lake Mohonk Conference, 1912,* 24-25.

28. Slayden, address, *Lake Mohonk Conference, 1906,* 60; Holt, *Federation of the World,* 1; Kirchwey, address, *Lake Mahonk Conference, 1908,* 75; Beals, *Higher Soldiership,* 10-11; Root, "Nobel Peace Prize Address," *Addresses on International Subjects,* 156-157.

29. "The Menace of the Navy," *Advocate of Peace,* LXVI (May, 1904), 77-78; Jefferson, "The New Navy," *Independent,* LVII (October 27, 1904), 972-974; Lucia Mead, "The Gentle Art of Making Enemies," *Advocate of Peace,* LXVIII (December, I906), 250-251; Jones, address, *National Peace Congress, 1909,* 308-815; Mead, address, *Report of the Proceedings of the New England Arbitration and Peace Congress,* Hartford and New Britain, *May 8 to 11, 1910,* ed. James L. Tryon (Boston, 1910), 105.107; [Holt] "Armament Scandals," *Independent,* LXXIV (May 1, 1915), 946; Slayden, "The Traffickers in War," *Farm and Ranch,* XXXII (November 22, 1913), 4-5; Jordan, *War and Waste; A Series of Discussions of War and* War *Accessories* (Garden City, N.Y., 1913), 52.89; Ginn, address, Lake Mohonk *Conference, 1913,* 24.

30. Bryan, address, *Proceedings of the National Arbitration and Peace Congress,* New York, April 14th to 17th, 1907, ed. Robert Erskine Ely (New York, 1907), 393-394; Lynch, *Peace Problem,* 120-127; Luda Mead, address, *Lake Mohonk Conference, 1902,* 64-65; Mead to Carnegie, Mar. 27, 1905, Edwin and Lucia Mead Papers, Swarthmore College Peace Collection, Box 1; Dutton, *Social Phases of Education in the School and the Home* (New York, 1900), 73-75, 140, 194-197, 236-237; First Annual Report of the American School Peace League (Boston, 1909), 28; Jordan and Edward Benjamin Krebbiel, Syllabus of Lectures on International Con-

ciliation, Given at Leland Stanford Junior University (Boston, 1912), esp. 133-143; Hull, "New Peace Movement," 50-51; Butler, address, *Lake Mohonk Conference, 1909*, 17-18; and Ginn, address, *Lake Mohonk Conference, 1913*, 26-29. For two students' acceptance of these values see Nasmyth, "The Peace Movement in the Colleges," *Independent*, LXVIII (February 7, 1910), 362-365; Lochner, "The Cosmopolitan Club Movement," *International Conciliation*, No. 61 (December, 1912).

31. *Address of* Hon. Richard Bartholdt, *President of the American Group*, at *the XIII Conference of the Interparliamentary Union at Brussels*, Aug. 29, *1903*, printed speech, Richard Bartholdt Paper, Missouri Historical Society; Scott, address, *Lake Mohonk Conference, 1910*, 71; Holt, "A World Legislature," 41.

32. Trueblood, address, *Lake Mohonk Conference, 1895, 9;* Hale, "The United States of Europe," *The Peace Crusade*, I (March 8, 1899), 5; Root, "Instructions to the American Delegates to the Hague Conference," May 81, 1907, in James Brown Scott, *The Hague Peace Conferences of 1899* and *1907* (2 vols., Baltimore, 1909), II, 191; Lucia Mead, address, National *Peace Congress, 1909*, 257; Butler, address, *Lake Mohonk Conference, 1910*, 20; Marburg, address, *ibid.*, 86-87; Holt, address, American *Peace* Congress, *1911*, 7-9.

33. Jordan to Ginn, Feb. 3, 1912, Jordan Papers, Supplementary Correspondence; Bryan, address, *Lake Mohonk Conference, 1910*, 166; Mead, address, *National Peace Congress, 1909*, 306; Paine, address, *Universal Peace Congress, 1904*, 34-86; Smiley, address, *Lake* Mohonk *Conference, 1917*, 17-21. On the decline of wars, see Hale, address, *Lake* Mohank *Conference, 1899*, 10-11; "Will War Ever Be Altogether Abolished?" *Advocate of Peace*, LXVII (Slay, 1905), 93; Lucia Mead, A *Primer of the Peace Movement* (Boston, 1905), [2]; Holt, "Federation of the World," 7; Mead, address, *National Peace Congress, 1909*, 41-42; Beals, address, *American Peace Congress, 1913*, 179-180.

34. Marburg, "Backward Nation," 1365-1368; Butler's addresses, *Lake Mahonk Conference, 1909*, 19, *and Lake Mohonk Conference, 1910*, 23. Also, Root, "Nobel Peace Prize Address," *Addresses on International Subjects*, 159-174.

35. "Battleships and Universities," *Advocate of Peace*, LX (August-September, 1898), 175; Hale, address, *Lake Mohonk Conference, 1899*, 12; Butler, address, *Lake Mohonk Conference, 1909*, 18-19; Slayden, "Millions Wasted for War," *Farm and Ranch*, XXXI (March 9, 1912), 1, and "What Armed Peace Costs the Nations," *ibid.*, XXXII (December 6, 1919), 5-6.

36. "Commerce a Peacemaker," *Peacemaker*, XXIV (March, 1903), 52-53; Bridgman, *First Book of World Law*, 299-300, 306-307, and *World Organization*, 82-86; Beals, *Higher Soldiership*, 20; Hull, *The New Peace Movement* (Boston, 1912), 44; Lucia Mead, *Swords and Ploughshares*, 481; Trueblood, "War A Thing of the Past," *Cosmopolitan Student*, I (April, 1910), 49-50.

37. See, for example, the addresses in *Lake Mohonk Conference, 1906*, 85-123; and the businessmen's bulletins, "Obligatory Arbitration and Business," and "The Business Man and International Law," *Lake Mohonk Conference, 1911*, 186, 188-189. The writings of Norman Angell, a British peace worker, bolstered the peace leaders' hopes that nationalism was declining and war was becoming outmoded. See his *The Great Illusion: A Study of the Relation of Military Power in the Nations to Their Economic and Social Advantage* (London, 1910). For the influence of Angell's views, see *After All: The Autobiography of Norman Angell (Lon*don, 1951), 147-158; Jordan, "Bankers as Peace Guardians," *World ToDay*, XXI (February, 1912), 1786-1789; and Luria Mead, *Swords and Ploughshares*, 139-152.

38. Harold and Margaret Sprout, *The Rise of American Naval Power, 1776-1918* (Princeton, 1939), 266-290, 308-309; David S. Patterson, "The Travail of the American Peace Movement, 1887-1914" (unpublished Ph.D. dissertation, University of California, Berkeley, 1968), 338-346. Arthur Henry Dadmun (field secretary of the Navy League), address, *American Peace Congress, 1913*, 234; and Jonathan Daniels, *The End of Innocence* (Philadelphia, 1954), 115.

39. Bryan's speech, quoted in *The Commoner*, Mar. 8, 1912, p. 3, col. 1; cf. *New* York Times, Dec 11, 1913, p. 1, col. 6. Also, Arthur L. Weatherly, discussion, *American Peace Congress, 1913*, 150; Beals, address, *ibid.*, 194; and John Wesley Hill, address, *ibid.* 380.

40. The International Peace Bureau Papers, United Nations Library, Geneva, and the Bertha von Suttner-Alfred Fried Correspondence, United Nations Library, Geneva, contain much correspondence between American and European peace workers. Also see Mead, "England and Germany," *Atlantic Monthly*, CI (March, 1908), 399-407; Jefferson, "The Delusion of Militarism," *ibid.*, CIII (March, 1909), 379-388; Kirchwey, address, *Lake Mohonk Conference, 1909*, 30-38; Carnegie, "A Silver Lining to War Clouds," *World ToDay*, XXI (February, 1912), 1793; Butler, address, Lake Mohonk *Conference, 1912*, 14-15; Lynch, "Peace and War in 1913," *Yale Review*, III, new series (January, 1914), 272-284; Nasmyth to Mead, Mar. 29/Apr. 11, 1913, Mead Papers, Box 1; Dutton, address, *Lake Mohonk Conference, 1914*, 80-84; and Jordan's report, "The World Peace Foundation: Work In 1914," *World Peace Foundation, Pamphlet Series*, IV, No. 7 (December, 1914), 23-24.

41. Jordan, "The Impossible *War*," *Independent*, LXXIV (February 27, 1913), 467-468; Addams, "Peace on Earth," *Ladies Home Journal*, XXX (December, 1913), 27; Nasmyth to Mead, Apr. 24, 1913, Mead Papers, Box 1; and Trueblood, *89th Annual Report of the Directors of the American Peace Society, 1915* (Boston, 1918), 15-18.

42. Louise Whitfield Carnegie, preface to *Autobiography of Andrew Carnegie*, v; "Secretary Trueblood's Retirement," *Advocate of Peace*, LXXVII (May, 1915), 105; Beals, *Benjamin Franklin Trueblood—Prophet of Peace* (New York, 1916), 14-15; Lucia Mead to Miss Trueblood, Aug. 2, 1915, Mead Papers, Box 1; Lucia Mead to Jordan, Aug. 24, 1918, Jordan Peace Correspondence, Box 11; and Lucia Mead to Jane Addams, July 13, 1919, Addams Papers, Box 7.

43. Henry F. May, *The End of American innocence: A Study of the First Years of Our Own Time, 1912-1927* (New York, 1959), esp. 9-56, 396-398.

44. For a good case study of the dilemma over sanctions see Martin David Dubin, "Elihu Root and the Advocacy of a League of Nations, 1914-1917," *Western Political Quarterly*, XIX (September, 1966), 439-463; also Kuehl, *Seeking World Order*, 184-195, 205-211.

45. *Ibid.*, 213-231, 336-339. For other accounts of new groups founded after 1914 see Bartlett, *League to Enforce Peace*, 28-82; Marie Louise Degen, "The History of the Woman's Peace Party," *The Johns Hopkins University Studies in Historical and Political Science*, LVII, No. 3 (Baltimore, 1939), 11-191; and Charles Chatfield, *For Peace and Justice: Pacifism in America, 1914-1941* (Knoxville, Tenn., 1971), 15-41.

CHAPTER THREE

WORLD WAR I AND THE LIBERAL PACIFIST IN THE UNITED STATES

Charles Chatfield

Considered one of America's foremost historians of the American peace movement, Charles Chatfield, H. Orth Hirt Professor Emeritus, Wittenberg University, details the transformation of pacifism from mere opposition to war to a great concern for social reform. This essay, later expanded into his popular study, *For Peace and Justice: Pacifism in America, 1914-1941* (1971), dispels many of the myths surrounding the pacifist's lack of political realism. Chatfield explores the emergence of liberal pacifism that was aroused in the wake of World War One. Peace advocates were essentially internationalist, politically active, and, indeed, influential. They became instruments ushering in the "modern" peace movement. Largely focusing on the liberal pacifism of the Fellowship of Reconciliation, a religious organization created during the war, Chatfield explores how the progressive values of the period defined their pragmatic approach to choices involving the ultimate worth of the individual in society. In light of Chatfield's analysis, consider the following questions: How should political power be distributed in a society largely characterized by the concentration of economic wealth?; In what ways did socialist theories influence the liberal pacifist critique of war?; How did liberal pacifists begin to address the issue of force as an instrument for social control and, in the process, reject its violent means?

54

The meaning of the word pacifist changed under the pressure for patriotic conformity in 1917-18. Having had the benign connotation of one who advocated international cooperation for peace, it narrowed to mean one who would not support even a "war to end war." Pacifists were linked with draft dodgers, socialists, and communists, portrayed in hues from yellow to red; a rude inscription in the lobby of 70 Fifth Avenue in New York, where some pacifist groups were housed, read, "Treason's Twilight Zone."[1] The word was thenceforth plagued with double meaning, and more than one prowar peace advocate hastened to explain that "those who are now called 'pacifists' here do not include all or most of those who were called 'pacifists' before the war."[2] Later, when it was respectable to be against the war, the word sometimes was used in its original, broader sense, but it would be used by pacifists themselves, as it is used here, to designate those who worked for peace and refused to sanction any given war—absolute and religious but also selective and political objectors.[3] The narrowness of this definition masked a new dimension in the American peace movement.

There had been pacifists in the strict sense before World War I, but for the most part they had been sectarians motivated by obedience to religious injunctions against killing and against complying with the military. Their churches supplied most of the conscientious objectors in the Civil War and both world wars, but these were nonresistants obedient to the claims of religious faith and not challenging governmental authority or social policy except in the specific cases of their military service.[4]

If sectarians had eschewed social reform, few progressives had stressed the war question, and even fewer seriously considered conscientious objection to war service. Indeed, the prewar advocates of peace hardly sensed the possibility of divided loyalties. They assumed that war was anachronistic. Reason, embodied in arbitration and law, in treaties and international juridical institutions such as The Hague Court, would obviate recourse to war, In this respect peace advocates were internationalists, and so they liked to think of themselves. But with few exceptions they were solid nationalists as well, for they assumed that America's virtues were unique and her interests paramount. If the nation ever should go to war, they believed, its democratic politics and humanitarian traditions would guarantee its cause to be just and necessary.

These peace advocates either were directors of business and educational institutions or accepted such men as models. They gave their movement a literary, patriarchal, and elitist quality, and relied on education and discussion rather than political action. They operated the Carnegie Endowment for International Peace (founded in 1910), the World Peace Foundation (1910), the Church Peace Union (1914), the American School Peace League (1908), the American Peace Society (1828), and various other groups organized to promote study, friendship, and arbitration. They were established men who valued order and distrusted radical challenge to authority, successful men who assumed that progress was inevitable and who aimed at the further perfection of society.[5]

Sarajevo shattered the doctrine of perfection, at least as it applied to Europe. The established peace movement faltered and fell into disarray; by April 1917 most of its leaders had joined the war effort, determined to establish a universal peace along American lines. Accustomed to look for evil on the surface, not in the heart of man, they identified it with one nation—Germany. Peace was held at bay by Prussianism, they said; victory became the prerequisite of progress.[6]

Those who rejected this view and advanced alternatives to it were the wartime pacifists. They reorganized the American peace movement, giving it much of the structure, leadership, social concern, and rationale that would characterize it for over a generation. Where it had been educational and legalistic, the peace movement became political as well; where it had been polite it also became aggressive; where it had been conservatively Brahmin, it also acquired a socialist base; where it had assumed progress, it would claim only possibility. The movement remained divided--perpetually, it seems--between competing points of view and programs, but the wartime pacifists gave it vital leadership and broad social concern.

They brought to it an unresolved dilemma, too, for their experience imparted both a more radical view of society and an ethic of conflict that proscribed the use of violence for social change. No less committed to liberal values than were the intellectuals who stoutly defended the war, pacifists interpreted it differently. No less fervent in their opinions than the patriots, they were virtually isolated from public opinion. When they were subjected to social pressure to conform, pacifists came to distrust authoritarianism itself and to connect it in their minds with violence. That is one reason why their leftward movement stopped short of revolutionary socialism. Associating injustice with war, they hobbled the drive for social justice with a commitment to peace.

Liberal pacifists were the remnant of a peace coalition composed largely of progressives who viewed the war as a threat to the values for which they had worked. War must not come to America, they agreed; and, moreover, its very existence in Europe challenged that notion of an open-ended world of social possibility in which these problem-solvers believed. This war was no abstraction. It was a compelling problem, they insisted, and its solution required concerted social action. This was the response of Louis Lochner who, with the help of George Nasmyth and the American Peace Society, had organized the Cosmopolitan Club movement in American universities, the man who before 1914 had personified internationalism to thousands of college students. After the outbreak of war he left the American Peace Society, tried to refashion the Chicago Peace Society, and together with Jane Addams and others launched a National Peace Federation.[7] It was one of several new organizations federating liberal and peace forces that emerged from such centers of social reform as the Henry Street settlement house founded in New York by Lillian Wald. There social workers, clergy-men, educators, and publicists who were conscious of a bond of social concern they had formed in response to industrialism and urbanism met in response to war.[8]

When the Woman's Peace Party was founded in Washington on January 10, 1915, it was clear that advocacy of peace "provided a common ground upon which could meet American women from almost every important section of their organizational life."[9] The women quickly joined hands with their counterparts in Europe; together they developed a plan for a conference of neutral nations that would stand ready to clarify the war aims of belligerents and to negotiate peace. They sent emissaries to the belligerent leaders and tried to induce President Wilson to adopt their program. He seemed unresponsive, and so their diplomacy evolved into a commission of private citizens to which Henry Ford gave funds and publicity. Ridicule of Ford's Peace Expedition obscured the serious purpose of a significant nongovernmental international organization. Still, the women who promoted it had forged organizational links with civic and professional groups, connections that would survive the war. They brought new leadership into the peace movement and created a modern pressure group of a kind familiar to progressive reformers.

Meanwhile, some Quakers, social gospel clergymen, and YMCA leaders responded to the organization of religious pacifists in England when, on November 11,1915, they created the Fellowship of Reconciliation (FOR), which became the central body for religious objectors for the next half century.[10] Moreover, liberal journals such as the *Survey,* the *Independent,* and the *Nation* opened their pages to proposals for a neutral conference for peace in Europe and to arguments against preparations for war at home. Indeed, by the time the Ford project became a laughingstock, peace workers from Henry Street were bringing the progressive peace coalition to its culmination in the American Union Against Militarism.[11] Historically important for its large-scale antipreparedness campaign of April and May 1916 and for its role in preventing a full-scale war with Mexico in June, the American Union became a model for postwar peace lobbies, and from its ranks emerged both the Foreign Policy Association and the National Civil Liberties Bureau. Its leaders included many of those active in domestic reform and Progressive politics who feared that militant nationalism would sap social progress and frustrate open diplomacy and world federation. Throughout 1916 they supported Wilson with alternating reluctance and enthusiasm as he seemed to act against or speak for their principles.

In 1917 three events shook the progressive peace coalition and reduced it to pacifism. First, when Wilson severed relations with Germany in February, the American Union lost one of its most ardent members, the influential rabbi of New York's Free Synagogue, Stephen Wise. Antiwar leaders who had valued his example included Paul Kellogg, editor of the *Survey,* and Emily Balch, founder of the Denison House settlement in Boston and active in the Woman's Peace Party. They were stunned, but nonetheless participated heartily in a new Emergency Peace Federation to keep America out of war. Throughout the spring pacifists enlisted much popular support, but when in April the United States entered the war, prominent peace leaders, including David Starr Jordan, the chancellor of Stanford University, left their ranks.[12] Even so, they were encouraged by the fact that six senators and fifty representatives voted against the war resolution and by the opposition voiced by the Socialist party after the resolution passed. There was still some basis for hoping that they might influence public policy, and so pacifists created the People's Council of America for Peace and Democracy in order to advance civil liberties and democratic peace terms during the war. By September 1917, however, the council had aroused so much public opposition by criticizing conscription and defending the Russian Revolution that it did not seem useful to Lillian Wald, Paul Kellogg, and some others who had initiated the new peace coalition.

The American Union Against Militarism was divided during the summer by the efforts of some of its leaders to commit it to the cause of conscientious objectors. Three pacifists were particularly active: Roger Baldwin, who came to the staff from a position as secretary of the Civic League of St. Louis and who shortly organized the Civil Liberties Bureau; Norman Thomas, who was a socially concerned Presbyterian minister and who later joined the Socialist party because of his pacifist beliefs; and vivacious Crystal Eastman, an expert on the legal aspects of industrial accidents who was active in the women's suffrage campaign and the New York branch of the Woman's Peace Party and who with her brother Max later edited the antiwar *Liberator*. The membership of the American Union was at no time entirely pacifist in the strict sense, and these driving leaders threatened to undercut its constituent base and respectability.

On August 20, in the absence of Miss Wald, the executive board of the American Union voted to send delegates to the People's Constituent Assembly of the People's Council of America. She eventually resigned from the board; others followed, and the Union was shattered. It continued to exist in nominal fashion, but the National Civil Liberties Bureau separated itself on October 1, 1917, and thereafter the American Union Against Militarism operated largely on paper only. [13] During the war liberal pacifists affiliated with several other groups that have lasted over half a century: the Civil Liberties Bureau, the Fellowship of Reconciliation, the Woman's Peace Party and its successor, the Women's International League for Peace and Freedom, and the American Friends Service Committee (founded in 1917 to provide humanitarian alternatives to fighting).

In their opposition to the war the remnant of the progressive peace coalition was linked with literary radicals (including most of the staff of *The Masses)* and with those Socialists who supported the antiwar resolution that their party made in St. Louis on April 7, 1917. The party convention had been largely middle class in composition, and although its majority report was cast in the language of anticapitalism, it advocated a platform like those of the peace groups rather than a program of revolution or general strike.

These opponents of war were joined by new recruits who in the long run were most important of all, since they virtually staffed the pacifist movement after peace was re-established. They included, among others: A. J. Muste, a Congregational minister who subsequently became a leader in the labor and Trotskyite movements, chairman of the Fellowship of Reconciliation, and the symbol of radical pacifism to a cold-war generation; John Nevin Sayre, an Episcopal minister who was never far from the center of the International Fellowship of Reconciliation or its American branch; Evan Thomas, an out-standing conscientious objector of World War I and chairman of the War Resisters League during the Second World War; Kirby Page, a YMCA worker who became the most influential pacifist speaker and writer of the interwar period; Ray Newton, active in Quaker relief work, who later directed the Peace Section of the American Friends Service Committee; Frederick Libby, Florence Boeckel, and Dorothy Detzer, who operated an influential peace lobby in Washington during the thirties; Devere Allen, a student at Oberlin College who became the chief advocate of war resistance in the Socialist party; and the subsequent leader of that party, Norman Thomas.

Few of those converted to pacifism during the war had been active in peace groups before 1917, and they thought through the war question by themselves. They had not been active in domestic reforms, but they were, indeed, just discovering social problems--some through college experiences, some through church work, and others in the fresh idealism of the YMCA, then promoting international concern through the Student Volunteer Movement. In short, the young pacifists encountered World War I when they were coming of age socially, just as progressives of a previous generation had awakened to contemporary problems when they were choosing personal directions. It is hardly surprising that many of those whose pacifism commenced in the war years made peace work a vocation.

There were liberal pacifists of various hues, then, and their language and experiences differed significantly. The very corollary of conscience is, in the apt phrase of Rufus Jones, "a final farewell to uniformity," so that any analysis of the movement is hazardous.[14] Moreover, pacifists' ideas appear more coherent in retrospect than they did when first published, because ideas that we now analyze in terms of common postulates were first advanced polemically by persons whose lives were strikingly dissimilar. This is not to suggest that pacifists acted altogether rationally. Rather, they were drawn together in action through their similar interpretations of their various experiences. If the history of ideas is the story of men's reflections upon their experiences, then it is the study of what meaning they assigned to life; and meaning, if not life, has logical form. What pacifists had in common that set them apart from war supporters was neither a covert conspiracy nor any discernible personality or set of social characteristics. They shared, instead, a distinctive view of the war and a disposition to elevate that view into a matter of principle.

To begin with, pacifists accepted such liberal values of progressivism as the pragmatic approach to choices, the democratic process, and the ultimate worth of the individual. These were hardly more than loosely defined notions, but they implied at least the following: that decisions should be made in the light of consequences rather than of a priori rules and that the meaning of social institutions is found by experiencing them; that political power should be distributed in a society in which economic power is highly concentrated and that decision making should be broadly based; and that individuals are the ends for wham society is ordered. Sentiments like these can be found in a wide variety of objections to the war, even among the disparate arguments of socialists.

The leaders of the Fellowship of Reconciliation put their notion of human value in religious terms, agreeing with Norman Thomas that war is "absolutely opposed to Christ's way of love and His reverence for personality."[15] Although they did not define personality, they often referred to it in the sense of a man's total being and latent possibility. They rejected the notion of prowar clergymen that combat or even death could leave men undefiled, could even ennoble them. War immolates personalities, they said. In the oldest tradition of their faith, religious pacifists revolted "not only against the cruelty and barbarity of war, but even more against the reversal of human relationships which war implied."[16] The doctrines of love, fatherhood, and brotherhood and such symbols as the cross expressed the normative value of personality for pacifists. Their rhetoric would sound formal to a later generation, but to them it expressed a long-neglected doctrine of Christian faith, the fundamental worth of each individual in the sight of God.

If human personality was sacred to religious pacifists, it had nearly absolute value for some who stood on secular grounds as well. Roger Baldwin, the director of the National Civil Liberties Bureau, spoke for them. On trial for refusing to take the physical examination required in the draft, he said, "The compelling motive for refusing to comply with the Draft Act is my uncompromising opposition to the principle of conscription of life by the state for any purpose whatever, in time of war or peace."[17] At the same time, he felt an intense social concern.

As Norman Thomas explained shortly after the war, the individual is a "product of the group, but the group is only valuable as it permits personalities, not automatons to emerge."[18] Liberal pacifists, unlike Spencerian individualists, supported social reform, but, unlike those whose individualism derived from concepts of natural law, they believed that every man is of intrinsic value. Some of them reconciled individualism and socialism, for example, by assuming that man is essentially a social animal and that an individual's personality is most fully realized in altruistic impulses.

The sense of the individual was muted for most socialists by awareness of class, but even so they argued that the organized proletariat itself was "proclaiming the glad tidings of the coming emancipation," freedom from the tyranny of class over men.[19] Socialists were most strongly united against military conscription. A few supported it, to be sure. William English Walling accused his opponents of accepting conscription by foreign governments that they favored while "leaving America helpless."[20] On the contrary, most socialists who opposed conscription believed that "it robs the individual of freedom" and is "the readiest tool of the military class."[21] As Emily Balch wrote, "It means conscription of mind, hierarchical stratification of society, industrial discipline on [a] military model, obedience as the prime virtue."[22] Even those socialists who could support a war to save the country from militarism could not conceive of "militarism to save us from war."[23] The commitment to individual worth and freedom permeated the publications of pacifists of all political views. For many this commitment was in itself sufficient reason to refuse military service; for all it guaranteed the right of conscientious objection.

Objection to military service was interpreted as the right to dissent by many pacifists who regarded that right as a corollary to the democratic process of majority decision. Like abolitionists before them, the pacifists won support on civil liberties that they could not get on the war issue. The American Union Against Militarism had come into being largely in the vague apprehension that preparedness, conscription, and war would undermine the gains of the Progressive era.[24] Its programs and techniques expressed the progressive faith in the power of public opinion and in government responsible to the people. Woodrow Wilson expressed the same political faith even as he pressed for policies that distressed the pacifists. Even in February 1917 most members of the American Union's executive board preferred to leave foreign policy in Wilson's hands. Increasing numbers of pacifists became apprehensive as the administration geared up for war, although Crystal Eastman wrote in June of the president's wartime appointments:

It [is] as though he said to his old friends, the liberals, "I know you are disappointed in me—you don't understand my conversion to the draft—my demand for censorship. I have reasons, plans, intentions, that I can't tell you. But as guarantee of good faith I give you Baker and Keppel and Lippman and Creel, to carry out these laws. No matter how they look on paper, they cannot be Prussian in effect with such men to administer them."[25]

The guarantee was not sufficient. The National Civil Liberties Bureau and related organizations expanded their work rapidly, insisting that the civil rights of conscientious objectors to the war were linked to the democratic process itself; majority decision that rested on the suppression of minorities would be a thinly veiled tyranny. This was exactly the premise of those who wanted to keep the Bureau within the American Union in the fall of 1917. As Norman Thomas said, no other national group was prepared to fight for the "tolerance of minority ideas" that "is absolutely necessary for reasonable social progress."[26] Blatant persecution of dissenters aroused in Eugene Debs the fighting qualities that had been depressed by his sensitivity to the tragedy and anguish of war. His devotion to the workers' cause had never lagged, but his anger was rekindled by the flagrant denial of "the constitutional right of free speech in a country fighting to make democracy safe in the world."[27] He had never ceased to condemn the war, but he stepped onto the platform again on behalf of socialists' freedom. So persistent was the value of democracy in his mind that in 1920 he denied that the Bolsheviks had really intended a dictatorship, even of the proletariat. For Debs "freedom and equal rights" were inseparable.[28]

Similarly, pacifists in the People's Council of America who supported the Russian Revolution during the war regarded it as a vindication of the democratic process and not of the Bolshevik party or even, on the whole, of

Marxist economics. As Max Eastman wrote, "what makes us rub our eyes at Russia . . . is the way *our own theories* are proving t r u e ."[29] These pacifists supported the revolution, too, because its peace planks accorded with their own demand for a "new diplomacy" embodying democratic principles such as freedom of press, petition, and speech, a progressive tax on war profits, and a "referendum on questions of war and peace."[30]

However impractical a referendum on war might appear to be (it proved no more plausible in 1917 than it would twenty years later as the Ludlow Amendment), most liberal pacifists were responsive to the pervasive currents of pragmatism. Norman Thomas heeded them at Union Seminary, Randolph Bourne at Columbia, Kirby Page at Drake and Chicago; but, in fact, pragmatism was construed to support opposing positions on the war. John Dewey and liberals aligned with the *New Republic* (like some prowar socialists) argued that since war prevailed, the intelligent thing to do was to participate so as to be present at that "plastic juncture" when history is being made--the peace settlement. [31]

Randolph Bourne called this a rationalization of intellectual default. By the time of his death in 1918 Bourne's ideas were as familiar to liberal pacifists as was the sight of his hunched back and tortured features. He distrusted religious moralism less only than complacent liberalism, but he came to conclusions similar to those of Christian pacifists, breaking with many of the assumptions and friendships of his past in order to do so. He tried to reach back beyond Dewey's instrumentalism--now a lever for preserving the old order, he thought--to the spirit of William James.

In a world "where irony is dead" he scored prowar intellectuals for their credulity. He was offended as much by the quality of their thought as by their conclusions. "The ex-humanitarian, turned realist, sneers at the snobbish neutrality, colossal conceit, crooked thinking, dazed sensibilities, of those who are still unable to find any balm of consolation for this war," he observed bitterly.

The so-called pragmatists had idealized the instruments of policy, he wrote; they had forgotten that "the real enemy is War rather than imperial Germany."[32] Did the realists think that they could control events by joining forces already in motion? Perhaps. But a more consistent pragmatism would be less sanguine: ". . . if it is a question of controlling war, it is difficult to see how the child on the back of a mad elephant is to be any more effective in stopping the beast than is the child who cries to stop him from the ground."[33] The tendency to judge things in terms of results typified all liberals. Bourne was atypical only because he was pessimistic about the consequences of national war.

A number of those who would become professional pacifists between the wars had been impressed in college by the developing field of sociology and the prospect of "discovering concrete ways of getting ideals incarnated in actual institutions." [34] Their disposition to value pragmatic criteria in decision making set them apart from sectarian nonresistants of the past. Kirby Page, working out his position while helping German prisoners of war through the English YMCA, argued that war had to be judged by what it does: War is not an ideal, it has an ideal; war is not a spirit, it is waged in a certain spirit; war is not a result, it produces results. War is always and everywhere a method, and it is as a method that it must be discussed.[35]

He concluded that it was unchristian, and so his judgment was perhaps not political, but his approach laid the foundation for empirical analysis of international affairs in the postwar years, if not for selective objection to military service. His friend Evan Thomas—Norman's brother--wrote that "on purely sociological grounds I would oppose the war."[36]

These values--pragmatism, democracy, and the sanctity of individual life --were shared in some degree by all liberals and many socialists. Pacifists universalized them. They applied them even to national policy, even in wartime. They made them "axioms of emotional nature" that lent special force to their distinctive view of the politics of the war.

Liberal pacifists concluded that World War I was a product of the European state system and that American national interests were best served by staying out. They identified the causes of the war in European rivalries, in long-standing "misunderstanding, suspicion, fear, diplomatic and commercial struggle to which all nations contributed."[37] All elements of later revisionist writing on the war question can be found in the antiwar literature of 1917-18. Pacifists and antiwar socialists alike stressed the role of commercial competition, imperialism, secret treaties, and war profits in producing international conflict.

Socialists found in the economic origins of the war clues to its class basis. The workers were as expendable in wartime as they had been in peace, and for the same selfish ends, it was said: "Wars bring wealth and power to the ruling classes, and suffering, death, and demoralization to the workers."[38] At the very least, fighting abroad would "neutralize the class struggle," as some socialists explained. [39] Everything they believed about the war's origins confirmed their view that it was an imperialistic conflict and "not the concern of the workers." Moreover, such leaders as Morris Hillquit and Eugene Debs sensed the power of nationalism with its psychological extensions of fear and pride even in the arguments of those socialists who supported the crusade. Hillquit later ascribed the "stifling terrorism" of a "morbid war psychology" to the circumstance in which the major political parties were rivals in promoting the war effort.[40] Several socialists distrusted the idea of holding a referendum on war precisely because they feared that popular agitation would increase jingoism. Their sensitivity to the power of militant nationalism drew these socialists close to less class-conscious pacifists.

Whereas socialists had a handbook in George Ross Kirkpatrick's unbridled Marxist indictment, *War, What For?*, liberal pacifists found their thinking reflected in Norman Angel's analysis of the fallacy of viewing national defense as security, *The Great Illusion*.[41] Conflict of economic interest was the underlying cause of the war, they agreed, but its catalyst was nationalism itself. In this sense, at least, all the belligerents shared the blame for spreading the war and for the injustice and deceit that characterized it. Indeed, Jane Addams, Kirby Page, and others found that their reports of Allied atrocities were resented by the public simply because it accepted that notion of exclusive national virtues that had led to war in the first place. Pacifists distinguished between the mean motives of all belligerent governments and the high idealism of all the peoples who fought, as did Woodrow Wilson, but they could not support Wilson's idealistic war on behalf of the Allies. Everything they knew of the war's origin pointed to a strictly nationalistic European conflict with which the United States had no business. Private business (war trade and finance) was involved, to be sure, but neither national security nor American ideals were entrenched on one side or the other of no-man's land.

American pacifists were not intentionally isolationist in this regard. They consciously identified with men from all belligerent nations who shared what John Haynes Holmes called an "international mind." Holmes had matched a brilliant record at Harvard University with vigorous leadership in the Unitarian church, where he helped to organize the Fellowship for Social Justice. In 1912 he had written of the revolutionary function of the modern church in America, and four years later he broadened his horizon to include the international scene. There, in the midst of war, he found kindred spirits in Karl Liebknecht, Romain Rolland, and Bertrand Russell, among others. With them he recognized that there were in the world intense struggles for human dignity and decency, for peace itself, but he found these issues active within each nation at war.

Some such transnational humanism characterized pacifists of every hue, from class-conscious socialists to social gospel clergymen--Walter Rauschenbusch, for example, or Paul Jones, an Episcopal bishop who was removed from his diocese because of his views. It was the organizing principle of the Fellowship of Reconciliation and of the American Friends Service

Committee. The St. Louis Resolution of the Socialist party implied that American intervention was "a crime against the people of the United States and against the nations of the world."[42] The war seemed irrelevant to the pacifists because, in short, it seemed artificial. Neither side epitomized the values in which pacifists believed, whether phrased socialistically or religiously. No victory promised political justice or the quality of life for which they had labored as progressives. For this reason the famous and radical reporter John Reed wanted to tell the soldiers of both sides, "This is not your war."[43] For this reason Max Eastman found the war "un-interesting for all its gore" and Bertrand Russell called it "trivial, for all its vastness."[44]

This interpretation of the war gained the force of moral commitment from the values that pacifists held. It set them apart from prowar internationalists (just as it would set them apart from isolationists after the war). One after another they described the anguish of being isolated in the midst of idealism about the war. They were able to endure only through the fellowship of other pacifists and their activity for war relief and civil rights,

But, in fact, many did more than endure, The generation of leaders whose pacifism matured between 1914 and 1919 were "as a man . . . awakened out of sleep," suddenly alive to the "moral confusion and disorder that lie concealed in a civilization heavily weighted with materialistic aims."[45] Heightened social responsibility and a more radical view of society led some men to participate in the labor movement after the war, A. J. Muste, for example, joined the strikers, was general secretary of the Amalgamated Textile Workers until 1921, and then became director of Brookwood Labor College and started his sojourn with radicalism. Other pacifists, including Norman Thomas, Devere Allen, and Kirby Page, were led toward active socialism. The sources of this leftward shift were varied; one was the pacifists' association with antiwar socialists, and another was their confrontation with the wartime state.

The radical peace and justice movement of the post-1914 era was international from its inception. A similar devotion to pacifism and social work by religious men and women from London, Berlin, Paris, and Prague led to Quaker relief projects and the creation of the International Fellowship of Reconciliation. A similar conception of the war's origin and of peace terms linked American pacifists with British left-wing labor, antiwar German socialists, and the Russian Petrograd Council. In the United States the chief agencies of this first united front were various civil liberties bureaus and the People's Council of America.

Launched at a huge Madison Square Garden rally May 30, 1917, the People's Council was organized by moderate socialists and the remnant of the progressive antiwar coalition. Its original program was familiar enough: from May to September it campaigned for a quick peace on liberal terms, for civil liberties and repeal of conscription, and for economic demands no more radical than fair labor standards, curbs on the high cost of living, and taxes on war profits. Hoping to supplant its socialist-pacifist base with a farm-labor coalition, its organizers formed local branches and affiliated labor groups. By August it claimed just under two million constituents, a measure of its aspirations more than of its power. Five large meetings were held across the country as the Council prepared for a grand constituent assembly on September 1.

Clearly, the Council was associated with international socialism on war issues. Just as clearly, it was billed as radical and subversive by fervent patriots and conservative labor leaders, who thwarted its plan to meet in Minneapolis. Amid great confusion, delegates aboard a special train from New York pulled into the one Midwest city willing to be their host--Chicago. Even there the meetings were hasty and almost covert. Throughout the fall the Council increasingly represented socialists and radical labor; it was the chief defender of Soviet Russia in 1918-19, but it never quite lost the marks of liberal progressivism. Its program remained virtually unchanged. Scott Nearing, a socialist economist who was dismissed from the Wharton School of Finance because of his reform activities, became chairman on the understanding that the Council would work for "industrial democracy," but when he was asked if that meant socialism, he replied, "No."[46] Nonetheless, pacifists who associated with socialists, in the Council or elsewhere, were tarnished with the radical image.

The nature of that so-called radicalism is important: it derived from the reflection of pacifists upon wartime society in terms of their own experience. Isolation was painful enough, but pacifists were, in fact, the target of persecution because of their opposition to conscription and their association with political radicals. They promised not to obstruct the war effort, but their skeptical neutralism was itself a crime. Pacifists found that their meetings were broken up; their friends were harassed, run out of town, and imprisoned; their literature was withheld from the mails; their headquarters raided; and the president they trusted kept his own peace. Early in the war, before nationalism was virulent, the People's Council printed in facsimile a Russian peace appeal, together with an English translation and this note: "The original copy of the Bulletin from which this reproduction is made was smuggled over to this country—though not, as in the old days—smuggled out of Russia, but, as in these strange, new days—smuggled into America!"[47] Pacifists now looked upon their earlier warnings as prophetic. The American Union had said in 1916 "militarism is the real danger" of the war, and Randolph Bourne was not alone two years later in describing the "inextricable union of militarism and the State," or in fearing that "War is the health of the State."[48]

Bourne assumed that the ruling classes use the instruments of the state and its military authority to exploit those whose allegiance it commands. There was nothing new in his description of economic injustice or even its connection with war, but he went on to identify violence as the essence of war and authoritarian-ism as the essence of the state. In a state that identifies itself with democracy, the authority of conformity takes the place of violent, physical force.

Wartime patriotism is, therefore, the obverse, the domestic counterpart, of military force. Violence and authoritarianism are essentially and equally objectionable.

Bourne made the most significant statement of this theme, but it was echoed in the diverse literature of liberal pacifism, introducing a political and ethical note into the antiwar socialism of Max Eastman, Scott Nearing, and Norman Thomas. Only three weeks before he applied for membership in the Socialist party, Thomas had written that he feared its tendency to bind the, individual to the class.[49] He did join because he feared more deeply "the undue exaltation of the State" and believed that "radicals ought to stand up and be counted."[50] He was a radical pacifist before he was a socialist, and his distrust of violence and authoritarianism would leave its mark upon the party in the future. Scott Nearing was becoming politically more radical in these years, but he declared that, in the name of liberty and humanity, he was against violence in any cause. Max Eastman was no absolutist--like most socialists he was against World War I specifically--but his fervor against that war modified his radicalism. Later he recalled, "A similar thing happened . . . to a good many American socialists. The reality of armed conflict in Europe dampened the proletarian-revolutionary part of their credo, and stepped up to a high pitch the antimilitary part."[51] They emerged all the more skeptical and alienated from society.

Bourne's understanding was reflected, too, in Kirby Page's influential analysis of war as the method of violence and in the declarations of pacifists in the Fellowship of Reconciliation. Their enemy was war itself, and they concluded that war was the result of the entire competitive economic system. War could be linked to the whole "causal circle," wrote Vida D. Scudder, a socialist professor at Wellesley who had ferreted out the social ideals of English literature, and the pacifist who saw his connection would be forced into a "constructive social radicalism."[52] Under the circumstances it was radical enough to express skepticism of the war or the social system of which it was a part. When conformity is an instrument of war, as in 1917–18 it was, then skepticism is a crime. The liberal pacifists stood accused as a group. In their alienation they discovered that what made their pacifism radical was their equal objection to violence and authoritarianism.

This discovery pointed toward a new ethic of conflict, one that looked for the implications of war as a method and related the instrument to its objectives, As Kirby Page wrote, war must be judged by what it does because that is inseparable from what it is for. John Haynes Holmes argued at length that although the logic of force is that it can defend and liberate men, the fallacy of force is that it actually brings new forms of conflict and is the sine qua non of tyranny. Jane Addams spoke repeatedly of the futility of using violence in order to deal with the causes of fighting. "Militarism can never be abolished by militarism," as the majority of socialists had agreed in St. Louis when the American government determined to "make the world safe." "Democracy can never be imposed upon any country by a foreign power by force of arms."[53] Their declaration was directed specifically to the international war and was based on a Marxist analysis, but it reflected the very liberal values that absolute pacifists took to imply a universal principle.

The religious pacifists of the FOR abjured fighting on the grounds that it is sinful in its consequences, and agnostic Max Eastman found himself mindful of the "mangled bodies and manic hatreds implied by that lyric word *violence* so dear to humdrum petty-bourgeois dreamers like George Sorel. . . ."[54] For a generation and more pacifists would evaluate choices in terms of the relationship of "ends and means" and, in fact, the phrase would acquire sanctity independent of tough-minded analysis. The new pacifist ethic was not fully articulated in its inception, in part because the war was brief; the fetters of conformity were shortly removed, and professional peace advocates felt free again to fight militarism without, it seemed, challenging the state.

The memory of World War I was an important consideration in the responses of Americans to foreign affairs for two decades. It was a formative influence upon the pacifist. He tended to universalize the war and apply its example to other events; he used it to popularize his view that wars are always futile and irrelevant to fundamental social issues and that the United States could stand aside from a European state system based on force of arms. Revisionist histories of the First World War provided a vehicle for inculcating that view, but they could not convey the internationalism that was a corollary of the pacifist's humanism. To the extent that his memory of the war was accepted by the public, it encouraged isolationism. There was a deeper dilemma. Pacifism was historically oriented to liberal values. The progressive background of the liberal pacifist reinforced these values even as it socialized them and added a disposition toward political action. In 1917–18 the pacifist began to view war as an integral part of an unjust social order. The instruments of political control involved at least the latent threat of violence, he discovered, and these were in the hands of classes opposed to change. Behind even the system of democratic majority decision he found the tacit sanctions of violent force. To his political right and left were activists for whom violence appeared to be the ultimate authority.

But if the pacifist remembered anything from World War I, it was that violence and authoritarianism were precisely what threatened his every liberal value. Against them he began to define an ethic of conflict, dealing with force as an instrument for social control and rejecting violent means.

Only a few pacifists perceived that their impulse to far-reaching reform might come into conflict with their refusal to sanction violence in any cause: Evan Thomas and his friends on a hunger strike at Ft. Leavenworth, perhaps; John Haynes Holmes trying to find ways to rationalize the passivity out of pacifism, looking for the example of a Gandhi; Kirby Page seeking nonviolent methods of social change; moderate socialists warding off a Bolshevik-communist line. Even these men forgot the dilemma once the war was over, and they returned to normality or took up again the traditional instruments of social change. Liberal pacifists would face it again, however, in the agony of defining the road to power that split the Socialist party in 1934 and in the fight against war and fascism; and their successors would meet it in the sixties in the civil rights movement and the opposition to the war in Vietnam. The terms of the dilemma were exposed in World War I. A willingness to grapple with them would characterize liberal pacifism in the twentieth century.

NOTES

1. This graffito is mentioned in "Memoir of Frances Witherspoon and Tracy Mygatt," p, 8, Oral History Collection, Columbia University. Both women were active in the peace movement and especially the civil liberties groups in New York during World War I.

2. Julia Grace Wales to Clark F. Huhn, Nov, 28, 1917, Wales Papers, Wisconsin Historical Society, Madison, Wisconsin (italics in the original are omitted). Julia Wales was an instructor in English at the University of Wisconsin and the author of a plan for continuous mediation by an international commission of citizen experts.

3. Pacifism is sometimes defined still more narrowly as the position of only those who are opposed to alt war. This is the basis for legal recognition of conscientious objection in the United States, and there is considerable merit in its usage, Philosophically and politically speaking, this is a tidy definition but it is not historically useful since the impact and significance of pacifism varied with its changing constituency and since pacifists of all persuasions responded to the same historical events.

4. The peace churches are traditionally designated as the Quaker, Mennonite and Brethren, but others important for pacifism include the Disciples of Christ and Jehovah's Witnesses, The definitive study of religious pacifism is Peter Brock, *Pacifism in the United States: From the Colonial Era to the First World War* (Princeton, 1968). See also Roland Bainton, *Christian Attitude; Toward War and Peace: A Historical Survey and Critical Re-evaluation* (Nashville, 1960), and, regarding the Quakers, Elbert Russell, *The History of Quakerism* (New York, 1942). Rufus M. Jones, *The Later Periods of Quakerism* (London, 1921) and *A Service of Love* in *War Time: American Friends Relief* Work in *Europe, 1917-1919* (New York, 1920), and Lester Jones, *Quakers in Action* (New York, 1929).

5. The prewar peace movement is studied thoroughly in David S. Patterson, "The Travail of the American Peace Movement, 1887-1914" (Ph.D. dissertation, University of California, Berkeley, 1968), and interpreted in Charles R. Marchand, "The Ultimate Reform: World Peace in American Thought During the Progressive Era" (Ph.D. dissertation, Stanford University, 1964). Varying strands of the movement's rationale are developed in Sondra R. Herman, Eleven *Against War: Studies in American Internationalist Thought, 1898-1921* (Stanford, 1969). The older and established histories of this movement are, of course, Merle Curti, *Peace or War; the American Struggle 1636-1936* (New York, 1936), and Devere Allen, *The Fight for Peace* (New York, 1930).

6. This argument is oversimplified in comparison with its most restrained and balanced presentation (Harry Emerson Fosdick, *The Challenge of the Present Crisis* {New York, 1917)), but it is underplayed in comparison with many contemporary slogans even those of religious and peace organizations. See Ray H. Abrams, *Preachers Present Arms* (New York, 1933), and Horace C. Peterson and Gilbert Fite, *Opponents of War, 1917-1918* (Madison, 1957).

7. Other organizations in which Lochner played a leading role included the Ford Peace Expedition {November–December 1915), the First American Conference for Democracy and the Terms of Peace (May 30–31. 1917), and the People's Council of America (May 30–31, 1917). He was also active in other peace movements of the period.

8. Groups whose primary impetus came from New York included the American Union Against Militarism (April 1916), the American Neutral Conference Committee (July 1916), the Emergency Peace Federation February 1917), the People's Council, and the National Civil Liberties Bureau (a separate organization as of October 1, 1917). The Woman's Peace Party (established January to, 1917) and the Fellowship of Reconciliation (November 11, 1915), although New York oriented, did not stem primarily from the Henry Street group but included many of its members.

9. Marie Louise Degen, *The History of the Woman's Peace Party* (Baltimore, 1939), 40. For the history of the successor to the WPP, see Gertrude Bussey and Margaret Tims, *Women's International League for Peace and Freedom: 1715-1966* (London, 1965). The story is told through biography in James Weber Linn, *Jane Addams, a Biography* (New York, 1937), John C. Farrell, *Beloved Lady: A History* of fare *Addams' Ideas on Reform and Peace* (Baltimore, 1967), Mercedes M. Randall, *Improper Bostonian: Emily Greene Balch* (New York, 1964), Jane Addams, *Peace and Bread in Time* of War (New York, 1945) and Second *Twenty Years* (New York, 1930), and Louis Lochner, *Henry Ford—America's Don Quixote* (New York, 1925). Regarding the role of Julia Wales, see William Trattner, "Julia Grace Wales and the Wisconsin Plan for Peace," *Wisconsin Magazine of History,* YLIV (1961), 203-61.

10. Membership in the *FOR* involved signing a declaration of principles. Consequently its membership rolls are the best index of pacifist intention for peace advocates, and its minutes and publications are the best sources on the rationale of religious pacifism. They are collected in the Swarthmore College Peace Collection (hereafter SCPC), but since much from the war period is missing, they must be supplemented with the papers of Gilbert Beaver, Norman Thomas (New York Public Library, hereafter NYPL), John Nevin Sayre (personal possession, Nyack, N.Y.), and others.

11. The Anti-Preparedness Committee, established in November 1915, became the American Union Against Militarism (AUAM) on April 3-4, 1916. Only the name changed in the context of a determined anti-preparedness drive from April 6 to May 6; the leadership and rationale of the organization remained the same. The best published account of the AUAM is in Donald Johnson, *The Challenge to American Freedom: World War I and the Rise of the American Civil Liberties* Union Lexington, 1963), but see also Robert L. Duffus, *Lillian Wald: Neighbor and Crusader* (New York, 1938), John Haynes Holmes, *I Speak for Myself* (New York, 1959) Rabbi Stephen S. Wise, *Challenging Years* (New York. 1949), Michael Wreszin, *Oswald Garrison Villard: Pacifist at War* (Bloomington, 1965) and David Starr Jordan. *Days of a Man* (New York. 1922), II, 690–707, 712-730.

12. *Ibid. 734-36.* Regarding Wise's change of view see Carl Herman Voss, *Rabbi and Minister: The Friendship of Stephen S. Wise and John Haynes Holmes* (New York, 1964) 141-43. The Emergency Peace Federation was formed out of the American Committee for a Neutral Conference, but its leadership overlapped with the AUAM. Lillian Wald and Paul Kellogg helped

to found a "Committee on Nothing at All" in April 1918, which had the nucleus of the original AUAM and which evolved into the Foreign n Policy Association. Sec Lillian Wald, *Windows on Henry Street* (Boston 1934) 311.

13. Minutes of Aug. 30, Sept. 13, and Oct. 1, 1917, and *passim,* AUAM Papers, SCPC.

14. Jones, *A Service of Love,* 105

15. Thomas, "Some Objections Considered," in *The Conquest of War: Some Studies* in *a Search for a Christian World Order,* ed. Norman Thomas (New York, 1917).

16. Jane Addams, *Peace and Bread,* 4. See also W. Fearon Halliday, *Personality and War* (New York, 1916).

17. "Statement in Court," Oct. 30, 1918, enclosed in a letter from Norman Thomas to Harry W. L. Dana, Oct. 31, 1918, Dana Papers, SCPC. It was subsequently printed as *The Individual and the State: The Problem as Presented by the Sentencing of Roger N. Baldwin* (New York, 1918). For other examples of this position see Ernest L. Meyer, *"HEY? YELLOWBACK?": The War Diary of a Conscientious Objector* (New York, 1930), and the discussion of nonreligious objection in Clarence M. Case, *Non-Violent Coercion: A Study in Methods of Social Pressure* (New York, 1923), 251–64.

18. Thomas, *The Conscientious Objector in America* (New York, 1923), 29.

19. *Voices of Revolt: Speeches of Eugene V. Debs,* introd. Alexander Trachtenberg (New York, 1928), 74

20. Socialists and the Problems of War: A Symposium," *Intercollegiate Socialist, V* (1917), 26. Socialist views on the war are interpreted in their diversity in James Weinstein, *The Decline of Socialism in America, 1912–1925* (New York, 1967), but see also Peterson and Fite, *Opponents of War,* and Morris Hillquit, *Loose Leaves from a Busy Life* (New York, 1934). The best sources for the period are pamphlet literature, notably *The American Socialists and the War,* ed. Alexander Trachtenberg (New York, 1917), and periodicals such as *The Masses, New Review,* and *Intercollegiate Socialist,* The latter is particularly useful as it printed reasoned arguments representative of both sides as a matter of editorial policy (see statement of May 7, 1917, Intercollegiate Socialist Society Papers, Taminment Institute, New York). The Socialist Party Collection of manuscript sources at Duke University is not strong for this period.

21. William E. Bohn and Randolph Bourne in "Socialists and the Problems of War," *Intercollegiate Socialist, V* (1917), 10.

22. *Ibid., 9.*

23. Joseph D. Cannon, *ibid.,* re, Cannon wrote that he could conceive of a legitimate war of national defense.

24. The theme of war as a threat to progressive gains pervades antipreparedness literature. Typical are the following: "Around the Circle Against Militarism," *Survey,* XXXVI (1916), 95; John Haynes Holmes. "War and the Social Movement." *ibid.,* XXXII (1914), 629–30; and Oswald G. Villard, "Shall We Arm for Peace," *ibid.,* XXXV (1915), 299.

25. Crystal Eastman to members of the executive committee, June 14, 1917, AUAM Papers, SCPC. Newton D. Baker, Mayor of Cleveland (1912–16), was appointed secretary of war on March 7, 1916; Frederick Keppel, dean of the College of Columbia University, became third assistant secretary of war: Walter Lippmann, liberal commentator for *The New Republic*, was assistant to the secretary of war, June to October 1917; and progressive newspaper editor George Creel became chairman of the Committee on Public Information on April 14, 1917.

26. Edward Evans to Crystal Eastman, Sept, 28, 1917, and Norman Thomas to Crystal Eastman, Sept. 27, 1917, AUAM Papers, SCPC.

27. Quoted in Ray Ginger, *The Bending Cross: A Biography of Eugene Victor Debs* (New Brunswick, 1949), 356.

28. *Speeches of Eugene V. Debs*, 55-56

29. Eastman, *Love and Revolution: My Journey Through an Epoch* (New York, 1964), 45.

30. "Resolutions of the First American Conference for Democracy and Terms of Peace," May 30–31, New York City, Organizing Committee, People's Council of America Papers, SCPC.

31. Regarding the *New Republic* group see Charles Forcey, *Crossroads of Liberalism* (New York, 1961), chaps. 7 and 8, and Christopher Lasch, *The New Radicalism in America, 1889–1963: The Intellectual as a Social Type* (New York, 1965), chap. 6,

32. Randolph S. Bourne. "War and the Intellectuals," in *War and the Intellectuals: Essays by Randolph S. Bourne, 1915-1919*, ed. Carl Resek (New York, 1964), 10. A fuller range of Bourne's thought is suggested in Lillian Schlissel, *The World of Randolph Bourne* (New York, 1965).

33. Bourne, *War and the intellectuals,* 12.

34. *Ibid.,* 10.

35. Kirby Page to Howard E. Sweet, Feb. 3, 1918, and especially the manuscript, "The Sword or the Cross." Page Papers, Southern California School of Theology, Claremont.

36. Evan to Norman Thomas, Nov. 5, 1916, Norman Thomas Papers, NYPL. This sentiment was an integral part of Evan Thomas' agonizing re-evaluation of religion.

37. John Haynes Holmes, *The International Mind* (New York, 1916), 7, but see his full argument in *New Wars for Old* (New York, 1916) and wartime, pamphlets, as well as in other pacifist literature, including especially the FOR journal, *The World Tomorrow,* edited by Norman Thomas.

38. The majority report of the Socialist party, adopted in St. Louis on April 11, 1917, is printed in full in Nathan Fine, *Labor and Farmer Parties in the United States, 1828–1928* (New York, 1928), 310–14. The report was written by Morris Hillquit and Charles Rutherberg, among others. A minority report by Louis Boudin is also printed in full in *ibid.,* 315–17.

39. Alexander Trachtenberg "Socialists and the Problems of War," *Intercollegiate Socialist, V* (1917), 25.

40. Hillquit, *Loose Leaves from a Busy Life,* 169.

41. About 150,000 copies of *War, What For?* were sold between its publication by the author in 1910 (West Lafayette, Ohio) and its suppression in 1917, and perhaps another 100,000 copies of Kirkpatrick's *Think or Surrender* (New York, 1916) were distributed. Angel's *Great Illusion* (London, 1913) had a great following among internationalists, including those who reluctantly supported the war.

42. Quoted in Fine, *Labor and Farmer Parties, 31.*

43. Granville Hicks, *John Reed: The Making of a Revolutionary* (New York, *1937),* 169.

44. Eastman, "The Uninteresting War," *The Masses,* VI (1915), *5–8;* Russell, *Justice in War Time,* quoted in Holmes, International *Mind,* 13,

45. Typed ms., unsigned, ca. 1917, a draft of a statement on behalf of the Fellowship, probably by Norman Thomas or Paul Jones, FOR Papers, SCPC. This sense of recognition appears not only in the literature of the Fellowship, but also among Quakers such as those in the Friends Service Committee and the Philadelphia Yearly Meeting Committee on the Social Order.

46. Minutes of the executive committer of the People's Council, Sept. 21, 1917, People's Council of America Papers, SCPC. See also the minutes of the organizing committee, June 21, July 19 and 26, and Aug. 16, *1917,* and the *Bulletin* of the People's Council, Aug. 7, 1917, p. 1, *ibid.* The assembly of September 1, 1917, is fully documented in the People's Council Papers. The best published versions are in Frank L. Grubbs, Jr., *The Struggle for Labor Loyalty: Gompers, the A. F. of L., and the Pacifists, 1917–1920* (Durham, 1968), and Peterson and Fite, *Opponents of War,* although these authors interpret the Council and also the American Union Against Militarism as being somewhat more radical than the manuscripts seem to warrant.

47. *Bulletin,* Aug. 7, 1917, [pp.] 2–3.

48. Bourne, "The State," in *War and the Intellectuals, 89,* 84.

49. Thomas to Mrs. Anne C. Brush, Sept. 24, 1918, Thomas Papers, NYPL.

50. Thomas to Alexander Trachtenberg, Oct. 18, 1918, and Thomas to Morris Hillquit, Oct. 2, *1917,* Thomas Papers, NYPL.

51. Eastman, *Love and Revolution, 26;* Henry May, *The End* of *American Innocence: A Study of the First Years of Our Time, 1912-1917* (New York, 1959) *368.*

52. Scudder, *On Journey (New* York, *1937), 285.* Miss Scudder joined the FOR after she realized that its members were integrating their pacifism with a demand for drastic social reorganization. Similarly, Jane Addams' autobiographical works can be read profitably as records of recognition of injustice on expanding levels of the social older, culminating in a view of the relationship of inter-national injustice and war.

53. Majority report of the Socialist party, St. Louis, quoted in Fine, *Farmer and Labor Parties,* 312.

54. Eastman, *Love and Revolution,* 26.

CHAPTER FOUR
THE MAKING OF THE MODERN PEACE MOVEMENT
Charles DeBenedetti

At the time of his untimely death, on his forty-fourth birthday, Chuck DeBenedetti had already established himself as a leading authority on American peace history. His initial research in the area of diplomatic history during the Vietnam War led to his interest in internationalism and the role of Columbia University historian, James T. Shotwell. This conclusion to his book, *Origins of the Modern American Peace Movement, 1915-1929*, expressly coins the phrase, "Modern American Peace Movement." According to the author, the modern peace movement has been defined by its focus on advancing peace as a process in human social relations. Such focus largely defined the role of the movement throughout the 20th century. The peace reformers in post-World War One America understood justice as the amelioration of social wrongs and not simply the adjudication of courts. Nationalism was now being viewed in terms of cultural diversity rather than some form of Anglo-Saxon exclusivity; war as a byproduct of militarism, nationalism, and imperialism and not merely as an irrational outburst of mass ignorance. These peacemakers, moreover, promoted a reformed and democratized international system by which responsible policymakers would manage peace through applied social justice and world agencies. After reading this essay consider the following: How did the modern peace advocate argue that reform must advance at home through the nonviolent extension of justice under order?; How did their arguments redefine the notion of peace as more than an antiwar position?

From THE ORIGINS OF THE MODERN AMERICAN PEACE MOVEMENT, 1915-1929 by Charles DeBenedetti. Copyright 1978 by KTO Press. Used by permission of the heirs of Charles DeBenedetti.

Although hopeful, American peace leaders were chary in backing the Kellogg-Briand Pact from the time of its signing in Paris in August 1928 until its ratification in Washington five months later. Most freely praised the treaty as a welcome sign of international reconciliation. But they complained just as readily of its more flagrant weaknesses and spoke of the work yet to be done. Rather than provide blind support for Washington's policies, liberal pacifists hammered at the incongruity of the administration's dual commitment to the peace pact and to an enormous program of naval expansion. Protestant peace progressives and pro-League inter-nationalists argued that Kellogg's ideals would become real only when integrated into an organized international structure. Even legalist leaders, who alone stood unreservedly for the pact's ratification, called for the further development of more comprehensive means of settling disputes. Altogether, American peace leaders well realized the limited value of the Paris pact. They were quire aware that the treaty essentially represented the most advanced approach toward world order that could be elicited from Republican realists who envisioned peace in terms of an American paramountcy that rested on arms limitation agreements, open economic competition, and moral suasion backed by United States Marines. They appreciated the pact for what it was: a vital element in the Republican triad of "preparation, limitation and renunciation" that encompassed what President Coolidge called "the only practical principles" upon which peace could be built.[1]

The Ratification of the Kellogg Pact and the Continuing Naval Controversy

Senate approval of the Kellogg Pact was accomplished with uncommon dispatch and a telling lack of rancor. Indeed, the very ease with which the treaty passed the Senate increased the skepticism felt by critical peaceseekers for the administration's handiwork. The ratifying process began on November 22, 1928, when Foreign Relations Committee chairman Borah announced that he and Frederick Hale, chairman of the Naval Affairs Committee, had agreed to a parliamentary arrangement by which the Senate would consider the Kellogg Pact before the naval appropriations bill that had already received House approval. Three months later, on January 3, 1929, Borah reported the treaty out of his committee after a minimum of serious debate.

On the Senate floor the pact was greeted with whimsy and cynicism by a bipartisan coalition of Republican and Democratic nationalists who pressed the administration to explain its importance. Determined to preserve unchecked the full decision-making freedom of future American policymakers, several senators demanded the formulation of reservations that would protect the Monroe Doctrine and the inviolability of national self-defense efforts and would ensure against any link with agencies of international collective action. The Senate's desire to clarify precisely the country's obligations under the antiwar treaty came as no surprise to Kellogg or Borah. Sympathizing fully with the nationalists' fears, the administration's two top treaty strategists offered repeated assurances that the pact entailed no political commitments, no compromise of the nation's right to determine its own defense, and no restriction upon the disposition of United States armed forces. The treaty demanded only that the United States undertake a "commitment for peace," Borah declared. It contained no "commitments for war."[2]

Borah and Kellogg refused, however, to gut the treaty publicly drafting a set of specific reservations that conveyed their narrow understanding of its reach. The pact was "brief and simple," Kellogg promised Coolidge. It contained "no reservations or exceptions, and there are no collateral understandings which detract from its effectiveness or qualify its high purpose."[3] Moreover, the secretary stated, the tangle of reservations and conditions that its European signatories had attached to the treaty were of no real relevance. The whole meaning and range of the pact was incorporated in its direct contractual terms. There were therefore no reasons to complicate matters by contriving a set of specific reservations.

Yet in deference to the powerful "clarificationist" sentiment of Senate nationalists, Borah did agree on January 15 to summarize the administration's understanding of the pact in a formal paper he attached to the Foreign Relations Committee report on the treaty. The senator's clarifying statement was "Significantly silent in regard to the attitude the United States will take toward the application of League sanctions against an aggressor," some pro-League advocates of neutrality revision whispered hopefully.[4] But it effectively accomplished its first purpose. The Idahoan's position paper immediately overcame nationalist opposition and opened the way toward affirmative congressional action. Within hours of his work, the treaty sailed through the Senate by a margin of 85 to 1. Two days later, President Coolidge signed the pact in a formal ratification ceremony at the White House.

In these same weeks, plans for enlarged naval construction hurtled toward Senate approval. Aided by the ominous Anglo-French naval agreement of July 30, the War Department and the semi-official Navy League waged a massive propaganda campaign in the last months of 1928 in order to secure Senate approval of the administration's sixteen-ship construction bill. The size of the navalists' propaganda blitz dwarfed the concurrent movement on behalf of the antiwar treaty and underscored Washington's primary reliance on unilateral national power as an instrument of world policy. The president supported the need for American naval expansion in a belligerent Armistice Day address that precipitated a flurry of international controversy, while Kellogg insisted that the peace pact and a new naval building program were fully compatible in spirit and practice. Republican leaders contended that the enforcement of the peace pact depended solely on the massed power of world public opinion and that the realization of America's peaceable international objectives depended in a complementary way on the ordering power of United States naval strength. The treaty would interfere in no way with Washington's decisions for overseas action, Kellogg maintained. It would neither compromise the country's pursuit of its independent police role in the Western Hemisphere nor impede its determination to protect American nationals and their property from Panama to the Yangtze.

In public and in private, American policymakers protested that there was no inconsistency between the moral outreach of the antiwar treaty and the unchecked application of American power anywhere in the world. The Senate evidently agreed. On February 5, it approved by an overwhelming majority the administration request for the sixteen-ship naval expansion program. Coming three weeks after its approval of the peace pact, the Senate action reinforced the Republican resolve to preserve America's independent global leadership through a combination of arms limitation, moral inspiration, maritime power, and industrial dynamism.

Within the American peace movement, legalists alone supported the Republican contention that the peace pact and the cruiser bill were compatible in spirit and practice. Although Edwin Borchard and others had some reservations, conservative legalists in the Carnegie Endowment for International Peace and American Peace Society generally praised the pact and congratulated Kellogg for extending the "due process of law" among nations. Arthur Deerin Call thought the treaty signified an uplifting "moral gesture" toward international reconciliation; but he and his like-minded compatriots in the American Legion and the Daughters of the American Revolution found it easier to support the pact as an adjunct to the administration's naval program.[5] Progressive legalists in the Outlawry of War crusade believed that the relationship was the reverse. Delighted with the peace pact but disturbed by the cruiser bill, Outlawry leaders supported the administration's position on the ground that the pact, "as international law, will abide when all these fifteen cruisers have become obsolete and have been sunk to the bottom of the sea as mere junk." And in all events, they added, the pact had nothing to do with the intricate needs of American naval policy. "The outlawry of war has nothing to do with any policy," Charles Clayton Morrison insisted, "it involves the renunciation of war as an instrument of every policy."[6] The naval policies of nations had no significance for a treaty that worked to delegalize war and crush it through the combined sentiments of the world's peace loving peoples.

Confident that no single nation could buck the world's moral will, Outlawry enthusiasts anticipated the organization of international relations along juridical lines plotted in American constitutionalism and rooted in the popular yearning for peace. The League of Nations theory of peace through fear and force was entering its final phase, Levinson believed. It would soon yield to a "no-sanction peace" whose value had been proven through the American example "running back into the foundation of the government in 1787."[7] Anxious for further action toward a true World Court, Outlawry leaders were disappointed with the lack of serious Senate discussion as to the larger meaning of the peace pact. But they took comfort in their conviction that the pact had finally vindicated the real value of progressive Irreconcilability. The treaty that excised war from law had saved Europe from itself, and, in the process, it had saved America from Europe and for the world.

Liberal pacifists were more circumspect in their reaction to Washington's double-barreled disposition of the peace pact and the cruiser bill. At their most sanguine, pacifist leaders dreamed that the treaty had transformed the legal and moral status of peacemakers, turning pacifists into national heroes and militarists into common criminals.[8] William Floyd's *Arbitrator* called ambitiously for cadres of "Peace Patriots" to work throughout the world in order to make real the spirit of the peace pact and denounced the Big Navy "War Patriots" who threatened the treaty's promise. Frederick Libby also thought the pact would revolutionize the social acceptability of pacifism. The National Council for Prevention of War sponsored the posting of thousands of copies of the treaty, strikingly reproduced in red, white, and blue, on post office bulletin boards throughout the country.

In the main, however the pacifist reaction to the Kellogg Pact was muted and mistrustful. Unfazed by Washington's peace rhetoric, social progressives of all persuasions perceived the peace pact as one phase of the "great moral battle" that was raging between them and militant nationalists over the direction of future United States foreign policy.[9] Viewed in the context of that struggle, the pact was a major victory. But the cruiser bill was a larger loss. Peace progressives were divided in confusion when confronted with Washington's dual commitment to the pact and to expanded naval construction. New York area peace activists were reportedly "in danger of being torn asunder" in quarrels over the politics of treaty ratification and naval expansion.[10] A good many followed the lead of William Floyd, who dismissed the treaty as a deceptive oversimplification and who refused to support it as long as it was tied to the administration's naval program. "It seems to me," agreed Dorothy Detzer of the Women's International League for Peace and Freedom, "that we had better lose the Kellogg Pact at this time if the Navy Bill is to go through and if the Pact is to be filled with reservations."[11] Others joined John Haynes Holmes and Frederick Libby in backing ratification of the pact but resisting the administration's naval building plans. And still others like John Nevin Sayre and Kirby Page tepidly accepted the peace pact as a suitable framework for European-American relations, but vowed to oppose Washington's "gun-boat imperialism" elsewhere.[12]

The peace pact worked no magic solvent upon American--let alone international--diplomacy; social progressives agreed. In fact, Emily Greene Balch declared late in 1928, there was "no country in which militarism appears to me to be on the increase in the way that it is here." The aggressive nationalism that was being spread through education, journalism, politics, and "military-minded films" was looming as a real "menace to peace."[13] On all sides, social progressives believed that the conclusion of the Kellogg Pact must not be permitted to lead peaceseekers to slacken their parallel efforts toward world order. More than ever, *The World Tomorrow* advised, "the occasion demands a tidal wave of public opinion."[14] Peaceseekers must use Washington's antiwar diplomacy as a driving wedge toward the World Court, League of Nations, disarmament, and arbitration. The Paris pact signaled "a mighty stride toward peace," declared Carrie Chapman Catt. But it would be an empty stride unless it was followed by a lockstep movement that aimed for international cooperation over competition and for consensus over conflict.[15]

Most resolutely, social progressives spoke of connecting the treaty to the world's ongoing peace "machinery;" a word revolutionary of their continuing fascination with the images of speed, efficiency, utility, and standardization that would accompany an organized system, of peace with justice. Undismayed by Washington's opposition to systematic forms of international cooperation, peace reformers reiterated their commitments to the World Court, League of Nations, international disarmament, and the withdrawal of American troops from Nicaragua and Haiti. "War cannot be outlawed by political fiat," warned Church Peace Union leader Henry Atkinson. "A treaty against it is a mere scrap of paper" unless it was followed by collective attempts to make it real through multilateral action.[16] Eminently sensitive to the realities of American as well as world politics, churchmen, feminists, and pacifists seldom permitted their public support of the treaty to mislead them into thinking that Kellogg's work represented the diplomacy of the apocalypse. "Because they are realists," Linsey Gordon said of the country's peace workers, "they are not foolish enough to imagine that the multilateral treaty is the beginning and the end, the Alpha and Omega of world peace."[17]

The most ambitious attempt to use the pact as a step toward fuller international cooperation was undertaken during the winter of 1928-29 by the pro-League advocates of American neutrality revision. Keenly aware of the integral connection between the pact and the cruiser bill, some of the brightest proponents of eastern establishment internationalism praised the antiwar treaty at the same time as they attacked Washington's refusal to explore naval arms limitation possibilities and complained of the tense state of relations with Great Britain. "The naval problem ranks with reparations as the most serious of pending and unsettled international problems," said Allen Dulles, former American delegate to the League Preparatory Commission for disarmament and legal adviser to the United States delegation at the 1927 Geneva Conference. The intensifying Anglo-American competition was, agreed one-time Associated Press European correspondent Frederick Moore, "one of the most wanton rivalries in armament it is possible to conceive" and the most likely escalator to "another gigantic conflict."[18]

Anxious to temper sharpening Anglo-American tension, internationalist spokesmen urged Washington to use the Kellogg Pact to end the unsettling ambiguity that American neutrality policy posed to British naval policy and to Britain's obligations under the League's sanction system. Former Democratic presidential candidate John W. Davis suggested that Washington and London conclude an agreement that would bar conflict between the two "in the event of constabulary action against a covenant-breaking state"; and retired State Department solicitor Charles Cheney Hyde proposed that the United States proclaim its "position where as a neutral, without violating any obligation to anybody, we may withhold aid and comfort at any time from a state which breaks its pledge to us and embarks upon a belligerent program which it has agreed with us to renounce."[19] Whatever the formula, pro-League sympathizers were clearly eager to seize upon the Kellogg Pact as a means toward closer Anglo-American relations and firmer United States ties to the League. Otherwise, they agreed, the pact stood as nothing more than a wispy gesture conjured up by Republicans as an alternative to the League in a cheap political maneuver so transparently callous that it was "enough to make the angels weep." "In this pact," warned Raymond Fosdick, "we are merely laying down a principle. How that principle shall be applied to concrete cases we do not know, and unless we get to work on that problem, this present gesture will be an empty and foolish one." [20]

In the most serious effort to apply the pact to concrete cases, Nicholas Murray Butler induced Arthur Capper to reintroduce in the Senate on February 11, 1929, his year-old resolution that proposed to define aggression and to withhold governmental protection from American nationals who aided foreign aggressors. To Butler and other League enthusiasts, the Capper resolution offered the most direct means of coming to grips with the Anglo-American naval rivalry as well as the most indirect but effective way of strengthening United States ties with the League. The proposal would "be of the greatest possible value in clearing up the equivocal position in which the Cruiser bill has placed us," ventured John Hessin Clarke, while Shotwell valued it as a camouflage pathway toward Geneva. Claiming that the Kellogg Pact had ended war's status as "the free prerogative of nations," Shotwell argued that the pact had reformed the international community by investing neutrality with "a moral character" that was incompatible with the crime of war. After the treaty, Shotwell said, every nation had a duty to stand by the world community "when crime is running rampant": and this duty was affirmed "in its smallest terms in the Capper Resolution: not to help the criminal." [21]

The 1929 Capper resolution thus appeared as the next logical step in leading America through the Kellogg Pact into more meaningful international cooperation. It was the ideal basis, said Capper himself, from which the United States could move "to underwrite the Peace Pact without compelling us to police the world." [22] Shotwell delightedly endorsed Capper's interpretation of the resolution in his public statements, and he was even more ebullient in private. The resolution was "a definite step towards the League and almost an open one," the professor told one intimate, and he urged his friends in Geneva to greet the senator's tentative outreach toward collaboration with low-keyed but constant encouragement. [23]

Butler and Shotwell found little support, however, for their plans in Washington. The general antipathy there to the cause of neutrality revision had been visibly bared in the Cruiser bill, which passed the Senate on February 5 with a special provision inserted by Borah that called for a series of maritime treaties guaranteeing the rights of neutrals and reiterating the traditional American understanding of the freedom of the seas. Pressed to define that understanding, Borah called freedom of the seas "the right of neutral nations to carry their commerce as freely in time of war as in time of peace," except when their ships bore munitions or sought to break a legitimate blockade. It was a classic defense of the historic American position on neutrality, stated firmly against revision and yet in a temperate tone that blunted the issue that everyone agreed was at "the crux of our naval controversy with Great Britain." [24] Borah's tact worked well in its immediate context, facilitating the passage of the naval bill while preserving the neutral base of America's maritime unilateralism. But it failed to quiet the groundswell of support that was building in these same months beneath the Capper resolution.

As Butler had anticipated, the Capper proposal won plaudits throughout the spring of 1929 for pointing "the way to the next step" and for suggesting the most feasible means of insuring the peace pact's working success. [25] The internationalist attempt to implant "teeth" in the infant antiwar treaty gained broad support. Feminists praised the Capper resolution as "a long step in the right direction," an attractive signpost for "the way for a further program of peace." Leaders of both the Federal Council of Churches of Christ in America and the League of Nations Non-Partisan Association pledged their support of the proposal, while Frederick Lynch of the World Alliance for International Friendship Through the Churches reported that his personal soundings had recorded a deep reservoir of support for the resolution. Sustained by pro-League sympathizers, the Capper formula passed through the last months of the decade generating interest as the most effective way of giving force to the peace pact and of aligning the United States with the forces of world order centered at Geneva. As Edwin Borchard recalled uneasily in 1937, the resolution continued "to command support in the highest quarters in this country" and "might have been adopted but for the turn of events in Europe and Asia during 1930 and 1931."[26] But then those events changed everything.

Altogether, the most striking feature of the reaction within the American peace movement to the conclusion and ratification of the Paris pact was that everyone believed that the treaty marked a turning point in postwar history—but few could agree which way history was turning. Social progressives and internationalists held that the pact hinted at Washington's emerging willingness to commit itself more deliberately to the preservation of organized world order. The treaty was "an opportunity rather than an achievement," observed Frederick Libby.[27] It was a precious new chant for American peaceseekers to overcome their failures in the League and Court fights and lead the country toward fuller cooperation in the organization of peace. Conversely, conservative legalists and orthodox Republicans respected the pact as an invigorating new expression of the nation's traditional willingness to use its independent moral influence to deter the outbreak of foreign wars and to substitute law for war. Kellogg's treaty affirmatively proposed "a policy of voluntary peace," one GOP elder submitted. It freshly articulated standards of morality and law that America had long observed and whose extension President Coolidge believed would do more than anything else "to stabilize and give expression to the peace sentiment of the world."[28] While most observers agreed that the pact might well dissolve into a meaningless gesture, few believed that it would have no effect on national politics. Hard-bitten conservative legalists like David Jayne Hill welcomed the treaty as "the expression of a new conception of international relations" that placed heavy new emphasis upon legal means of resolving disputes.[29] More skeptical treaty backers like James Shotwell interpolated their pro-League hopes into the literal terms of the treaty and argued that the pact bound the United States morally to "benevolent neutrality" toward League attempts to contain the spread of modern total war.

And less cautious pro-League enthusiasts applauded the pact as, "in fact, though not in form," a treaty between Washington and Geneva, an interpretation in which a few worried conservative legalists like Edwin Borchard concurred.[30] But few peace workers went this far. The "general feeling" of the country, estimated the *Literary Digest,* was that the pact bore little more than some indeterminate "moral influence."[31] Clean of commitments and obligations, the treaty was accepted as a plastic--and not a paper--device that Washington chose to mold about its unilateral pursuit of naval expansion, arbitral compacts, and arms limitation agreements. Most peaceseekers shared in this general judgment, and they looked to the pact's very plasticity as its main value. It might yet be shaped in ways that would draw the American people into fuller cooperation toward the international organization of peace.

The pact was not reshaped in these ways, due to the desires of its draftsmen and not of its distant supporters. Partly an expression of nationalist pride in the success of the American experience, the treaty was designed by Republican leaders who were anxious to demonstrate that an independent America could do more for world order through the free exercise of its wealth and power then it could through any peace agreement to act in concert with foreign powers. The Kellogg Pact was not a Republican trick to beguile a gullible public into expecting war's end. Nor was it the result of the American public's irresponsible preference for a cheap peace. It was rather the upshot of the Republicans' combined determination to offset the negative political impact of expanding naval arms competition, to restore American leadership in the field of arbitration, and to demonstrate the formidable global power of America's independent moral and economic energy. A product of many forces, the Kellogg Pact was the most advanced expression of the postwar Republican goal of tying the popular dream of world peace to its partisan vision of organizing world of law and economic cooperation free of political precommitment. It was the fulfillment of that faith that Republicans and conservative legalists shared that "out of justice grows peace" and that "the object and the aim of the United States is to further the cause of peace, of strict justice between nations with due regard for the rights of others in all international dealings."[32]

Ambiguous but meaningful, the Paris pact was wholly appropriate to the attitudes and expectations of Washington policymakers who operated in the late twenties according to their understanding of the American national interest. The pact failed to fulfill their hopes of sustaining the peace not so much because of the naïveté of their hopes as the fact that the conditions and assumptions that under girded the treaty in 1928 were revolutionarily transformed after 1929. A product of Coolidge's America, the antiwar treaty became an embarrassing anachronism as soon as the two interrelated bases of its promise—unchallenged United States economic hegemony and European political stability—collapsed in the face of the generalized crises of the thirties. The treaty failed after 1931 because it was irrelevant. It was as irrelevant to the world of depression diplomacy as the rugged individualism of Herbert Hoover was to the depressed American economy.

The same Republican policymakers who skillfully devised a treaty formula appropriate to their needs in 1928 flailed helplessly before a succession of shocks after 1931. And as they flailed, a corrosive disillusionment cut through the body of liberal nationalists who made up the bulk of the postwar peace movement, moving them to look back with contempt upon the twenties and to equate uncritically its idealism with weakness and its hope with befuddlement. Whether called "neo-orthodoxy" or "Christian realism," there spread across the liberal nationalist backbone of reform America a censorious attitude that Charles Clayton Morrison prophetically anticipated as early as September 1928, when he warned:

> If this pact does not end war it would be better for humanity had it never been signed. The moral chaos that would ensue upon a major violation of this treaty would be worse than the devastation of war itself... It must mean a new world, a world of permanent peace on the basis of justice.

And if it does not mean that, it will mean nothing less than a new epic in the fall of man.

Morrison prayed that the treaty pointed the way upward a new era in international relations. It would "only be cast down by the inconceivable lapse of humanity into anarchy and barbarism," after which peace would be known only as predominance.[33]

Some Concluding Thoughts

The modern American peace movement originated between 1915 and 1929, as the traditional liberal faith in the emergence of peace through advancing industrial interdependence and national self-determination collapsed in the face of the World War and spreading social revolution. Headed by a youthful combination of liberal world-order planners and Social Gospel pacifists, there arose instead an energetic new movement that conceived of peace as a process that progressed through the deliberate application of social scientific knowledge and adherence to nonviolent values.[34] Less nationalistic than their prewar predecessors, leaders of the new movement perceived peace in the age of total war as the most necessary of reforms. Yet they also recognized after the war-borne surge of American superpatriotism and the success of the Bolshevik Revolution that peace detached from raw American power appeared increasingly to their countrymen as a subversive reform. Caught between the necessity of peace and its subversive connotations, peace activists proceeded between 1915 and 1929 to invent the modern American peace movement in three critical ways. Tactically, they created a host of enduring new organizations and mobilized the largest number of citizens in peacetime American history in campaigns for disarmament and the World Court. Ideologically, they resisted modern right-wing radicalism (which granted life in the counterrevolutionary American reaction to Bolshevism's success) in its attempts to turn the United States into a military juggernaut that identified international change in terms of Soviet conspiracy. Intellectually, they forsook the traditional liberal faith in industrial interdependence and national self-determination and they inquired seriously for the first time into the implications for international peace or societal modernization. The reality of their times was that growing material interdependence was intensifying rather than easing tribal antagonisms and integral nationalism. And they worked to explain that reality in order to change it. The first purpose of the modernizing peace movement was to drive the United States government into leading the international effort to trap the menace of modern total war in a web of global order. Organized principally through the efforts of an eastern urban middle-class intelligentsia, the country's peace workers shared a sense of genuine excitement with the historic significance of their part in "the greatest struggle of the ages of social reform"--the elimination of the war system and "the wholesale legalized slaughter of human beings."[35] Peaceseekers well knew that they had no institutionalized political base in the country. Yet they prepared resolutely to advance their cause through the force of a moral and intellectual dynamic that drew generating power from a shared set of common convictions.

Postwar peace activists resolved first of all to prevent the reappearance of those factors that they felt were mainly responsible for the Great War, especially secretive cabinet diplomacy and calculating balance-of-power politics. Contemptuous of the Old Diplomacy, they tried uniformly to institutionalize a democratic diplomacy that would give force to what they were sure was the popular will to peace. Out of this persuasion, peace leaders worked to promote peace education and international understanding in order to disperse the ignorance and fear that clouded the common people's search for global harmony. Confident of the primacy of human reason and goodness, the liberal activists who dominated the movement believed that a spreading familiarity with war's costly horror and with peace's real benefits could not help but fortify people in their general will to peace. Peace education provided a vital impetus to peace progress; and peace progress, in turn, provided a working example of the larger law of progress that movement activists saw at work in human affairs. Peace and its realization comprised a central phase in man's irrepressible movement toward his highest potential. "Peace is inevitable," said the National Council for Prevention of War's Florence Brewer Boeckel in a common expression of the 'seekers' sentiment. And it was the job of the postwar peace movement to protect the immediate future against war "so that the sentiments and institutions of a generation could be massed impenetrably in defense of global law and order."[36]

American peace workers also moved forward during and after World War I out of the common conviction that Western man was passing through a critical watershed. With the old European order wrecked and the colonial world shaken, American peace leaders realized that the international structure that had largely determined the world's destiny for five centuries was crumbling into disrepair and ready for replacement. These were the "decisive years," declared the pacifist Henry Pinkham. They were the years that would prove either to be a "breathing-spell" between cataclysms or a healing period of reconstruction.[37] And what direction these years would take, peace leaders agreed, depended on the way in which industrial peoples responded to the phenomenon of modern total war. Raging at the intersection of scientific technology, machine industrialism, and mass nationalism, total war represented a devastating new force in world affairs. Its indiscriminate violence raised war for the first time into a veritable threat to the species. Its very destructiveness signaled "a revolution not only in the art and science of warfare, but, also, in the use of war itself as an instrument of politics."[38] Total war meant that war had escaped calculation and control; that conquering peoples suffered almost as severely as did the conquered; that the means of violence had consumed the end of advantage. With the advent of this new phenomenon, the whole relationship between war and statecraft had been revolutionized, "and it is this revolution in the character of war today which makes the movement for international peace a necessity."[39]

Alert to the critical nature of their times, American peaceseekers continually employed their sense of historical self-consciousness to prod themselves into action against war's ominous new meaning. "No more thrilling challenge confronts the people of this generation," exulted Kirby Page, "than that inherent in the crusade to abolish war and to create adequate international organization. We can do, it if we will!"[40] The realization of this "greatest of all revelations in the world's history," proclaimed James Shotwell, truly figured as the high privilege and task of this generation. It is an unescapable responsibility placed upon us by the fact that to us at least, war under modem conditions has been revealed to us in such fullness of tragedy as to offer for the first time a chance to mobilize the intelligence as well as the material forces of society, for not only the outlawing but the ending of war itself.[41]

These were "great times," agreed Raymond Fosdick. "I would not want to live in any other generation."[42] Brimming with the hopes and apprehensions of pioneers, American peace workers crossed the twenties in a common determination to put war on the road toward its final end. The world to them was fragile but malleable, and whether it would break or bend depended mostly on the work that they and other progressive-minded people did in the exhaustion and euphoria that followed upon the greatest blood letting in Western memory. Finally, American peace workers operated after 1915 out of the common conviction that the prospects of saving the world from total war in their generation turned essentially on America's willingness to discharge its proper global responsibility. America's enormous power "will really tip the balances finally toward peace or toward war," most peace leaders believed. It alone could "break the vicious spell which an evil past has placed upon the world." It was "the key to world peace."[43] Firmly nationalistic, American peace workers felt sure that the United States had an obligation to save mankind from the horror of renewed total war and to reorder international politics in a system of purified nationalism that joined the uniqueness of different peoples within a community of peace and justice. They felt much less sure, however, as to what precise form the fulfillment of the American peace mission must take. Some believed that America's chief peace contribution involved the voluntary extension of its constitutional and federal principles. Others felt that it should encourage the spread of it disciplined democratic processes. Still others thought that it could best share the productive efficiency of its capitalistic economy.

Yet beyond all these differences, nearly all assumed that the dedicated pursuit of America's global mission would work for the sake of peace with a three-sided effectiveness. First, it would blunt the sharp competitiveness of international politics. Secondly, it would liberate other nations for the job of realizing their highest individual destinies through peaceable means. And finally, it would serve to pacify and free the peoples of the world directly at the expense of revolutionary socialism, which had expanded so tremendously in the war's turbulence. American peace leaders generally opposed outside interference with the Soviet experiment in Russia. But they definitely favored its containment and spoke uneasily of the threat of larger revolutionary violence. The United States had a vital and manifest interest in the international peace reform, peace leaders agreed. It must act as the master organizer of the world's disordered politics so that all might be liberated from the twin dangers of total war and social revolution.[44]

In spite of these shared sentiments, however, the common front evinced by the postwar American peace movement was split along several fault lines. Peace leaders clashed often with one another because of temperamental differences and personal animosities. They quarreled over matters of political partisanship, proper tactics, and realizable ends, and they permitted many of their differences to be aggravated by the larger struggle that ranged reformers against standpat nationalists throughout the twenties.

But perhaps the largest single source of friction within the postwar movement flowed from the varying social, economic, and cultural attachments of the country's major peace leaders. Joined by those slender tendons of common conviction, peace leaders operated not so much as members of a movement as they did as defenders of a cause that stretched across a continuum of committed groupings, each of which was distinguished by a unique conception of peace, a singular vision of the American world role, and a special socioeconomic appeal. Conservative legalists moved from their Old Guard Republican alignments and their juridical sense of peace as courtroom justice to stand in defense of postwar Republicanism and to speak politely of the need for spreading international law. Guided by Elihu Root and other highly respected leaders of the prewar peace movement, conservative legalism appealed to those eastern metropolitan businessmen and lawyers who treated war as a real if unpleasant fact of international life and who aimed to limit its reach through voluntary international ordinances and domestic controls on excitable mass democracies. Tactful and discreet, conservative legalist leaders slid with smooth influence along the inner rims of Republican policymaking circles. They praised the politics of stability, defended United States military interventions as policing operations, and disdained more ambitious peaceseekers who sought to hurry the laws of evolutionary progress that eventually would bring peace. The American Society of International Law, the American Peace Society, and the Carnegie Endowment for International Peace all operated well in line with their needs.The liberal internationalist leadership, on the other hand, generally consisted of those progressive lawyers, journalists, and social scientists who resolved during the Great War to extend the organizational techniques by which they were managing the American military effort to the management of the postwar peace. Committed to the purposeful control of social and industrial change, pragmatic progressives like Raymond Fosdick and James

Shorwell viewed war as a systemic malfunction and argued for the fuller assembling of international peacekeeping machinery and the improved administration of a better engineered world order. Peace to them was the dynamic produced as peoples cooperated under expert direction in the rational management of change. Jarred after 1915 by the exponential growth of war's destructiveness, liberals intended first to effect systematic order through the League of Nations among those great industrial powers lying along the Euro-American axis. Working through the League of Nations Non-Partisan Association and the Foreign Policy Association, they criticized Washington policymakers for ignoring the Geneva experiment and any other attempts to organize cooperation among the great industrial powers; in a more positive vein, they undertook actions, like the struggle for neutrality revision, that were designed to draw the United States into fuller responsibility for preserving Europe's peace. In all these things, liberal internationalists found themselves at odds with the most vocal exponents of the conservative legalist approach and, in many of them, they also differed with the social progressives who made up the great bulk of the postwar peace movement.

Across the broad base of the postwar American peace movement were those social progressives who had enlisted in the peace crusade after service in a variety of progressive reform causes. Working with special strength in church and women's organizations, the social progressive grouping claimed the support of victorious Prohibitionists and women suffrage activists, plus a vibrant new breed of liberal pacifists that had appeared in opposition to the barbarism of the Great War. Inveterately moralistic, social progressives saw modern total war as a social sin, and they sought to expel it through the rime-honored reform techniques of popular exhortation, general condemnation, and legal reformation. They were preachers and pontificators par excellence. Appealing to a national audience, social progressives organized public constituencies, moved congregations, and defined various approaches toward the peace reform. Some like Kirby Page plotted out approaches that were remarkably realistic. Others like the Women's Peace Union embarked on enterprises that were painfully utopian. Yet all shared in a sense of the overriding immediacy of the peace reform. And all expressed an unsettling ambivalence toward the relationship between the American global mission and a working peace reform. Peace progressives felt sure that the American people had a peculiar responsibility to advance the cause of peace through means of trade, moral encouragement, and limited acts of cooperation. What confused them was the nature of the American peace responsibility in Europe. Commonly convinced that America's highest spiritual duty was to be played out in Asia, the social progressives' desire to save Europe from the institutionalized evil of the war system clashed consistently with their determination to avoid absorption in Europe's ancient hatreds.

Caught in this dilemma, peace progressives haggled over the most appropriate means--a noncoercive League of Nations, a World Court, arbitration, disarmament, the Outlawry of War--by which America might smash the war evil in Europe and free itself for its larger organizing/liberating purpose in the rest of the world. "The only practical issue" before American peaceseekers, declared the progressive philosopher John Dewey, "is whether there is some means of engaging the action of the United States on the side of cooperation for international peace that does not tie us in advance to support the existing European settlement."[45] It was not only the most practical issue for peace progressives; it was also the most divisive. Crackling at the center of tensions that ranged pro-League progressives against Outlawry of War reformers, the question of how the United States might save Europe from the war evil without entanglement swung like a downed high-tension wire among social progressives throughout the postwar decade, scattering them across various issues and preventing them from uniting behind any coherent formula that might reconcile the American world mission and real peace reform.

The ambivalence felt by social progressives toward the American role in Europe aggravated the more serious divisions within the postwar peace movement and ensured the movement's failure to affect American foreign policy. But there were other reasons for that failure as well. Leading a voluntaristic movement for moral reform, top peaceseekers wielded little influence in Republican Washington, a sweaty Southern town where major policy decisions emerged from a welter of personal ambitions, party needs, and propertied interests brokered by men of power and connection. In this environment, the moral and intellectual orientation of the volunteer middle-class peace reformers did them little good. In fact, that very orientation actually impeded them in the pursuit of infrequent suggestions that they team with the angry farmers, disorganized wage-earners, oppressed ethnics, and other aggrieved forces in American life who were pressing for change out of sheer material necessity. The International Association of Machinists voted to withdraw from the NCPW in September 1926, for example, because of fear that its continuing connection would handicap its members in their contract negotiations with military officers of the army and navy installations across the country. [46] Though curt and abrupt, the Machinists action provided an accurate reflection of the real distribution of political power in postwar America and a sharp reminder of the peace movements limited political effectiveness. Movement activists might as well face the facts, peace leaders concluded by mid-decade. The American government would support institutions of world order only when American business decided that those institutions could "bring stability to the world, which is what business interests require more than any other factor." There was little use in appealing to Washington's finer moral sensibilities. Business interests and business considerations were "governing national policies everywhere now-a-days," peace reformers agreed. They constituted "the decisive factor" in effecting a more cooperative American international policy.[47]

At the same time, the effectiveness of postwar peace reformers diminished as they were swept up in the war-borne battle between progressives and traditionalists over the very definition of American nationhood. Ignited in Wilson's crusade and flashing intermittently thereafter, there took place throughout the decade an ugly firefight between the forces of order and the forces of movement, between a newly invigorated Right and an irrepressible Left. At its base, the struggle between militant nationalists and liberal reformers represented the latest phase in the fifty-year-old conflict in America over the tolerability of flagrant social and economic injustices in an industrial capitalist society. But that conflict took on new form in the twenties, metamorphosing into a cultural struggle between traditionalists and modernists over the custodianship and reordering of the nation's values in a time of rapid demographic and economic change.[48] Epitomized in courtroom melodramas like the Scopes "monkey" trial and the Sacco-Vanzetti case, the battle between the forces of tradition and the forces of modernity ranged over matters of national loyalty, racial integrity, and religious truth with a virulent intensity that distracted and confused peace reformers. The combined class, religious, and cultural struggle was broad in scope and penetrating in power. It opened many wounds and closed many minds. And it produced a climate most inhospitable to peace reformers anxious for harmony and reconciliation.

Almost as frustrating to dedicated peace activists was the indifference with which they and their cause were met by the great majority of Americans in the twenties. The campaigns for the League, disarmament, World Court, arbitration, and the Outlawry of War proved little more than "mere chips and foam on the surface of the stream of American life" in the twenties, said one sympathetic contemporary.[49] They seemed random and adrift, so light and ephemeral that they were incapable of reaching the great body of the American public consciousness. Optimistic peace leaders argued that more and more people were discovering an immediate personal interest in the organization of world peace. But most had to agree that it was extraordinarily difficult to interest the masses in the politics of peace as long as they were engrossed in the far glossier—and less controversial—worlds of sports, motion pictures, and high finance. No matter how avidly they spoke of the new democratic diplomacy, peace activists could not escape the general indifference that the masses exhibited toward international issues. They simply had to cope with a public attitude that was best captured by the *Detroit News as* it analyzed popular reaction to the 1929 Cruiser bill: "Great enthusiasm for the bill on the part of a few Senators, a few people; great enmity to the bill on the part of a dozen Senators, a few people; and great apathy toward the bill on the part of the overwhelming majority."[50]

Faced with internal division, antipathy in Washington, enmity on the Right, and apathy in the general electorate, the modernizing peace movement was unable to shove American foreign policy into directions that would help industrial peoples to resolve the problem of total war and pave the way toward total peace. Yet peaceseekers succeeded in at least three vital ways in forging the bases of a new reform movement. In the first place, they successfully established a host of new organizations and agencies, including the Foreign Policy Association, the WILPF, the War Resisters League, and the League of Nations Non-Partisan Association (linear antecedent of the modern United Nations Association of the United States), which worked to keep the peace issue far forward in the public consciousness and which demonstrated their effectiveness by their very durability over the rest of the century. Peace workers in the twenties constructed the organizational substructure for the long-term upbuilding of peace.

In the second place, postwar peace leaders defined and articulated the most intelligent critiques of Washington's ongoing foreign policies and mounted in their writings and speeches the best reasoned attacks on the unilateralist and imperialist underpinnings of American diplomacy. Whether phrased in the arguments of Edwin Borchard, James Shotwell, or Jessie Wallace Hughan, the peacemakers as a group demonstrated the most realistic understanding of Washington's postwar purposes and issued the most incisive challenges to Republican priorities. If the peace movement failed to alter national policy, it succeeded in doing the next best thing that can be expected of a movement for change and reform: it questioned prevailing dogma and advanced fresh alternatives. It cut and cleared other paths. Finally, the peace movement became modern as it framed new perspectives. Perhaps the greatest breakthrough effected by postwar American peace activists involved their recognition of the synergism at work in their time among nationalism, advancing modernization, and a war-organized society. Peaceseekers had long suspected that integral nationalism and interdependent industrialism--the two elements traditionally upheld by Western liberals as the main ingredients of lasting peace--actually constituted an explosive admixture that produced more strife than harmony. Yet peace leaders in the early twenties thought for a brief time that they could overcome this threat. While sharply aware of the volatility of modern nationalism, peace workers tried to link it and the multiple loyalties that it contained to the kind of stable international institutions that would uphold a lasting peace. In this vein, they spoke most hopefully of the need for a "Christian Patriotism" or "a newer and higher conception of nationalism," some emotional coupling that would connect individual national loyalties to the general interest that everyone shared in interdependent material prosperity.[51]

Increasingly, however, more critical peace activists came to believe that what was happening around them involved no mere interplay between nationalism and industrial interdependence, but an unprecedented synergism between nationalism and a modernization process that was assuming a more militaristic cast. Like their contemporaries, peace leaders felt the pervasive power of postwar American nationalism and marveled at the country's incredible lunge toward greater modernization through corporate social forms and institutions. Unlike their contemporaries, however, they also felt a fuller sensitivity to the nation's enlarging fascination with things military. Annual United States military expenditures in the twenties averaged more than twice the level of the last (1916) peacetime budget, while the War Department wielded extraordinary new influence in matters of civilian preparedness and public education. The number of American men under arms by 1925 had nearly doubled within fifteen years; the navy stood at full treaty strength; and a rudimentary "Industrial-Military Complex" proceeded to rationalize relations between government war planners and civilian contractors.[52] While hardly signs of an emerging warfare state, these developments definitely reflected the deepening desire felt by American political and business leaders for the creation of a corporatist society that exalted the values of orderliness, purposefulness, and discipline--a society that found natural reinforcement in a popularized military ethic. Working within a highly nationalistic culture, the country's civilian leaders consistently lauded these values and that ethic as vital to continued modernization through a corporatist order that would save individual freedom from the twin threats of state socialism and monopoly capitalism.[53] With their encouragement, the forces of nationalism, modernization, and fuller militarization thus evolved in postwar America in a highly interactive and mutually supportive manner. And as they did, they were an extremely ominous portent to postwar peace leaders as to the possibilities of a living peace in the modern world.

Confronted with the force of this fresh social synergism, postwar American peaceseekers came gradually to speak of nationalism and modernization less as harmonizing elements in world politics, and more as the highly divisive sources of rank imperialism and conflict. Kirby Page concluded that the seeming anomaly between growing economic interdependence and deepening nationalist sentiment actually constituted the chief stimulus to competing Great Power imperialisms that, in turn, fired national self-consciousness and the urge toward militarized social modernization among colonial peoples. It promised to be a violently expansive cycle. Jessie Wallace Hughan similarly observed that "the focus of national devotion had unmistakably shifted away from the ideal of nationality to the far wider principle of imperialism." The nineteenth-century dynamism of nationality or cultural identity, Hughan asserted, no longer found "an outlet in constructive nationalism" that came through the development of a political state. Instead, it was being diverted by sharpening industrial competition as more states modernized "along the new channels of imperialism." [54]

Without doubt, warned the leading Protestant theologian Harry Emerson Fosdick, the "sheer paganism" of mass nationalism was gaining influence with such speed that it threatened to be "the chief rival of Christianity." "The supreme object of devotion for multitudes is the nation. In practical action they know no higher God." Frightened by nationalism's burgeoning mass power, Fosdick called upon his generation to take "the next great step, the most momentous step in human history"--the step toward superseding "belligerent nationalism with co-operative international substitutes for war!"[55] It was the only way in which the world's most powerful social dynamic could be separated in the modernizing process from the overhanging menace of war. It was the only practicable way by which the threat of modern total war could be mitigated. More acutely than anyone, postwar American peaceseekers perceived the greatest paradox of our century, that nationalism "is at the same time the most unifying and the most divisive force in our modern world," the most contributive to modernization and the most destructive of cooperation.[56] How that paradox was to be resolved for the sake of a peace that persisted in order and diversity was the most baffling problem of their times. And it remains ours.

NOTES

1. New *York Times,* 12 November 1928, p. 2.

2. Borah, in speech before the Foreign Affairs Press Association, 7 March 1928, p. 4, Box 308, William E. Borah Papers, Manuscript Division, Library of Congress, Washington, D.C.

3. Kellogg to Coolidge, 1 December 1928, 711.0012 Anti-war/565, Record Group 59, "Records of the Department of State" hereafter cited as State Department Records, National Archives, Washington, D.C.

4. M.S.W., "With Interpretations," *News Bulletin* of the Foreign Policy Association 8, no. 12 (25 January 1929): 2.

5. James Brown Scott, in Yearbook of the Carnegie Endowment for International Peace, 1930 (Washington, 1930), p. 102; Arthur Deerin Call, "'Only a Moral Gesture,'" *Advocate of Peace Through Justice* 90, nos. 10-11 (October—November 1928): 598.

6. Charles Clayton Morrison, "The Senate and the Peace Pact," *Christian Century* 45, no. 50 (13 December 1928): 1522. Italics in original.

7. Levinson to Raymond Robins, 20 February 1929, Box 22, Raymond Robins Papers, State Historical Society of Wisconsin Library, Madison, Wis.; or, "Prostituting the Peace Pact," *Christian Century 46*, no. 8 (21 February 1929): 257.

8. "The Treaty Is Ratified!" *Christian Century 46,* no. 4 (24 January 1929): 99; "Exit the Pacifist, Enter the Patriot," *ibid.*, no. 13 (28March 1929): 415.

9. *Annual Report* of the Federal Council of Churches of Christ in America (New York, 1929), p. 43.

10. John Haynes Holmes to Mrs. Gertrude Winslow, 27 November 1928, Box 1, John Haynes Holmes Papers, Manuscript Division, Library of Congress, Washington, D.C.

11. Dorothy Detzer to Emily Greene Balch, 26 November 1928, Box 5, Records of the U.S. Section of the Women's International League for Peace and Freedom, Swarthmore College Peace Collection, Swarthmore, Pa.

12. Kirby Page et al., form letter, 27 October, 1928, Box 2, Emily Greene Balch Papers, Swarthmore College Peace Collection, Swarthmore, Pa.,; see also Norman Thomas, "Advances in the Quest for Peace," in *Recent Gains in American Civilization,* ed. Kirby Page (New York: Harcourt, Brace, Inc., 1928), pp. 94-95.

13. Balch to Mrs. Maud Stockwell, 27 November 1928, Box 2, Balch Papers.

14. "Epoch-making Pact of Futile Gesture?" *The World Tomorrow* 11, no. 9 (September, 1928): 357.

15. Carrie Chipman Catt, "A Mighty Stride Towards Peace," *Woman's Journal* (September 1928): 28.

16. Henry Atkinson, Report of the General Secretary to the 15th annual meeting of the board of trustees, December 1928, p. 9, Box 1, Records of the Church Peace Union, Swarthmore College Peace Collection, Swarthmore, Pa. For similar expressions of Protestant sentiment, see report of the Committee on Messages and Recommendations, pp. 15-16, 11-13 November 1928, Box 2, Records of the World Alliance for International Friendship Through the Churches, Swarthmore College Peace Collection, Swarthmore, Pa; and *The Churches and the World Covenant of Peace: A Declaration of Policy,* pamphlet, December 1928, Box 1, Records of the Federal Council of Churches of Christ in America, Swarthmore College Peace Collection, Swarthmore, Pa.

17.Gordon, in World Alliance for International Friendship Through the Churches *News Letter 5, no.* 3 (12 September 1928): 2.

18. Allen Dulles, "The Threat of Anglo-American Naval Rivalry," *Foreign Affairs* 7, no. 2 (January 1929): 173; Frederick Moore, *America's Naval Challenge* (New York: Macmillan, 1929), p. 1.

19. John W. Davis, "Anglo-American Relations and Sea Power," *Foreign Affairs 7,* no. 3 (April 1929): 354; Charles Cheney Hyde, "An American Substitute for British Blockades," *ibid.*, no. 4 (July 1929): 631.

20. Fosdick on the peace pact, attached to Fosdick's secretary to Mrs. O. Henry Fredkin, 2 November 1928, Raymond B. Fosdick Papers, Firestone Library, Princeton University, Princeton, N.J.

21. John Hessin Clarke to Shotwell, 11 February 1929, League of Nations Association Box, A-L, James T. Shotwell Papers, Butler Library, Columbia University, New York, N.Y.; James Shotwell in New York *Times,* 11 February 1929, p. 2; idem, "Neutrality and National Policy," *Outlook* and *Independent* 151, no.16 (17 April 1929): 620. See also idem, "Memorandum on the Relation of the Kellogg Pact to Naval Disarmament," attached to Herbert Hoover to Frank Kellogg, 21 May 1929, p. 6, 711.0012 Anti-war/815, State Department Records; and "Conversation with Professor James Shotwell," 10 May 1929, 711.9412 Anti-war/127, *ibid.*

22. Capper press release, in Box: Bills introduced by A. Capper, folder: arms embargo, Arthur Capper Papers, Kansas State Historical Society, Topeka, Kans.

23. Shotwell to Manley O. Hudson, 11 March 1929, Fosdick Papers.

24. "The Issue Behind the Cruiser Controversy," *Literary Digest* 100, no. 7 (16 February 1929): 9-10.

25. Butler to M. Georges Lechartier, 15 February 1929, folder: A. Capper, Nicholas Murray Butler Papers, Butler Library, Columbia University, New York, N.Y.

26. "Steps to Peace," *Women's Journal*, March 1929, p. 26; Annual Report of the Federal Council of Churches of Christ in America (New York, 1929), p. 177; minutes of the board of directors, 28 March 1929, Records of the League of Nations Non-Partisan Association, in the possession of the United Nations Association of the United Stares, New York, N.Y.; Frederick Lynch, in World Alliance for International Friendship Through the Churches News Letter S, no. 9 (16 March 1929): 2-4; Edwin Borchard and William Potter Page, *Neutrality for the United States* (New Haven: Yale University Press, 1937), pp. *295-96.*

27. Libby to Mrs. John F. Moors, 30 July 1928, Records of the National Council for Prevention of War (hereafter cited as NCPW Records), Swarthmore College Peace Collection, Swarthmore, Pa.

28. David Jayne Hill, "The Multilateral Treaty for the Renunciation of War," *American Journal of International Law* 22, no. 4 (October 1928): 825 ; Calvin Coolidge, 15 January 1929, in *The Talkative President: The Off-the-Record Press Conferences of Calvin Coolidge,* ed. Robert H. Farrell and Howard Quint (Amherst, Mass.: University of Massachusetts Press, 1964), p. 219.

29. Hill, p. 825.

30. For the last, see David Hunter Miller, *The Peace Part of Paris; A Study of the Briand-Kellogg Treaty* (New York: G.P. Putnam's Sons, 1928), p. 132; Borchard to John Bassett Moore, 7 January and 11 January 1929, Box 60, John Bassett Moore Papers, Manuscript Division, Library of Congress, Washington, D.C.; and Borchard to William Borah, 6 September 1928, Edwin M. Borchard Papers, Sterling Library, Yale University, New Haven, Conn.

31. "'The Pact of Paris' Opening a New World Era," *Literary Digest* 98, no. 10 (8 September 1928): 5.

32. 1928 Republican party campaign platform, New York *Times*, 25 June 1928,p. 8.

33. Charles Clayton Morrison, "The Treaty is Signed," *Christian Century* 45, no. 36 (13 September 1928): 1070; and "The Senate and the Peace Pact," *ibid.*, no. 50 (13 December 1928): 1521.

34. Peter Brock, *Pacifism in the United States: From the Colonial Era to the First World War* (Princeton: Princeton University Press, 1968), p. 869; Charles Chatfield, "World War I and the Liberal Pacifist in the United Stares," *American Historical Review* 65, no. 7 (December 1970); 1920-22, 1930-37; and Charles DeBenedetti, "James T. Shotwell and the Science of International Politics," *Political Science Quarterly* 89, no.2 (June 1974); 380-90.

35. Anna Garlin Spencer, "Organizing Peace," manuscript attached to Spencer to John Haynes Holmes, 4 June 1923, Box 1, Anna Garlin Spencer Papers, Swarthmore College Peace Collection, Swarthmore, Pa.

36. Florence B. Boeckel, *Between War and Peace: A Handbook for Peace Workers* (New York: Macmillian, 1928), p.5.

37. Henry Pinkham form letter, 6 October 1927, Box 1, Records of the Association to Abolish War, Swarthmore College Peace Collection, Swarthmore, Pa.

38. James T. Shotwell, "Plans and Protocols to End War. Historical Outline and Guide," *International Conciliation,* no. 208 (March 1925): 7.

39. *Ibid.* See also Shotwell in New York *Times,* 20 April 1925, P. 5; and idem. "Locarno and After," *Association Men* 51, no. 6 (February 1926): 269-270

40. Kirby Page, *An American Peace Policy* (New York: H. Doran & Co.,1925), p. 84.

41. Shotwell to Kirby Page, 18 August 1925, Box 2, Kirby Page Papers, Southern California School of Theology, Claremont, Calif.

42. Fosdick to Newton Baker, 8 September 1925, Fosdick Papers.

43. Frederick Libby, *What Price Peace? A Theory of World Peace,* pamphlet in *NCPW* Records; idem, "Only America Can Lead," National Council for Prevention of War *News Bulletin* 8, no. 1 (1 January 1929): 2; and idem, "The American Peace Movement—An Interpretation," *ibid.* 7, no. 6 (June 1928); 3.

44. As the FPA's James McDonald put it, the next war "would so disastrously disorganize the elaborate and delicate mechanism of modern industry, commerce and finance, as to provoke that widespread discontent which the communists believe will make possible the world revolution"; and it was "against this danger the capitalist states have set up the League of Nations" (James G. McDonald at meeting of Chicago Council on Foreign Relations, 10 March 1928, Box 477, Series I-E, Anita McCormick Blaine Papers, State Historical Society of Wisconsin Library, Madison, Wis.)

45. John Dewey, letter to editor, *New Republic* 54, no. 695 (28 March 1928): 195.

46. International Association of Machinists form letter co NCPW members, September 1926, NCPW Records.

47. Libby to William Hard, 29 April 1926, ibid. See also Newton D. Baker to Raymond Fosdick, 20 January 1928, Box 99, Newton D. Baker Papers, Manuscript Division, Library of Congress, Washington, D.C.; Edwin Borchard, "Common Sense in Foreign Policy," *Journal of International Relations* 11, no. 1 (July 1920): 27-44. Furthermore, for evidence of the mutuality of interests between the government and private arms manufacturers and the rudimentary beginnings of an "industrial-military complex," see Secretary of War John Weeks to Charles Evans Hughes, 26 September 1923, 511.3 B 1/128, State Department Records; and Paul A. C.

Koistinen, "The Industrial-Military Complex in Historical Perspective: The Inter-War Years," *Journal of American History* 56, no. 4 (March 1970): 819-39.

48. Don Kirschner, "Conflicts and Politics in the 1920's: Historiography and Prospects," *Mid-America* 48, no. 4 (October 1966): 233.

49. Merle Curti, *Peace or War: The American Struggle, 1636-1936 (New York:* W.W. Norton & Co., 1936), p. 262.

50. Quoted in "A Cruiser Victory That May Aid Disarmament," *Literary Digest* 100, no. 7 (16 February 1929): 5.

51. Sidney Gulick, *The Christian Crusade* for *a Warless World* (New York: Macmillan, 1922), pp. 46-47; Kirby Page, "Working Toward a Warless World," *The Christian-Evangelist 62,* no. 24 (11 June 1925): 745.

52. United States Bureau of the Census, *Historical Statistics* of *the United States: Colonial* Times *to 1957* (Washington: GPO, 1960), p. 718; Donald R. McCoy, *Coming of Age: The United* States *During the 1920's and* 1930's (Baltimore: Penguin Books, Inc., 1973), p. 44; and Koistinen, pp. 819-35.

53. Corporatism is here used to signify that form of political economy that "calls for the organization of society along the lines of functional economic units that include both labor and management, that are voluntary and decentralized ... self-governing and self-regulating, cognizant of the eroding distinctions between public and private sectors (i.e., national political institutions and the marketplace), and theoretically committed to harmonious cooperation out of a sense of community, social responsibility, and devotion to efficiency" (Joan Hoff Wilson, *Ideology and Economics: U.S. Relations with the Soviet Union, 1918-1933* [Columbia, Mo.: University of Missouri Press, 1974], pp. ix-x; and Charles S. Maier, *Recasting Bourgeois Europe: Stabilization in France, Germany, and Italy in the Decade After World War!/*Princeton: Princeton University Press. 1975] pp. 9-15). See also Cyril E. Black, *The Dynamics of Modernization* (New York: Harper and Row, Inc., 1966), pp. 27-29, 55, 131-133; John P. Diggins, *Mussolini and Fascism: The View from America* (Princeton: Princeton University Press, 1972), pp. 144-61, 262-67; and William E. Leuchtenburg. "The New Deal and the Analogue of War," in *Change and Continuity in Twentieth Century America*, ed. John Braeman et al. (New York: Harper Colophon edition, 1966), pp. 81-144.

54. Kirby Page, *An American Peace Policy*, pp. 10-17; idem, *Dollars and World Peace* (New York, 1927), pp. 9-11; and Jessie Wallace Hughan, *A Study of International Government* (New York: Thomas Crowell Co., Inc., 1923), pp. 124, 13'4.

55. Harry Emerson Fosdick, "A Christian Conscience About War," *Christian Work* 119, no. 13 (26 September 1925): 254-55.

56. Page, *Dollars and World Peace*, p. 9.

CHAPTER FIVE

THE PEACE MOVEMENT IN THE THIRTIES

Lawrence S. Wittner

Originally published in 1969, Wittner's revised work carries the story of the struggle against war to the 1980s. Wittner, one of the most distinguished historians in the field of peace history, recently achieved notoriety for the completion of his massive trilogy, *The Struggle Against the Bomb*. In this introductory chapter to his revised edition, Wittner offers an extensive and thorough examination of the principles and methods, successes and failures of the leading figures and organizations of the interwar peace movement. His unique contribution to the field is the way in which he attempts to explain how the peace movement of the 1930s combined moral influence with political relevance. He connects it to the struggles involving organized labor, civil rights, and social justice movements. His overview of the pre-World War Two peace movement raises some interesting questions to ponder. After reading the essay consider the following: How did charges of Communism and Socialism thwart their appeal?; What tensions existed between pacifists and non-pacifists seeking to avoid another world war?; What impact did the rise of Fascism and Nazism have on the dynamics of peace efforts in the thirties?; and, How has the movement's structural fluidity account for both its repeated weakness in times of international tension and peculiar resiliency once war does break out?

I am a pacifist. You, my fellow citizens . . . are pacifists, too.
FRANKLIN A. ROOSEVELT, 1940[1]

In 1910, when Andrew Carnegie set aside ten million dollars in bonds "to hasten the abolition of international war," the optimistic Scottish immigrant assured his trustees that "when war is abolished," they could "consider what is the next most degrading evil." A quarter century later, although that contingency had not yet arisen, the cause of world peace could boast an unprecedented organization and popularity in the United States. One writer estimated at the time that the peace movement had twelve million adherents and an income of over one million dollars.[2]

The pacifist ideal, while possessed of a long and distinguished history, never took hold in the United States until the aftermath of World War I, when a wave of disillusionment with that conflict swept across the country. A series of gruesome books, often written by the participants themselves, turned Wilsonian rhetoric on its head. Henri Barbusse's *Under Fire*, Siegfried Sassoon's *Counter-Attack*, Ernest Hemingway's *A Farewell to Arms*, John Dos Passos' *Three Soldiers*, Laurence Stallings' What *Price Glory?*, and the most popular war story in America, a translation of Erich Maria Remarque's *All Quiet on the Western Front*, portrayed a gory and senseless slaughter. The redeeming features of this bloodshed were undermined for the public by scholars and publicists who pointed to selfish war aims and deception on the part of the Allies. Arthur Ponsonby's *Falsehood in Wartime*, Harold D. Lasswell's *Propaganda Technique in the World War*, and Sir Philip Gibbs' *Now It Can Be Told* helped to convince Americans that their emotions had been skillfully manipulated by the masters of war.[3]

As the circle of discontent widened, many Americans, convinced of their betrayal, found the culprit in the villain of the depression-scarred decade--the avaricious businessman. In the spring of 1934 an article entitled "Arms and Men," appearing in the conservative *Fortune* magazine, together with two books, George Seldes' Iron, *Blood and Profits* and Helmuth Engelbrecht and Frank Hanighen's *Merchants of Death,* stimulated interest in the machinations of munitions makers. *Merchants of Death* soon became a best seller and a Book-of-the-Month Club selection, while the thesis that traffic in armaments led to war gained widespread currency. It was thereafter repeated by the President of the United States, two former Secretaries of State, the Christian *Science Monitor,* the *Wall Street Journal,* and members of Congress. When the Nye Committee investigations, born themselves of popular outrage, were completed, the new mood had received its official sanction.[4]

It did not require many publicists to show that the war's aftermath failed to measure up to wartime promises. As the black-shirted legions drilled in Europe who could believe that the war had made the world safe for democracy, or that it had ended war? William Allen White, the Kansas newspaper publisher, wrote in an editorial of November 11, 1933:

Fifteen years ago came the Armistice and we all thought it was to be a new world. It is! But a lot worse than it was before.

Ten million men were killed and many more maimed, fifty billion dollars' worth of property destroyed, the world saddled with debts.

And for what? Would it have been any worse if Germany had won? Ask yourself honestly. No one knows.

. . . The boys who died just went out and died. To their own souls' glory, of course—but what else? . . . Yet the next war will see the same hurrah and the same bowwow of the big dogs to get the little dogs to go out and follow the blood scent and get their entrails tangled in the barbed wire.

And for what?

. . . . .

War is the devil's joke on humanity.[5]

In the early Thirties, stunned by the new perspective on World War I, millions of Americans vowed "never again." The Reverend Harry Emerson Fosdick recalled that he "went through the disillusionment of it aftermath, confronting with increasing agony the anti-Christian nature of war's causes, processes and results." He concluded that he would "never again put" his "Christian ministry at the nation's disposal for the sanction and backing of war," and consequently "became a pacifist." Clergymen "committed a sin when they blessed war banners," Rabbi Stephen Wise told a Paterson audience in 1931, "and I for one will never again commit that sin." The Jewish leader, who had deliberately taken a job in a naval shipyard during World War I, now declared that "war never ends war. War ends nothing but peace." In February, 1937, when Americans were asked, "If another war like the World War develops in Europe, should America take part again?," 95 per cent answered "no."[6]

With war and the military under fire, thought of disarmament flourished and achieved unprecedented respectability. "Secretary [of the Navy] Wilbur says the Navy is unready for war," laughed the *New Yorker* in 1929, and "by an amazing coincidence there is no war ready for the Navy." A total of 22,165 different plans for world peace were submitted in one year in the Bok Peace Award Contest. Albert Einstein told a pacifist meeting: "You must convince the people to take disarmament into their own hands and to declare that they will have no part in war or in the preparation for war." Young men who resisted conscription and refused arms served as "the pioneers of a warless world." Scientists should "refuse to co-operate in research for war purposes," while every newspaper should "en-courage its readers to refuse war service," Einstein declared. This was "not the time for temporizing. You are either for war or against war." [7]

In reality the issue was far less sharply defined than the distinguished mathematician thought. Participants in the peace movement found unity solely in their collective opposition to war, although, even on this point, disagreement existed between pacifists and those, no less sincere, to whom military force represented a dreadful, but possible, alternative. On other issues the peace movement, like other mass movements, was hopelessly divided. And yet, despite their many differences, peace activists frequently shared a common faith, often unspoken, in the potentialities of a disarmed world. They saw feuding nations displaced by international authority, economic and racial injustice giving way to a more equitable social order, and fear and hatred replaced by harmony and joy. When Americans dreamed of a world without war, the vision shimmered hazily before them of the restoration of the human community.

A social cause with a variegated constituency, the peace movement appealed perhaps most strongly to women. In the decades following the granting of women's suffrage, politicians kept a wary eye on the peace issue, convinced that it exercised a strong influence over the feminine ballot. When the President hedged in 1935 on neutrality legislation, Representative Fred Sisson of New York angrily informed the White House that "thousands and thousands of women's votes have been lost by this stalling." A visit to Washington in the cause of world peace by Mrs. Carrie Chapman Catt, who represented the eleven largest women's organizations in the country, occasioned considerable attention and respect from the uneasy legislators. Nor was the legend of Lysistrata primarily a matter of folklore. Frederick J. Libby, a leading figure in pacifist circles during this period, argued in 1930 that women "constitute the backbone of the peace movement in America," while a more recent student of the era has maintained that a large percentage of individuals involved in the peace effort were women. As one of their number has observed: "They were not women of the leisure class but professional women—doctors, lawyers, professors, editors of periodicals, journalists, social workers, reformers, and some public officials."[8]

In the decade before the European war clouds darkened the horizon, the American peace movement experienced some of its most dazzling successes within the Protestant churches. A conference on the Churches and World Peace of the Federal Council of Churches resolved in 1929 that "the churches should condemn resort to the war-system as sin and should henceforth refuse to sanction it or to be used as agencies in its support." In 1931, when the religious pacifist magazine *The World Tomorrow* polled Protestant ministers in the United States on the question of military service, 12,078 of the 19,372 respondents declared that the church should never again sanction any war. Three years later, a similar poll found pacifism among the clergy on the rise.[9]

As pacifism swept through the Protestant churches in the Twenties and Thirties, condemnations of war also increased in Catholic literature. Arguments developed by Catholic peace proponents usually questioned whether modern warfare could be compatible with the requirements in natural law for a just war. Outright pacifism remained weak, however, for few took the position that Catholics should refuse participation in all wars.[10]

Jewish religious opinion, formerly not as concerned as Protestant theology with the question of peace, veered sharply toward pacifism in these years. In 1935, when the Central Conference of American Rabbis was canvassed by mail on whether it should "recommend to its members that they refuse to support any war in which this country or any country may engage," 91 voted "yes," 31 voted "yes" with reservations, and only 32 voted "no." Until the late Thirties, the Central Conference of American Rabbis, the National Council of Jewish Women, and the National Federation of Temple Sisterhoods belonged to a militant peace organization.[11]

College students joined women and the clergy as the third great force in the peace effort of the mid-Thirties. In 1933, when the Brown University *Daily Herald* polled 21,725 students in 65 colleges on the issues of peace and war, it found that the largest number, 8415, pledged themselves to absolute pacifism; another 7221 would bear arms solely in the event of an actual invasion of the country; and only 6089 would serve in any war involving the United States. The following year, nationwide "strikes" against war commenced on American campuses. In April 500 Vassar College girls in caps and gowns, led by the president of the college, paraded through the

Poughkeepsie streets, chanting "no more battleships, we want schools." This antiwar demonstration represented a radical turn about from 1917, when undergraduates had similarly paraded, but in favor of war.[12]

On April 12, 1935, 60,000 students in the nation's colleges participated in a "strike" against war. Sponsored by religious pacifist and left-wing student groups, the demonstrations drew large numbers, especially in New York, where an estimated 10,000 gathered for denunciations of war and fascism. At Columbia University 3000 students cheered speeches by Roger Baldwin of the American Civil Liberties Union (A.C.L.U.), Professor Reinhold Niebuhr of Union Theological Seminary, and James Wechsler, editor of the Columbia *Spectator*, many taking the Oxford Oath of absolute refusal to serve in the armed forces. In November demonstrations in New York drew 20,000 students. At City College 3500 crowded into the Great Hall, booing the college president when he objected, unsuccessfully, to a reading of the Oxford Oath. At Columbia a meeting of 2000 students on South Field heard Professor Harry J. Carman, chairman of the college history department, urge "spreading the anti-war gospel." New York University's two campuses played host to 4500 cheering demonstrators. "It will take more than flagwaving and bugle calls to empty the colleges for another war," reported one observer of the campus protests.[13]

If the peace movement appealed strongly to professional women, clergymen, and college students, it found less support in other elements of the population. American farmers had displayed moderate interest in opposition to war since the days of William Jennings Bryan, and the three major agricultural organizations accordingly endorsed the work of peace groups. In the autumn of 1934 petitions to the President against increased armaments were signed by ninety-six thousand farmers within three weeks. Nonetheless, rural pacifism, perhaps because it clashed with another agrarian tradition of insular pride and bellicose nationalism, remained only lukewarm. The peace movement stirred even less fervor within business circles, while veterans' organizations regarded it with unveiled hostility. American labor, perhaps repelled by the upper middle class tone of the typical peace worker, exhibited only the mildest of interest, although a few left-wing unions occasionally participated in antiwar demonstrations.[14]

Arguing that wars merely reflected the imperialism of the capitalist order, American radicals became prominent proponents of peace in the mid-Thirties. At its 1934 convention the Socialist Party adopted a resolution by a 99 to 47 vote declaring its opposition to "militarism, imperialism, and war." Neither war nor "preparedness for war" could "be tolerated by Socialists," proclaimed the convention, and if war came, Socialists would attempt to break it up by "massed war resistance" in the form of "a general strike." American Communists took a similar position, emerging as the loudest advocates of a "united front" of the working class against war. Large numbers of liberals and unaffiliated radicals, members of neither left-wing party, nevertheless believed that wars were nothing more than the expression of an exploitative economic system.[15]

Unlike the Communists, however, many American Socialists had a strong ethical commitment to pacifism. As the peace movement moved left in the radical climate of the Thirties, pacifism and democratic socialism increasingly overlapped. Socialists who also belonged to absolute pacifist organizations included Devere Allen, Socialist candidate for the United States Senate in Connecticut; Jessie Wallace Hughan, Socialist candidate for several state offices in New York; Harry Laidler, director of the League for Industrial Democracy; Clarence Senior, national secretary of the Socialist party; Powers Hapgood and Darlington Hoopes, members of the party's national executive committee; as well as Kirby Page, Sherwood Eddy, Vida Scudder, John Haynes Holmes, and Reinhold Niebuhr. Perhaps the leading pacifist Socialist of the period was the party's Presidential standard-bearer, Norman Thomas. Thomas had joined the Fellowship of Reconciliation, a religious pacifist organization, when, as a minister in New York, he perceived "an irreconcilable gulf between Christian ethics and participation in war." In 1917 he resigned his parish to become executive secretary of the organization, maintaining close connections with it thereafter as titular bead of the Socialist Party.[16]

Attempting to give some form to burgeoning peace interest throughout the United States, thirty-seven peace organizations united in 1933 to form the National Peace Conference, a loose federative effort. On the political Right were the "conservative" peace organizations, headed by the Carnegie Endowment for International Peace, the World Peace Foundation, the Woodrow Wilson Foundation, and the Church Peace Union. Old, wealthy, and compromised by their support of World War I, they failed to draw the new generation of pacifist militants but instead continued their patient efforts through established channels in educational work, in the promotion of international good will, and in the strengthening of legal and judicial machinery for the peaceful resolution of international conflict. The League of Nations Association, usually classified with these groups because of the scope of its concern, differed in that it did not possess independent economic resources but maintained a membership as a source of income and support.[17]

Perhaps the most vigorous and effective of the groups in the peace movement's militant wing was the National Council for the Prevention of War (N.C.P.W.), founded in 1921 by the Quaker pacifist Frederick J. Libby. The organization had no membership of its own, but brought together pacifist groups with such peace-minded but non-pacifist ones as the American Federation of Teachers, the Young Women's Christian Association, and the National Education Association. Libby made the first concerted efforts to attract farmers and organized labor to the cause of peace, efforts which were re-warded with a moderate degree of success in the form of organizational endorsements of the N.C.P.W. and printing of its press releases. *Peace Action*, the monthly newsletter of the N.C.P.W., achieved a circulation of over twenty thousand, while the N.C.P.W.'s Washington headquarters distributed between one and two million pieces of literature yearly throughout the Thirties. In 1935 the N.C.P.W. sent regular press releases to six hundred publications, maintained reliable newspaper contacts in over three hundred Congressional districts, and began a radio program for which Congressmen and Senators came to its studios to deliver speeches often written by the N.C.P.W. staff.[18]

Operating out of an old building across the street from the State Department under Libby's tutelage, the N.C.P.W. in 1935 consisted of twenty-one participating organizations and ten cooperating ones, a staff of eighteen, five branch offices throughout the country, and an annual budget of well over one hundred thousand dollars. Jeannette Rankin, a former leader in the woman's suffrage and Progressive movements, and a former member of the House of Representatives who had voted against American entry into World War I, served as its well-known Congressional lobbyist. The largest and most aggressive of the peace organizations, the N.C.P.W. enabled the peace movement to exercise a moderate influence in Washington affairs.[19]

Around the corner from the Washington headquarters of the N.C.P.W. stood the offices of the United States section of the Women's International League for Peace and Freedom (W.I.L.P.F.). Founded in 1915 by Jane Addams and other feminine reformers active in the quest for social justice and world peace, the international organization expanded rapidly, although the American section remained the most powerful and vigorous. Swept forward by the wave of pacifist sentiment among American women in those years, the W.I.L.P.F. in 1937 had a paid staff of eleven, one hundred twenty branches throughout the country, and over thirteen thousand members.[20]

Thanks to the efforts of its lobbyist and executive secretary Dorothy Detzer, the W.I.L.P.F. sparked a number of Congressional activities in the Thirties, including the famous investigation of the munitions industry. Miss Detzer successfully persuaded Senators Norris and Nye and even Secretary of State Cordell Hull, to his later regret, of the necessity, of the investigation. Eventually, when the W.I.L.P.F.'s lobbyist was accorded the opportunity to select the Nye Committee's chief investigator, she chose the zealous and radical Stephen Rauschenbush, who did much to initiate the Committee's sensational revelations.[21]

If the W.I.L.P.F. catered to the women's constituency, the Fellowship of Reconciliation (F.O.R.) ministered to the Protestant churches. Founded in England in 1914 as an international Christian fellowship, this religious pacifist organization developed into one of the leading spokesmen for radical Protestantism in the United States. The membership, largely recruited from the younger clergy and the religiously motivated professional classes, reached over four thousand in 1935. F.O.R. leaders included John Haynes Holmes, Harry Emerson Fosdick, and John Nevin Sayre, but after 1936 it came strongly under the influence of its most brilliant and daring thinker, A. J. Muste.[22]

Time magazine referred to Muste in 1937 as "lean, sparse. . . America's Number One pacifist." After careers as a minister, union organizer, "labor-college" administrator, and Trotskyite, Muste returned to the F.O.R. refreshed, "knowing from experience in the revolutionary movement," he stated in 1936, "that he who denies love betrays justice." His shift from Marxism to pacifism represented not a turn to the Right, but a revival of the utopian Left--an attempt to reunite the diverging strains of love and justice through the conversion of pacifism into a radical action movement.[23]

The War Resisters League (W.R.L.), established as the outgrowth of a F.O.R. enrollment committee in 1923, was designed by its founder, Jessie Wallace Hughan, to unite political, humanitarian, and philosophical objectors to war. Developed as the secular counterpart to the F.OR., the W.R.L. sought to enroll conscientious objectors with the credo: "War is a crime against humanity. We therefore are determined not to support any kind of war and to strive for the removal of all causes of war." By February, 1937, over twelve thousand Americans, many of them socialists, anarchists, and independent radicals, had signed the W.R.L. pledge. Throughout the decade the W.R.L., with its offices in

New York, played a relatively insignificant role in the peace movement; annual income never reached five thousand dollars and the active membership lagged below one thousand.[24]

An organization with pacifist principles but rarely considered part of the Thirties peace effort was the Catholic Worker movement. Launched on New York's Lower East Side in 1933 by Peter Maurin, itinerant French peasant philosopher, and Dorothy Day, a graduate of the University of Illinois, former Hollywood scenario writer, suffragette, and contributor to the Socialist *Call* and the *New Masses*, the Catholic Worker movement combined religious, radical, and anarchist concerns. By the mid-Thirties it maintained a remarkable newspaper the *Catholic Worker* (one cent per issue, circulation 110,000), Houses of Hospitality for the poor in thirty cities, and a series of Farming Communes. In 1935 members organized a branch of the English *Pax* movement at its Mott Street headquarters to study Catholic teachings on the morality of war. Catholic religious leaders lectured there and around the country, while the Catholic Worker began a long documentation of its peace position, interspersed with articles on the immorality of war and conscription. Although it devoted its prewar efforts largely to charitable works, the Catholic Worker movement provided the leading voice in American Catholic circles for militant pacifism.[25]

The so-called Historic Peace Churches contained the largest numbers of traditional religious pacifists. In 1936 there were 114,337 Mennonites, 93,697 Friends, and 188,290 Brethren residing in the United States. Their outlook on war was simply but firmly expressed by a group of Quakers (Friends) to Charles II, King of England, in 1660: "We utterly deny all outward wars and strife, and fightings and outward weapons, for any end, or under any pretence whatever; this is our testimony to the whole world. The Spirit of Christ by which we are guided, is not changeable. . . . Therefore, we cannot learn war any more." Yet despite the pacifist heritage of these churches and the ongoing humanitarianism of their action organizations—the American Friends Service Committee (A.F.S.C.), the Brethren

Service Committee, and the Mennonite Central Committee -- time and assimilation had gradually eroded much of their corporate peace testimony. For this reason, and because of a strong strain of religious quietism among the Mennonites and the Brethren, they never constituted as great an influence in the Thirties peace movement as their numbers might suggest.[26]

Left-wing groups made their own attempts to develop "mass" action for peace. The American League Against War and Fascism, established in 1933 by a coalition of liberal and left-wing organizations, drew together a paper membership of several million Americans in a "united front" against war. Members of its arrangements committee of that year, for example, included Communist leader William Z. Foster, as well as pacifists Devere Allen and Ray Newton. Groups of such divergent tendencies found it difficult to cooperate, however, and in 1934 Communists broke up a Socialist demonstration at a League meeting in New York. Shortly thereafter, Socialist elements, the National Association for the Advancement of Colored People (N.AAC.P.), and most pacifists began withdrawing from the organization. Nevertheless, the League Against War and Fascism remained vigorous throughout the decade, maintaining close ties with the Communist-influenced American Student Union and the American Youth Congress, holding mammoth demonstrations, and sending press releases to eight hundred farm, labor, and Negro newspapers across the country.[27]

Although in no sense mass organizations, these groups exercised considerable influence during the mid-Thirties. Through a maze of supporting organizations and interlocking committees, and buoyed on a cushion of favorable public opinion, pacifists were able to reach out to some forty-five to sixty million Americans.[28] The American peace movement had reached its zenith. Yet probably after 1935 and certainly after 1937 the pacifist impulse began to ebb, its strength declining in direct proportion to the rise of European fascism.

Ironically, and tragically, the renunciation of war by Americans coincided with Mussolini's seizure of power in Italy, the Nazi triumph in Germany, and the growth of Japanese militarism. But the discrepancy proved short-lived, for as the Axis powers began their series of military conquests--China and Ethiopia, Spain and Albania, Austria and Czechoslovakia--successive layers of the American peace movement broke away in anguished response. Moreover, those with an ethical revulsion to war could not fail to reserve a special shudder for the peculiar horrors of fascism. The destruction of individual liberty, the glorification of hatred, and, perhaps the ugliest of all, a series of anti-Semitic attacks that raised the ancient pogrom to the status of a State religion, sickened American peace activists, and led many to conclude that war represented the lesser of two evils.

Leading the assault upon the antiwar establishment was the brilliant ex-pacifist clergyman Reinhold Niebuhr. "History has so vividly proven" the "worthlessness" of war, he wrote in 1929, "that it can hardly be justified on any moral grounds." Chairman of the F.O.R. from 1932 to 1933, he resigned from that organization in 1934 because of his belief that violence on the part of the working class in its quest for a new social order was justifiable. War between nations, however, Niebuhr considered quite another matter, until the onset of Axis expansion. Blasting pacifist support of mandatory neutrality legislation in late 1937 at the time of Japanese aggression in Manchuria, Niebuhr declared: "We can justify the refusal to take such risks only if we believe that peace is always preferable to the exploitation of the weak by the strong." After the Munich settlement, he made his final break with pacifism. "Modern Christian and secular perfectionism, which places a premium upon non-participation in conflict, is a very sentimentalized version of the Christian faith," he wrote in 1940. And "modern Christian pacifism" was "simply a version of Christian perfectionism." On February 10, 1941, Niebuhr published the first issue of his journal *Christianity and Crisis*, which was designed to combat pacifism and neutralism within the churches.[29]

Americans now renounced pacifism with the same fervor with which they had previously renounced war. "Present-day world political conditions demand ...

a new attitude toward the problem of peace," wrote Albert Einstein, an active pacifist since 1914. "The existence of two great powers with definitely aggressive tendencies, (Germany and Japan) makes an immediate realization of movement toward disarmament ... impracticable. The friends of peace must concentrate their efforts rather on achieving an alliance of the military forces of the countries which have remained democratic." Sherwood Eddy, one of the foremost propagators of religious pacifism until this period, abandoned his pacifist faith. "Nothing . . . could stop them," he later remarked sadly, "except the use of force." Rabbi Judah Magnes, a prominent pacifist during World War I but a convert to force in 1939, typified the despair in the ranks of the peace movement. War against Germany might be immoral, he observed with sorrow, but "we do not know what else to do." [30]

Those Americans who remained committed to peace were not unaware of the evils of fascism; indeed, they were among the first to warn of them. In the spring of 1933 the first large-scale protest in the United States against Hitlerism was led down Broadway by pacifist leader John Haynes Holmes.[31] When the Reverend Harry Emerson Fosdick spoke on Nazi crimes in 1933 at the Riverside Church, some of his parishioners grew extremely upset, contending that he was too politically aggressive. He recalled with irony, several decades after the incident: "Later they were ready enough to go to war with Hitler; in 1933 they . . begged me to speak more softly even in talking about him." With the opening of the anti-Semitic drives of the Nazi regime, leaders of the peace movement worked desperately to overcome public opposition and save the helpless victims. "America is big enough to find a refuge for persecuted Jews," argued Peter Maurin in the *Catholic Worker*. Norman Thomas, urging that the United States serve as the asylum for European refugees, was sharply criticized. Polls in 1938 and 1939 reveal that less than 8 per cent of the American people were willing to admit Hitler's victims into the country. Thomas later remarked ruefully: "I learned first hand how many Americans preferred to fight or have their countrymen fight for the rights of Jews in Europe than to give them asylum in America."[32]

Nor did pacifists advocate or applaud the appeasement of the fascist powers. Oswald Garrison Villard, the pacifist editor of the *Nation*, labeled Chamberlain's pressure upon France to close its borders to Spanish Loyalists "an act so undemocratic, so base, and so perfidious as to deserve the bitterest condemnation." It was merely "another proof of the utterly heartless and ruthless way in which he pursues his shameful and stupid policy of keeping peace in Europe by wholesale surrenders to the dictators." "Has any British government in all history sunk so low?" asked Villard. Chamberlain's course was not one of pacifist humanitarianism, he wrote, but "of cowardly compromise, of buying off the dictators and thereby confirming them in their wrongdoing." [33]

Munich, the litmus test of appeasement, found peace workers astonishingly hostile, considering that President Roosevelt, the paragon of collective security, reported himself "not a bit upset over the final result" of the negotiations. Dorothy Detzer, scornful of the pact, asserted that "anyone who knows the nature of fascism knows that fascism must expand and Hitler has obligingly laid out his plans for all to read in *Mein Kampf*." Norman Thomas termed it "a logical kind of deal for capitalist powers." It was A. J. Muste, however, who presented the complete pacifist position, replete with all its difficulties. "Those people are probably right who think the four-power deal at the expense of Czechoslovakia and other lands is unlikely to accomplish any good," he wrote. "They lapse into sentimentalism, however, if they think war would accomplish more. There is only one course that will not lead to practically certain disaster: It is a renunciation of the game of power politics." [34]

Pacifists harbored no sympathies for fascism, but remained unconvinced that war represented a solution to the problem which it posed. Villard contended that the "cure" of military resistance resembled the disease. "Great armaments" are the "Road to Fascism," he warned. "They bring with them increased worship of the State, increased nationalism, increased State service, and therefore play into the hands of those like Hitler and Mussolini who declare that the citizen is made for the State and not the State for the citizen." Kirby Page, a leading pacifist publicist, feared that "the very nature of modern war necessitates the abrogation of democracy as an essential condition of success." The pacifist wanted security and peace, too, remonstrated John Haynes Holmes, "but how will they be attained through fighting? Where runs the connection between this violence and hate and the constructive policies which hold mankind together?" War might stop Hitler, they admitted, but would it stop Hitlerism? [35]

The organized peace movement underwent the beginning of a disastrous split in 1935, when the obvious collapse of the League of Nations and heightened European militarism presaged another great war. The N.C.P.W., the W.I.L.P.F., and staunchly pacifist groups, realizing their inability to prevent war in Europe, turned their attention to insulating America from that war; "conservative" elements, on the other hand, including the Carnegie Endowment for International Peace, the Church Peace Union, the World Alliance for International Friendship through the Churches, the Catholic Association for International Peace, the League of Nations Association, and Mrs. Catt's Committee on the Cause and Cure of War, gradually shifted to doctrines of collective security. In the heated neutrality debates, the former groups supported the maintenance of mandatory neutrality, while the latter worked for the modification of the neutrality provisions and, eventually, for their repeal.[36]

Joining the conservatives in the collective security camp after 1937 were important elements of the peace movement's left wing. The Spanish Civil War, the resurgence of German militarism, but especially the quest by the Soviet Union for a military alliance with the Western powers, signaled the end of the pacifist phase for American Communists. They now became dutiful New Dealers and supporters of the President's foreign policy, deftly swinging the League Against War and Fascism around to a collective security stance, and changing its name to the

American League for Peace and Democracy. One of the leading sponsors of the campus protests, the American Student Union, captured by a coalition of Communist elements and the followers of its nominally Socialist secretary, Joseph Lash, veered from pacifism to collective security, dropping the Oxford Pledge. Student demonstrations thereafter repudiated the Oxford Oath and lauded President Roosevelt's handling of the international situation, although a sizable minority, led by the non-Communist Youth Committee Against War, clung to the pacifist faith.[37]

Other segments of the American Left, while straying from the absolute pacifist position, nonetheless proved more steadfast in opposing the participation of the United States in war. During the Spanish Civil War the Socialist Party recruited the Eugene V. Debs Column for service with the Loyalists. Replying to pacifist critics, Norman Thomas explained that the party would "use to the uttermost non-violent methods consistent with true democracy. But . . . it will not yield to fascism anywhere without a struggle and . . . non-violence is not its first and last commandment." Thomas personally gave up his pacifist commitment at this time, both because he could not bear the prospect of a Spanish Republican defeat and because of a turn toward what he considered greater sophistication in his religious faith. Although he did not desire American intervention, he castigated the Roosevelt Administration for its embargo of arms for the Loyalists. In January, 1937, he wrote: "The whole record shows that with impunity and without rebuke established governments if they are conservative or Fascist have been allowed to buy what they needed ... when not actually at war with another nation. It is only when the Spanish Government fights against Fascism for the peace and freedom of mankind that the President's scruples are suddenly aroused."[38]

The outbreak of war in Europe, however, cooled Socialist ardor, wrecking the Party in the bargain. In 1940 a Socialist Party convention supported absolute neutrality and opposed military appropriations, arguing that although "the cause for which Hitler has thrown the German masses into war is damnably unholy," the "war of Chamberlain and Reynaud is not thereby rendered holy." As a result of the Party's firm anti-interventionist position, it rapidly disintegrated after 1939. Leading Socialists broke with the Party's antiwar position or resigned in what is referred to in Socialist circles as the "silent split." Half of the *Call* editorial board spoke out for full economic aid to Hitler's opponents. One group of New York Socialists joined the Committee to Defend America by Aiding the Allies, while another formed the Union for Democratic Action, which later became Americans for Democratic Action.[39]

The Party's leader, Norman Thomas, was torn by conflicting beliefs. A longtime opponent of fascism, he watched its military victories with horror. "I felt terrible when France fell," he recalled. "It shook me as very few things ever shook me." Yet, the suffering of modern warfare appeared to him as a poor palliative. "The certain evils of American involvement in war seemed greater than the uncertain good we might accomplish in a war which was still without . . . positive aim," the Socialist leader declared. In the 1940 election campaign, "we still thought we ought to keep out of war and we still said so." Members of his family disagreed, and Thomas and his wife sadly packed their youngest son off to the American Field Service a month before Pearl Harbor.[40]

Pacifism in the churches, relatively strong until 1939, began a slow decline thereafter. With the outbreak of war in Europe, Dr. George A. Buttrick, president of the Federal Council of Churches, asked Americans to maintain their neutrality "because ... war is futile and because we are eager through reconciliation to build a kindlier world," while the executive committee of the Federal Council denounced war in a unanimous resolution one month later as "an evil thing contrary to the mind of Christ." Fear of succumbing to patriotic frenzy, as in World War I, led most clergymen to take a disinterested stance in the initial months of the conflict. Gradually, however, clerical pacifism waned. Although pacifists could still rally the religious figures with greatest prestige, many prominent churchmen now commenced taking an active role in the various aid-to-the-Allies committees. As in World War I, Episcopalians and clergy with British and Canadian ancestry appear to have been most involved in these ventures.[41]

After 1939 the conflict between "radical" and "conservative" peace groups heightened. The N.C.P.W., the W.I.L.P.F., and the small pacifist groups vigorously opposed the Roosevelt Administration's foreign policy, aid to Britain, and conscription. The "conservatives," on the other hand, of the opinion that peace could be achieved only by curbing the "aggressor nations," worked closely with the Roosevelt Administration in sponsoring programs of American military assistance to the British and in securing Congressional passage of the Selective Service law. Firmly committed to collective security policies, they formed the nucleus of the Committee to Defend America by Aiding the Allies.[42]

Symptomatically, the director of the Committee, William Allen White, was a former pacifist, while he was recruited for the post by Clark Eichelberger, the director of the League of Nations Association. "With many a conflict, many a doubt," White wrote to his niece, "I who am a philosophical pacifist have yielded to my practical sense of the realities of a terrible situation," Indeed, although he sought to convince himself that aid to Britain was not, in fact, war, he had already grimly and unhappily accepted America's inevitable participation in the struggle, In May, 1941, White wrote to his old friend Oswald Garrison Villard: "I hoped I would never see another war. I shall never encourage the coming of another war. But if it comes, this summer or next summer . . . I see nothing to do but to fight it with all our might and all our hearts. And that's not a pleasant prospect for a man who realizes the utter futility of wars in the past and who can only hope rather vainly that, out of this war, men may learn wisdom in the end."[43]

With the signing of the Molotov-Ribbentrop Pact of August, 1939, American Communists, seriously embarrassed by their former bellicosity, launched another peace campaign, this time under the slogan "The Yanks Are Not Coming." The conflict in Europe, now an "Imperialist War," was not the business of the workers, and Communists obediently scuttled the American League for Peace and Democracy to make way for the American Peace Mobilization. The comrades proceeded to carry out crippling strikes against the Vultee Aircraft Corporation, the tank-producing Allis-Chalmers plant in Milwaukee, and the North American Aviation factory in California. Dalton Trumbo's antiwar novel *Johnny Got His Gun* (1930) was serialized in the Party press. Antiwar pickets ringed the White House on June 21, 1941, as the American Peace Mobilization called for National Peace Week.[44]

This proved to be strategically poor timing, however, for on the very day, Hitler's armies invaded Russia, thereby transforming the "Imperialist War" into a "People's War for National Liberation." The *Daily Worker* proclaimed the change of line to the faithful the following morning, but the organized campaign for peace and disarmament was not disposed of quite so easily. Meeting the challenge, the Party announced two weeks later that the American Peace Mobilization would henceforth be known as the American People's Mobilization and would begin an intensive campaign "for all-out aid to the Soviet Union and Britain." The new slogan: "Victory over Fascism." National Peace Week, of course, was never mentioned again.[45]

The rapid shifts of the Communist Party from war to peace to war again had little effect upon the peace movement, although they disillusioned many intellectuals closer to the Party itself.[46] Most pacifists had had nothing to do with the Communists' latest "peace front," and consequently were relatively untouched by its collapse. "It was not possible," wrote one peace worker, "for pacifists to associate themselves with a group whose peace-mindedness depended upon the policy of a foreign dictator." A. J. Muste warned in 1940 against the "Communists' fake anti-war campaign and its dangers." Some Party members, like Bayard Rustin, a member of the Young Communist League, turned to pacifism.[47]

In their resistance to the armaments apparatus of war, peace workers had as little in common with their temporary allies, the isolationists, as with the Communists. America First never advocated disarmament, but consistently endorsed the growth of American military power; its statement of principles called upon the United States to "build an impregnable defense for America. With such a defense no foreign power, or group of powers, can successfully attack us." "Keep Out, Keep Ready" ran the isolationist American Legion's slogan. Isolationist Senators, inflamed by any thought of entering "Europe's wars," usually voted for American military appropriations. America First opposed the Roosevelt Administration's foreign policy, explained its program director, because it allegedly squandered American resources upon foreign nations, thus failing to put America first. Isolationists, Communists, and collective security advocates, unlike pacifists, all believed in a strong military defense; they simply advocated different defensive lines.[48]

Furthermore, pacifists were alienated by isolationism's right-wing aura. Led for the most part by conservatives, financed by businessmen, and cheered by the reactionary Chicago *Tribune* and the New York *Daily News*, the forces of isolation seemed the epitome of the "masters of war." [49] Even more odious in the eyes of pacifists were isolationism's links to anti-Semitism and racism. Christian Front members poured into America First, despite the efforts of its leaders, while other neo-fascist groups seriously infiltrated isolationist ranks. Many of America First's leaders held strikingly racist views. Explaining his anti-interventionist position, Charles Lindbergh wrote that a European war was "not a question of banding together to defend the White race." Although America First contained a sprinkling of prominent liberals, its tone smacked of the political Right.[50]

American peace groups, on the other hand, generally promoted relatively advanced social and economic doctrines. A 1934 W.I.L.P.F. convention announced that "a real and lasting peace and true freedom cannot exist under the present system of exploitation, privilege and profit," and that consequently it would seek "a new system under which would be realized social, economic and political equality for all without distinction of sex, race, or opinion." In 1939 it declared: "There can be neither peace nor freedom without justice. The existing economic system ... is a challenge to our whole position." During the depression years pacifists were extremely active in the labor movement—although the concern was not reciprocated—leading strikes, marching on picket lines, and campaigning for social justice. While some elements in the Historic Peace Churches tended toward a more conservative position, or were simply apolitical, most pacifists tied themselves closely to radical causes. When F.O.R. members were polled in 1932 on their choice, for President, 75 per cent favored the Socialist candidate.[51]

Finally, at the core of much isolationism lay a belligerent nationalism, indifferent or hostile to the existence of foreign nations. The leading newspaper of Los Angeles boasted in 1927 that "a change of Ministers in France is of less importance to the residents of Los Angeles than a change of grade on an important thoroughfare." Paralleling isolationist indifference was often an attitude that suggested disdain for alien societies. "To hell with Europe and the rest of those nations!" declared a Senator from Minnesota during a 1935 debate on the World Court.[52] Isolationists rather appropriately named their leading organization America First.

The peace movement marched to a different drummer, During the Thirties, when the country turned fervently isolationist and even Franklin Roosevelt stated his opposition to the League of Nations, every major American peace organization supported American entry into the World Court and the League of Nations (although some favored restrictions on the latter's warmaking powers).[53]

Frederick J. Libby estimated that 90 per cent of the movement's adherents favored this policy. In 1925 Kirby Page undertook a twelve-week speaking tour on behalf of the World Court, and he was joined by John Nevin Sayre for five weeks and Norman Thomas and John Haynes Holmes for shorter periods. The Peace Section of the American Friends Service Committee promoted the League idea "so assiduously that in 1934 the League of Nations Association financed two of its New England peace caravans." Meeting in October, 1941, the national board of the W.I.L.P.F. reported itself "deeply concerned by a spirit of isolationism on the part of a large body of American public opinion—an isolationism which manifests itself in a narrow and hard nationalism, an unscientific racism, a disastrous militarism and an unthinking acceptance of an armaments economy." It added: "We believe that the world has developed into a single economic unity, and that only as nations develop . . . political world organization can we be spared from the continuance of war and violence." [54]

Obviously, then, the peace movement, despite its anti-interventionist position, was not "isolationist." This is a recurrent theme in the movement's literature. "The neutrality policy," observed Florence Brewer Boeckel of the N.C.P.W. in 1938, is "a policy of isolation from war, not of isolation from world affairs." Norman Thomas wrote in 1939: "Neutrality is concerned solely with avoiding war." In July, 1938, Oswald Garrison Villard told readers of the *Nation* that pacifists. "are isolationists only as to war, and are opposed only to such measures of international cooperation as would lead to war." There is "no form of activity . . , in which we are not willing to cooperate with all nations, save . . . war." [55]

Yet in spite of their extreme ideological differences, a few members of the peace movement tried unsuccessfully to cooperate with isolationists in their common struggle to keep America out of war. When the America First Committee was organized in September, 1940, pacifists Albert W. Palmer and Oswald Garrison Villard were on its national board. Within a month, however, they had resigned, objecting to the Committee's endorsement of military defense measures. This, in addition to Villard's pacifism, prompted Secretary of the Interior Harold Ickes to include him in a list of "Nazi Fellow Travelers" in a speech given in April, 1941. Norman Thomas spoke at meetings sponsored by America First, although he refused to join and emphasized his differences with the organization's backing of "armament economics." After Lindbergh's Des Moines speech containing anti-Semitic overtones, Thomas would have nothing further to do with the Committee. With these few exceptions, most pacifists stayed clear of America First.[56]

Of all the peace groups, the N.C.P.W. strayed furthest down the isolationist path. "With the defeat of the World Court in the Senate," Libby wrote in 1935, "those who believe in the collective systems began searching with the isolationists for temporary expedients: to keep the United States out of war." In 1939, carried away by an almost fanatical opposition to the Administration, the N.C.P.W, veered sharply into the isolationist camp. It distributed hundreds of thousands of copies of speeches by isolationists Senators Borah, La Follette, Nye, McCarran, and Walsh, as well as by the very symbol of nationalist isolationism, Charles Lindbergh. America First donated $1000 to the N.C.P.W. in 1941 for its assistance in opposing the President's Lend-Lease program.[57]

The only other peace group to receive a large contribution from isolationist sources was the W.I.L.P.F., to which the America First Committee donated $500. Hard-pressed for funds in the lean days after 1939, the W.I.L.P.F. accepted this assistance from its anti-interventionist ally with discomfort. Three weeks before Pearl Harbor, when a local chapter president of the W.I.L.P.F. reported her members uneasy about any link with the America First Committee, Miss Detzer assured her that there was none whatsoever. An executive committee member pointed out that the stand of the two organizations so clearly diverged on such matters as national defense and international cooperation that no connection was possible.[58] A close analysis of the ties between isolationists and the peace movement proves her essentially correct.

After 1935 pacifists took heart at the strong opposition of public opinion to American participation in war, but it is evident that this opposition was both on the decline and indicative of isolationist rather than pacifist motivations. A poll in November, 1935, found 75 percent of the American people in favor of obtaining the approval of a national referendum before any declaration of war; by March, 1939, support for this plan dropped to 58 per cent of respondents. Although at no time prior to the attack upon Pearl Harbor did more than 25 per cent of the American people wish to enter the war, perhaps more reflective of popular sentiment were polls indicating that 68 per cent thought it more important to defeat Germany than to stay out of the conflict.[59] That pacifists comprised but a small percentage was evident from a *Fortune* poll in 1939, which found only 2.1 per cent of the country opposed to maintenance of armed forces by the United States. Indeed, throughout the late Thirties, but especially with the outbreak of war in Europe, polls recorded Americans consistently in favor of enlarging the country's military forces. The President faced only the mildest of legislative opposition to his army and navy appropriations bills. In 1940, alone, Congress appropriated seventeen billion dollars for the military.[60] Thus despite their desire to avoid war Americans readied themselves for it.

Analyzing this situation, Evan Thomas, a pacifist leader in the W.R.L. and brother of the Socialist Party chieftain, sought to understand why people armed and went to war, although most "hate war and believe no good can come from it." The "answer," he contended" was that "the world is organized on the acceptance of war as the only possible court of last appeal." Too many opponents of war accepted the fact that "if all else failed, militarism must be met with militarism." Yet what else could be done? It was with more than a little justice that a 1941 editorial in the *Presbyterian Tribune* asked "what practicable alternative" pacifists "have to offer to the political courses framed .

. . by statesmen which they condemn." "What do pacifists propose," the journal inquired, "while the world is under the German terror?"[61]

Unfortunately, by 1941 American pacifists had no "practicable alternative" in the tragic context of the time. Their message had a moral but not a political relevance. "Positively," Norman Thomas recalled, pacifists "had nothing to offer in the problem of stopping Nazism.... Nothing that is, except for a religious faith." In Germany, at least, there was no evidence that ethics were honored by the conquerors; thousands of pacifists had already been placed in concentration camps. Nor, in the last analysis, did the pacifist belief demand political success. As William Penn had once declared, the pacifist choice was "not fighting, but suffering." Such a creed had its moral advantages, but surely could not be judged a "practicable alternative." "Pacifism is an obligation, not a promise," conceded the Friends Peace Committee in 1940. "We are not guaranteed that it will be safe. We are sure that it is right."[62]

Only the faintest stirrings of political interest broke the surface of moral concern [63] among pacifists in the years before Pearl Harbor. In 1918 John Haynes Holmes discovered Mohandas Gandhi, whom he lauded three years later in his widely discussed address "Who Is the Greatest Man in the World Today?" Gandhian *satyagraha*, or soul force, thereafter attracted considerable attention among pacifists interested in non-violent change. English pacifist Aldous Huxley commended it to public attention as the only option for oppressed people in the modern industrial age. Pamphlets of the F.O.R. made mention briefly of its use, while a W.R,L. pamphlet by Jessie Wallace Hughan argued in 1939 that resistance tactics could successfully halt an invasion of the United States. The only occasion on which non-violent resistance was actually tried by the theorists came in November, 1936, when two pacifist members of the American Federation of Full-Fashioned Hosiery Workers organized a "lie down" by members of their local in front of the factory gates. Despite an excellent response on the part of the workers, the strike failed when local law officials imprisoned all the strikers. A. J. Muste was exultant, especially after the national union appointed "a standing commission to study the merits and possibilities of using non-violent resistance in labor disputes"; however, nothing appears to have come of it."[64] *Satyagraha* remained a matter for talk and not for action.

The leading theorist of non-violent resistance was a Quaker lawyer, Richard Gregg. One day, quite accidentally, he read an article about Gandhi, and was greatly impressed with the few excerpts of the Indian leader's writings. After studying Gandhi's works, Gregg traveled to India in 1925, where he remained for the next four years, seven months of which he passed at Gandhi's ashram, or spiritual retreat. Arriving home, Gregg gave up his law practice and began to write and lecture on the subject of non-violence. His pioneering study *The Power of Non-Violence* proved immensely influential; he followed it by a series of short pamphlets sketching in details on non-violent discipline and modes of living. The message of the book was revolutionary: non-violent resistance had a political and social significance. Not only was non-violence "right," but it "worked."[65]

Strangely enough, despite the popularity of Gregg's book, pacifists were slow to see that he had given them an alternative to violence in conflict situations. Perhaps the idea seemed too new; perhaps the task of converting the world to a different kind of struggle appeared too awesome. In any event, even Gregg, when attempting to answer the question "How Can Hitler Be Stopped?," omitted any mention of non-violent resistance. His outlook was pessimistic. "Now the fat is in the fire," he wrote, "and European peoples and governments are paying for previous obstinate mistakes of their ruling classes. Our country will have to pay its share." Non-violent resistance represented at least an alternative, however problematical, but one, which was never explored.[66]

That pacifism remained almost solely a moral imperative is evident from the ebb and flow in the strength of peace organizations during the last years before the war. In general, those with absolute pacifist constituencies grew, while those with a broader membership rapidly faded. The religious pacifist F.O.R. increased from 4271 to 12,426 members between 1935 and 1941, with 4000 of the new members entering between August, 1940, and August, 1941. Similarly, the secular pacifist W.R.L. had its busiest year just before the war, enrolling the greatest number of new members, employing its largest staff, and spending the most money in its history. The N.C.P.W., which had garnered the support of many non-pacifist groups, saw them gradually fall away as the European crisis heightened, its income drastically declined, forcing it to pare salaries and drop staff members. Especially hard hit was the reformist W.I.L.P.F., whose chapter membership melted away in interventionist areas of the country. Between April, 1940, and April, 1941, membership in Manhattan dropped from 428 to 160, in Brooklyn from 334 to 148, in Santa Barbara from 125 to 55. Only in pacifist centers did it retain strength; in heavily Quaker Delaware County membership rose from 613 to 621, while in Philadelphia it fell only slightly from 1490 to 1432.[67] As Pearl Harbor approached, the peace movement grew increasingly pacifist.

The peace movement's dilemma of the late Thirties thus centered about the problem of the rise of fascism. Although the peace movement offered a long-term program of disarmament and social justice, it had no immediate solutions to cope with the aggressive world of angry power relationships it confronted. Its position was never adopted by any of the "great" nations, of course, but it seems unlikely that it could have met the military challenge posed by Hitler; pacifists would almost certainly have perished in the fiery hatred of the black-shirted legions. And while this may have been an ethically superior position, it was a bleak choice for men and nations.

On the other hand, pacifists quickly spotted the flaw in the logic of the collective security advocates. If the enemy was the cult of violence, nationalism, and racism, then war was obviously an inadequate method for its defeat. A world war might suffice in the short run, deposing Hitler, Mussolini, and their followers; but in the long run it offered little hope for a new type of relationship among men. Indeed, the hatred, brutality, and chauvinism churned up by modern warfare exacerbated the long-term problem as it alleviated the short-term one. Wars did not end this way, the peace movement understood; but then, how did they end?

****

Editor's Note: Among peace historians, Wittner has, in many ways, provided new and challenging interpretations. As a first book it was warmly received within the historical profession. He also provided one of the most interesting analogies regarding consistency within the various peace movements. In essence, he likened it to an onion, with the absolutists at the center and the less committed outside layers. At times of popular enthusiasm for war the less committed outside layers peel off, leaving the pacifist core; in times of strong aversion to militarism new layers appear, and the onion grows in size. This structural fluidity describes both the peace movement's repeated weaknesses in times of international tension and for its peculiar resiliency.

NOTES

1. New York *Times*, May 11, 1940.

2. Stanley High, "Peace, Inc.," *Saturday Evening Post*, CCX (March 5, 1938), 8; Merle E, Curti, *Peace or War: The American Struggle, 1636-1936*, p. 262; Robert H. Ferrell, "The Peace Movement," *Isolation and Security*, ed. Alexander DeConde, pp. 82-83; Marcus Duffield, "Our Quarrelling Pacifists," *Harper's*, CLXVI (May, 1933), 688-96.

3. Earl Charles Chatfield, Jr., "Pacifism and American Life, 1914 to 1941" (unpublished Ph.D. dissertation), pp. 72-73; Curti, *Peace or War*, pp. 288-70; Ferrell, "The Peace Movement," pp. 83-84; Robert E. Osgood, *Ideals and Self-Interest in America's Foreign Relations*, p. 330.

4. John E. Wiltz, *In Search of Peace: The Senate Munitions Inquiry, 1934-1936*, pp. 19-23, 227-31; Walter Johnson, *The Battle against Isolation*, pp. 14-15. Seldes' book was a sensational account, which proclaimed itself "An Exposure of the World-Wide Munitions Racket," while its jacket carried a blurb telling of "the Frenzied Years of 1914-17 when a peace-loving democracy, muddled but excited, misinformed and whipped to frenzy, embarked upon its greatest foreign war. . . Read it and blush! Read it and beware!" George Seldes, *Iron, Blood and Profits*; R. E. Osgood, *Ideals and Self-Interest*, pp. 365-68.

5. William Allen White, *The Autobiography of William Allen White*, p. 640.

6. Harry Emerson Fosdick, *The Living of These Days: An Autobiography*, p, 293; New York *Times*, November 18, 1931; Hadley Cantril (ed.), *Public Opinion, 1935-1946*, p. 986; Francis Sill Wickware, "What We Think about Foreign Affairs," *Harper's*, CLXXIX (September, 1939), 404.

7. Thomas A. Bailey, *The Man in the Street: The Impact of American Public Opinion on Foreign Policy*, p. 69; Edith Wynner and Georgia Lloyd, *Searchlight on Peace Plans: Choose Your Road to World Government*, p. 9;. Otto Nathan and Heinz Norden (eds.), *Einstein on Peace*, pp. 141-42. A collection of the early pacifist writings of Einstein is: *Albert Einstein, The Fight against War*.

8. Ferrell, "The Peace Movement," p. 104; William E. Leuchtenburg, *Franklin D. Roosevelt and the New Deal, 1932-1940*, p. 219; Frederick J. Libby, *The American Peace Movement*, p. 2; Robert Edwin Bowers, "The American Peace Movement, 1933-1941" (unpublished Ph.D. dissertation), p. 242; Mercedes M. Randall, *Improper Bostonian: Emily Greene Balch*, pp. 309-310; personal interview with Mercedes M. Randall, April 28, 1985. Mrs. Catt, a strong believer in the unique responsibility of women on the question of war or peace, told a women's delegation at the 1939 New York World's Fair that "we are responsible for the continuation of war, and for not making this a better world." New York *Times*, July 14, 1939.

9. Doniver A. Lund, "The Peace Movement among the Major American Protestant Churches, 1919-1939" (unpublished Ph.D. dissertation), p, 107; Devere Allen, *The Fight for Peace*, p. 50; "The Church Pacifist," *Nation*, CXXXII (May 6, 1931), 494; Kirby Page, "20,870 Clergymen on War and Economic Injustice," *World Tomorrow*, XVII (May 10, 1934), 222-56.

10. Vernon Howard Holloway, "American Pacifism between Two Wars 1919-1941" (unpublished Ph.D. dissertation), pp. 178-82.

11. Holloway, "American Pacifism," p. 200; Allan A. Kuusisto, "The Influence of the National Council for Prevention of War on United States Foreign Policy, 1935-1939" (unpublished Ph.D. dissertation), pp. 55-56. A compilation of statements by religious bodies illustrating the development of pacifist sentiment within the church is: Walter Van Kirk, *Religion Renounces War*.

12. *Nation*, CXXXVI (May 24, 1933), 571; "A Student Strike against War," *Literary Digest*, CXIX (March 23, 1935), 17; Joseph P. Lash, *The Campus Strikes against War*, p. 3.

13. New York *Times*, April 13 and November 9, 1935; Harold Seidman, "The Colleges Renounce War," *Nation*, CXXXVI (May 17, 1933), 554-55.

14. Kuusisto, "The Influence of the National Council for Prevention of War on United States Foreign Policy," p. 92; Libby, *The American Peace Movement*, p. 2; Bowers, "The American Peace Movement," pp. 428-29; Curti, *Peace or War*, p. 288; M. M. Randall, *Improper Bostonian*, p. 310. One pacifist wrote in dismay: "Labor's leadership is working-class, but inclined to ignore the values of organized peace effort; the peace movement Is 'high hat' or upper middle class when not positively blue blooded." Allen, *The Fight for Peace*, pp. *163-64.*

15. Devere Allen, "The Peace Movement Moves Left," *Annals of the American Academy of Political* and *Social Science*, CLXXV (September, 1934), 154-55; John W. Masland, "Pressure Groups and American Foreign Policy," *Public Opinion Quarterly*, VI (Spring, 1942), p. 119; James Peck, We Who Would Not Kill, pp. 60-64. See also: Norman Thomas, *War; No Glory, No Profit, No Need.*

16. Chatfield, "Pacifism and American Life," pp. 482-83; Philip G. Altbach, "The American Peace Movement, 1900-1962: A Critical Analysis" (unpublished), pp. 16-26; Vera Brittain, *The Rebel Passion; A Short History of* Some *Pioneer Peace-makers*, p. 110.

17. Merle E. Curti, "The Changing Pattern of Certain Humanitarian Organizations," *Annals of the American Academy of Political and Social Science*, CLXXIX (May, 1935), 61; "A Brief Review of Thirty-Five Years of Service toward Developing International Understanding," *International Conciliation*, No. 417 (January, 1946), 17-39; Elton Atwater, "Organizing American Public Opinion for Peace," Public *Opinion Quarterly*, I (April, *1937),* 114; Ferrell, "The Peace Movement," pp. 99-103; Bowers, "The American Peace Movement, " pp. 12-25.

18. Kuusisto, "The Influence of the National Council for Prevention of War on United States Foreign Policy," pp. 27, 70-72, 77, 81, 94; Atwater, "Organizing American Public Opinion for Peace," p. 118; War Resisters League, "National Council for the Prevention of War," *Peace Calendar and Appointment Book, 1985;* High, "Peace, Inc." p. 91.

19. Ronald Schaffer, "Jeannette Rankin, Progressive-Isolationist" (unpublished Ph.D. dissertation); Ferrell, "The Peace Movement," p. 93; Kuusisto, "The Influence of the National Council for Prevention of War on United States Foreign Policy," p. 61.

20. Gertrude Bussey and Margaret Tims, *Women's International League for Peace* and *Freedom, 1915-1965*; A *Record* of *Fifty Years' Work*, pp 77-78, 152; *History of the Women's International League for Peace* and *Freedom,* U.S. Section, 1915-I940 (1940), Women's International League for Peace and Freedom Manuscripts, Swarthmore College Peace Collection (WILPF MSS), Box 1.

21. Wiltz, *In Search of Peace*, pp. 24-25; Dorothy Detzer, *Appointment on the Hill*, pp. 151-88; Robert A. Divine, *The Illusion of Neutrality*, pp. 63-66.

22. Fellowship of Reconciliation, *What Is the Fellowship of Reconciliation?;* Masland, "Pressure Groups and American Foreign Policy," p. 115; "Membership Statistics" (1954), Fellowship of Reconciliation Manuscripts, Swarthmore College Peace Collection (FOR MSS), Box 4.

23. R. Alfred Hassler, *Conscripts of Conscience,* p. 15; A. J. Muste, Columbia Oral History Collection (COHC); *Christian Century,* LIII (October 14, 1936), 1374; Nat Hentoff, *Peace Agitator; The Story of A. J. Muste,* p. 9.

24. Jessie Wallace Hughan, *Three Decades of War Resistance,* p. 15; Frank Olmstead, "A Brief Biography: The War Resisters League" (January, 1945), Devere Allen Manuscripts, Swarthmore College Peace Collection (Allen MSS), Section C4, Box 1; Chatfield, "Pacifism and American Life," pp. 255-58; Atwater, "Organizing American Public Opinion for Peace," pp. 120-21; Evan Thomas to Members, December 26, 1944, War Registers League Manuscripts, Swarthmore College Peace Collection (WRL MSS), Box 3.

25. Histories of the Catholic Worker movement include: Dorothy Day, *Loaves and Fishes* and Dwight Macdonald, *Memoirs of a Revolutionist: Essays in Political Criticism,* pp. 349-68. Peter Maurin's biography is: Arthur Sheehan, *Peter Maurin: Gay Believer,* while an autobiography of Miss Day is: *Dorothy Day, The Long Loneliness. Pax* is discussed briefly in: Sheehan, *Peter Maurin,* pp. 127-28, and Catholic *Worker* (February, 1937).

26. U.S. Bureau of the Census, *Religious Bodies: 1936,* I, 346-48; *Why They Cannot Go to War,* n.p. Studies of the pacifist witness of the Historic Peace Churches are: Howard H. Brinton, *Sources of the Quaker Peace Testimony;* William D. S. Witte, "Quaker Pacifism in the United States, 1919-1942" (unpublished Ph.D. dissertation); Rufus D. Bowman, *The Church of the Brethren and War, 1708-1941*; Guy Franklin Hershberger, *War, Peace, and Nonresistance;* John Horsch, *The Principle of Nonresistance as Held by the Mennonite, Church.*

27. Irving Howe and Lewis Coser, *The American Communist Party: A Critical History, 1919-1957,* pp. 448-55; Chatfield, "Pacifism and American Life," pp 312-16; Altbach, "The American Peace Movement," p. 26; Hughan, *Three Decades of War Resistance,* pp. 16-21; Atwater, "Organizing American Public Opinion," p. 118. When Socialists left the organization they formed the Keep America Out of War Congress in 1938, which attracted a distinguished group of liberals, labor officials, and Socialists. It does not appear to have been very influential, however. Norman Thomas, COHC, pp. 136-37; Albert Horlings, "Who Are the Appeasers?" *New Republic,* C1V' (January 27, 1941), 112.

28. Ferrell, "The Peace Movement," p. 101.

29 Reinhold Niebuhr, "The Use of Force," *Pacifism in the Modern World*, ed. Devere Allen, pp. 18-17; Reinhold Niebuhr, "Why I Leave the F.O.R.," *Christian Century*, LI (January 3, 1934), 17-19; Lund, "The Peace Movement among the Major American Protestant Churches," pp. 119-20; Reinhold Niebuhr, *Christianity and Power* Politics, pp. ix, 4; Donald B. Meyer, *The Protestant Search for* Political *Realism, 1919-1941*, pp, 360-61; R. E. Osgood, *Ideals and Self-Interest, pp.* 381-83.

30. Albert Einstein to Jessie Wallace Hughan, August 12, 1933, WRL MSS, Box 15; Sherwood Eddy, *Eighty Adventurous Years: An Autobiography,* p 104; Judah L. Magnes, "A Tragic Dilemma," *Christian Century*, LVII (March 27, 1940), 406-407; New York *Times*, October 28, 1948. A member of the War Resisters League wrote to Jessie Wallace Hughan: "I know that the Treaty of Versailles was a terrible mistake. I know that Britain, France, and others are responsible for the rise of Hitler. I know that he is a symptom and not a personal devil. My deepest sympathy goes out to the German people, as to all others of the world. Having said this, however, I must add that I do not see how the Allies can now lay down their arms." Edwin L. Clarke to Jessie Wallace Hughan, May 27, 1940, WRL MSS, Box 14.

31. Rabbi Stephen Wise had arranged the anti-Hitler protest as an all-Jewish event, thinking that few other Americans would be interested, but he was joined, to his surprise, by his friend John Haynes Holmes. Down Broadway, from Columbus Circle to Union Square, marched the silent parade of thousands Jews, preceeded by Stephen Wise and pacifist minister John Haynes Holmes, the only Christian present. Carl Hermann Voss, *Rabbi and Minister: The Friendship of Stephen S.* Wise *and John Haynes Holmes*, pp. 285-86.

32. Fosdick, *The Living of These Days,* p. *282; Catholic Worker,* July-August, 1939; Harry Fleischman, Norman Thomas; *A Biography,* p. 195; Bailey, *The Man* in *the Street,* p. *25;* Cantril, *Public Opinion,* p. 1150. A particularly shocking display of American indifference came in response to a poll of January, *1939.* Americans were asked if the United States should permit the admission of "10,000 refugee children from Germany- -most of them Jewish"; only 30 per cent replied "yes," while 61 per cent said "no." Cantril, *Public Opinion,* p. 1081. Thomas wrote in *1938:* "The American who has studied the vogue of the Ku Klux Klan should understand some of the sources of Nazi strength." Norman Thomas, *Socialism on the Defensive,* pp. 85-86.

33. Oswald Garrison Villard, "Issues and Men," *Nation,* CXLVII (July 2, 1938), *18.*

34. Elliott Roosevelt (ed.), *F.D.R.: His Personal Letters,* 1928-1945, II, 818; Dorothy Detzer, "Dirge for Collective Security," *Fellowship*, IV (November, 1938), 6-7; Fleischman, *Norman Thomas*, p. 191; A. J. Muste, "Forth—to, War?" *American Scholar*, VII (Autumn, 1938), 402n.

3 5 Oswald Garrison Villard, *Our Military Chaos: The Truth about Defense,* p 124; Kirby Page, *How to Keep America Out of War,* p. 39; John Haynes Holmes, *Out of Darkness,* p. *83.* The chairman of the A.F.S.C. later explained: "Friends may sympathize with the alleged ends of a war; they may recognize as fact the situation which seems to others to recommend war. But that war is the way to deal with this situation or to strive toward these ends does not automatically follow. If flagrant abuse of its own citizens or of other peoples I practiced by a foreign power, violence on our part may involve other innocent persons and may not reduce the evil results" Henry J. Cadbury, "Peace and War," *The* Quaker *Approach to Contemporary Problems,* ed. John Kavaugh, p. 10.

36. Divine, *The Illusion of Neutrality*, pp. 93-94, 182; New York *Times*, January 30, 1937; Ferrell, "The Peace Movement," pp. 104-105; Kuusisto, "The Influence of the National Council for Prevention of War on United States Foreign Policy," pp. 103-282; Bowers, "The American Peace Movement," pp. 301 3 7. Howe and Coser, *The American Communist Party*, pp. 348-55; Daniel Bell, "The Background and Development of Marxian Socialism in the United States," *Socialism and American Life*, Vol. 1, ed. Donald Drew Egbert and Stow Persons, pp. 360-81; Masland, "Pressure Groups and American Foreign Policy," p. 119; New York *Times*, April 21, 1839.

38. Norman Thomas, "Norman Thomas Replies," *Fellowship, III* (February, 1937), 13; personal interview with Norman Thomas, October 4, 1966; Murray B. Seidler, *Norman Thomas: Respectable Rebel, pp. 203-205;* Norman Thomas, *COHC*, pp. *124, 135.*

39. David A. Shannon, *The Socialist Party of America: A History*, p. 255; Bell, "Backround and Development of Marxian Socialism," pp. 393-94; Fleischman, *Norman Thomas*, p. 199; Seidler, *Norman Thomas*, pp. 210-11; Norman Thomas, COHC, p. 77.

40. Norman Thomas, COHC, p. 127; Fleischman, Norman Thomas, pp. 194-95, 201. Thomas was extremely suspicious of the war aims of the parties involved in the European struggle. See, for example: Norman Thomas and Bertram D. Wolfe, *Keep America Out of War*.

41. Ray H. Abrams, "The Churches and the Clergy in World War II," *Annals of the American Academy of Political and Social Science*, CCLVI (March, 1948), 111-14; Meyer, *The Protestant Search for Political Realism*, pp. 350-54; New York *Times*, December 31, 1939.

42. W. Johnson, *The Battle against Isolation*, pp. 31-32, 41-42, 59; Divine, *The Illusion of Neutrality*, p. 304; John W. Masland, "The 'Peace' Groups Join Battle," *Public Opinion Quarterly*, IV (December, 1940), 664-73.

43. W. Johnson, *The Battle against Isolation*, p. 150; W. A. White, *The Autobiography of William Allen White*, p. 642; Divine, *The Illusion of Neutrality*, p. 304.

44. Howe and Coser, *The American Communist Party*, pp. 348-55; Earl Browder, *The Second Imperialist War*; Masland, "Pressure Groups and American Foreign Policy," p. 119; Basil Rauch, *Roosevelt: From Munich to Pearl Harbor*, p. 351; Bell, "Background and Development of Marxian Socialism," p. 396; Daniel Aaron, *Writers on the Left: Episodes in American Literary Communism*, p. 386.

45. Howe and Coser, *The American Communist Party*, p. 395; *Daily Worker*, June 23, 1941; Masland, "Pressure Groups and American Foreign Policy," p.119; Earl Browder, *Victory—And After*, p. 29.

46. Norman Holmes Pearson, "The Nazi-Soviet Pact and the End of a Dream," *America in Crisis*, ed. Daniel Aaron, pp. 327-48; Aaron, *Writers on the Left*, pp. 309-90; Bell, "Background and Development of Mandan Socialism," p, 395.

47. *Conscientious Objector*, February-March, 1941; A. J. Muste to Jessie Wallace Hughan, February 6, 1940, WRL MSS, Box 18; Hentoff, *Peace Agitator*, p. 113.

48. Wayne S. Cole, *America First: The Battle against Intervention,* 1940-1941, p. 95; Alexander DeConde, "On Twentieth-Century Isolationism," *Isolation and Security,* p. 24; Bailey, *The Man in the Street,* p. 293; Selig Adler, *The Isolationist Impulse: Its Twentieth Century Reaction,* p. 274; Leuchtenburg, *Franklin D. Roosevelt and the New Deal,* p. 287; radio interview with Charles A. McLain, former Program Director, America First Committee, WBAI-FM, New York City, September 6, 1966; R. E. Osgood, *Ideals and Self-Interest,* pp. 377-80.

49. Cole, *America First,* pp. 32, 60; Adler, *The Isolationist Impulse,* pp. 285-74, 283-84; Rauch, *Roosevelt,* p. 10; Leuchtenburg, *Franklin D. Roosevelt and the New Deal,* p. 311; Foster Rhea Dulles, *America's Rise to World Power, 1898-1954,* p. 200.

50. Morris Janowitz, "Black Legions on the March," *America in Crisis,* p. 316; W. Johnson, *The Battle against Isolation,* pp. 161-67; Cole, *America First,* pp. 131-54; Paul Comly French (ed.), *Common Sense Neutrality: Mobilizing for Peace,* p. 178.

51. Mercedes M. Randall, *High Lights in W.I.L.P.F. History: From* the Hague *to Luxembourg, 1915–1946;* "Principles and Policies" (1939), WILPF MSS, Box 1; Chatfield, "Pacifism and American Life," pp. 459–83; Bowers, "The American Peace Movement," pp. 153–236; Altbach, "The American Peace Movement," pp. 16–26; J. B. Matthews, "Pacifists Prefer Thomas," *World Tomorrow,* XV (October 26, 1932), 402.

52 Bailey, *The Man* in *the Street,* pp. 121-22, 213.

53. Ferrell, "The Peace Movement," pp. 85–90, 94–98; Norman Thomas, COHC, pp. 124–25; Kuusisto, "The Influence of the National Council for Prevention of War on United States Foreign Policy," p. 48; *The History of an Idea: The Women's International League for Peace and Freedom* (1955), WILPF MSS, Box 1; Schaffer, "Jeannette Rankin," pp. 163–64.

54. Chatfield, "Pacifism and American Life," pp. 288–95; Libby, *The American Peace Movement,* p. 6; *Four Lights, I* (December, 1941); C. B. Marshall, "Organized Groups," *Public Opinion Quarterly,* IV (March, 1940), 154.

55. Florence Brewer Boeckel, "The Peace Movement in the U.S.A.," Peace *Year Book 1938,* p. 159; French, *Common Sense Neutrality,* p. 221; Villard, "Issues and Men," p. 18.

56. Cole, *America First,* pp. 75, 78, 90–91, 147–48; Michael Wreszin, *Oswald Garrison Villard: Pacifist at War, pp. 265, 269;* New York *Times, May 24,* 1941; Norman Thomas, *What Is Our Destiny,* p. 36; Chatfield, "Pacifism and American Life," p, 680; Masland, "Pressure Groups and American Foreign Policy," pp, 116–17. According to the leading student of America First, some pacifist, were found on the local chapter level of the organization, as well as in the national speakers bureau. None appear to be figures of any prominence in the peace movement, however. Cole, *America First,* pp. 75, 90.

57. Schaffer, "Jeannette Rankin," P. 201; Kuusisto, "The Influence of the National Council for Prevention of War on United States Foreign Policy," p. 228; Cole, *America First,* p. 227; C. B. Marshall, "Organized Groups," pp. 154-55.

58. "Minutes of the W.I.L.P.F. Executive Board, February 26, 1941," WILPF MSS, Box 11; "Minutes of the Executive Committee Meeting, Women's International League for Peace and Freedom" (November 19, 1941), WILPF MSS, Box 11.

59. Cantril, *Public Opinion*, pp. 969–77, 1025–26; Wickware, "What We Think about Foreign Affairs," p. 406; Hadley Cantril, "Opinion Trends in World War II: Some Guides to Interpretation," *Public Opinion Quarterly*, XII (Spring, 1948), 37; R. E. Osgood, *Ideals and Self-Interest*, pp. 408-409; William A. Lydgate, *What America Thinks*, pp. 32, 35.

60. Cantril, *Public Opinion*, pp. 939–43; Dulles, *America's Rise to World Power*, p. 191.

61 *Conscientious Objector*, November, 1939; "What Do Pacifists Propose?" *Presbyterian Tribune*, LVI (August, 1941), 4.

62. Bell, "Background and Development of Marxian Socialism," p. 401; Cadbury, "Peace and War," p. 9; Witte, "Quaker Pacifism," p. 310. Dr. Emil Maurer, chairman of the Socialist Party in Vienna, told a London newspaper reporter that when he was sent to the Buchenwald concentration camp in September, 1938, one fifth of the inmates were pacifists, placed there for their refusal to serve in the *Wehrmacht*. Reprinted from the *London Tribune*, April 27, 1945, in: Jan Levcik, "Buchenwald before the War," *Politics*, II (June, 1945), 173-74.

63. One writer has succinctly phrased it: "Some people ... tend to ask first, 'What kind of world would I like to make?' and these we may call 'political' people. Others ask first, 'What kind of action is right for me to undertake?' and these we may call 'moral' people." Arthur I. Waskow, *The Worried Man's Guide to World Peace*, p. 49.

64. *Voss, Rabbi and Minister*, pp. 198–208; John Haynes Holmes, *My Gandhi;* Hentoff, *Peace Agitator*, p. 102; Aldous Huxley, *Ends and Means*; *Fellowship of Reconciliation, As War Comes Nearer*, p. 6; *Fellowship of Reconciliation, What Is the Fellowship of Reconciliation*, p. 5; Jessie Wallace Hughan, *If We Should Be Invaded;* Herbert C. Bohn, "We Tried Non-Violence," *Fellowship*, III (January, 1937), 7–8; A. J. Musts, "Sit Downs and Lie Downs," *Fellowship*, III (March, 1937), 5–6.

65. Chatfield, "Pacifism and American Life," pp. 548–49; Hassler, *Conscripts of Conscience*, p. 50; Richard B. Gregg: *The Power of Non-Violence; The Value of Voluntary Simplicity; Training for Peace: A Program for Peace Workers; Pacifist Program in Time of War, Threatened War, or Fascism; A Discipline for Non-Violence*. Another work that became a textbook for non-violent actionists at this time was: Krishnalal Shridharani, *War without Violence: A Study of Gandhi's Method and Its Accomplishments*.

66. Richard B. Gregg, "How Can Hitler Be Stopped?" *Fellowship, V (Oc*tober, 1939), 6. Emily Balch later acknowledged that World War II was inevitable, given mankind's "failure to have ready any effective technique for constructive non-violent action, such as Gandhi had arrived at." M. M. Randall, *Improper* Bostonian, p. 341.

67. "Membership Statistics" (1954), FOR MSS, Box 4; Brittain, *The Rebel Passion*, p. 58; War Resisters League, *Our Busiest Year!* (1940), WRL MSS, Box 3; Kuusisto, "The Influence of the National Council for Prevention of War on United States Foreign Policy," pp. 54–56, 63, *65, 226–27;* "Local Branches and Their Membership," WILPF MSS, Box 11; personal interview with A. J. Muste, June 2, 1966.

CHAPTER SIX
DIRECT ACTION, 1957-1963
James Tracy

James Tracy, a more recent student of the peace movement, demonstrates in this essay the impact of the "modern" movement in its attempts to stop the development of hydrogen and nuclear bombs. Prior to the confrontational tactics that were widely publicized during the Vietnam War, numerous peace activists and peace groups were already employing the strategies of direct action and nonviolent civil disobedience. In this essay from his book, Tracy explains how movement leaders rekindled the rebirth of American radicalism and social protest during a time when Cold War suspicions labeled such attempts disloyal and un-American. These radical pacifists developed an experimental protest style marked by nonviolent direct action. Their tactical commitment to such a strategy enabled them to become "the principal interpreters of Gandhism on the American left." In terms of radical pacifism, how did their actions highlight the strengths and weaknesses of American individualism in 20th century America? How did their tactics, well-suited among small groups, not prove particularly feasible when it came to building mass-based movements? How did they manage to succeed in remaining active in the face of Cold War realities and Red Scare hostilities?

NUCLEAR FALLOUT

Just before sunrise, the hills were lit by a blinding flash. Slowly, as nineteen pacifists looked on, a mushroom cloud rose to towering heights above a military installation in the Nevada desert. Eleven of those observing the detonation had been arrested for trespassing on the base the previous day, August 6, 1957, the twelfth anniversary of the atomic bombing of Hiroshima. After being released later from a local jail, Lawrence Scott, Jim Peck, Albert Bigelow, and eight other trespassers joined [A.J.] Muste outside the base just in time for the predawn explosion. One of the group remembered that, looking into the plume of a hydrogen bomb, "our conviction was made firm that it would be infinitely better to suffer death by a nuclear bomb than commit the blasphemy of dropping it on other men."[1] Jim Peck wrote that "it was as if you were to see a certain monster in your dreams and then one day were suddenly to come upon it in reality."[2]

Albert Bigelow had become a pacifist exactly twelve years before the day of his arrest. Born into a wealthy Boston family, Bigelow had attended Harvard before entering the navy. During World War II, he served with distinction as captain of a ship in the Pacific. When he first learned of the atomic bomb dropped on Hiroshima, however, Bigelow immediately concluded that modem war is morally unsupportable. This belief was later confirmed for him when he and his wife housed survivors of the Hiroshima blast who had been brought to Boston for reconstructive surgery.[3]

Bigelow and the others had come to Nevada in the summer of 1957 as members of a group led by Lawrence Scott, a Quaker pacifist. Scott's activism stretched back to the 1940s. He had worked with James Farmer on desegregation issues in 1941 and had participated in CORE's Kansas City local in 1943. He had also attended the founding conference of Peacemakers in Chicago in 1948 and since 1954 had worked for the American Friends Service

Committee in Chicago. In 1957, Scott left the AFSC because the organization would not support his decision to resist tax payments.

Scott had become increasingly concerned about the dangers to world health posed by fallout from nuclear testing. In early 1957, he wrote an article (later published in *Liberation*) entitled "Words Are Not Enough," in which he called for bold action against nuclear testing and blasted the "effete, middle-class Friends [Quakers] of today" for not doing enough against the arms race. Articulating a long-standing radical pacifist assumption, Scott called for a privileging of action over analysis, asserting that "speaking words has become so cheap in this age that only the literal act has much meaning."[4]

In April 1957, Scott organized a meeting in Philadelphia of pacifists interested in active opposition to nuclear testing. Among those in attendance was Homer Jack, a World War II prison absolutist who had worked closely with George Houser in Chicago during the early 1940s. The Philadelphia group decided to meet again in Washington the following month at the Prayer Pilgrimage for Freedom organized by Martin Luther King, because the pilgrimage would draw activists from around the country. Before King delivered the keynote address to a crowd of about thirty thousand, a group of pacifists and liberals met in a small office to discuss Scott's ideas for a campaign against nuclear testing. It was at this meeting that Muste suggested the Nevada Action for the upcoming anniversary of the Hiroshima bombing.

Out of these two meetings in April and May of 1957, two organizations emerged that were designed to have separate but complementary tactical foci. One group was to push forward the radical pacifist agenda, concentrating on direct action. Originally named Non-Violent Action Against Nuclear Weapons (NVAANW), it later became the Committee for Non-Violent Action (CNVA).[5] The other group was to reach out to the middle class and intellectuals by pursuing more moderate avenues of challenging above-ground nuclear testing. This group, led by Norman Cousins, editor of the liberal *Saturday Review* was called the

Committee for a Sane Nuclear Policy (SANE). Homer Jack, active in the leadership of both organizations, would become the de facto organizational link between these two groups established in tandem by a coalition of radical pacifists and liberals in 1957.[6]

Scott had touched a nerve with a public increasingly concerned about the effects of nuclear fallout. Despite official assurances that fallout from the above-ground nuclear tests being conducted by the United States, the Soviet Union, France, and Great Britain posed no health risks, increasing numbers of people feared that the "experts" were misleading them. SANE, using moderate methods to tap into a growing public fear of nuclear fallout, grew at an expansive rate. By July of 1957, SANE's leaders were able to present President Eisenhower with a petition signed by ten thousand people asking for a test ban.[7] Even more dramatic was the response to a full-page advertisement taken out in the *New York Times* by SANE on November 15, 1957, calling for an end to nuclear testing. Thousands of letters flooded SANE's office, and by the following summer it could boast 130 chapters and 25,000 members.[8] In the late 1950s, SANE became synonymous in the popular mind with the campaign against nuclear testing.

Meanwhile, Scott was busy organizing SANE's radical pacifist fraternal twin. He and Muste organized the action against the nuclear test in Nevada for August of 1957. The following year, CNVA engaged in its most influential action when Bigelow and three other CNVA members (Orion Sherwood, William R. Huntington, and George Willoughby, who had been imprisoned as a C.O. during World War II) attempted to sail a thirty-foot ketch they had christened the "Golden Rule" into a restricted zone in the Marshall Islands where the United States military was scheduled to detonate a hydrogen bomb. In the Gandhian tradition of openness, Bigelow announced his intentions ahead of time. He even published an article on his intentions the previous February.[9]

The "Golden Rule" managed to sail from San Francisco as far as Hawaii. While docked in Hawaii, however, a judge issued a restraining order demanding that the crew not leave port to continue to the Marshall Islands. Bigelow, who was captain of this ship, hesitated, prompting Muste to fly out to Honolulu to urge him to defy the judge's order. Bigelow finally agreed and set out from port with his original crew and a late addition, Muste. They got less than a mile out from shore before being intercepted by the Coast Guard.

The "Golden Rule's" crew entered a plea of guilty when arraigned in Honolulu on May 7, 1958. Bigelow, Willoughby, Huntington, and Sherwood gave eloquent statements at their arraignment about the dangers nuclear weapons posed to humanity. CNVA's leaders at this time carefully crafted their public statements to address concrete issues, such as the health effects of nuclear fallout while avoiding more controversial ideological issues such as pacifism or the radical politics motivating many of CNVA's members.[10]

After the crew received suspended sentences, Bigelow placed a large sign on the stern announcing that the "Golden Rule" would set sail again at noon on June 4. Because Bigelow and Huntington were the only crew members with navigational skills, the group decided to keep Huntington in reserve on shore. Huntington's replacement was Jim Peck, who had been in Hawaii throughout the action for just such a contingency.

Ten minutes before their planned departure on June 4, federal marshals arrived to arrest Bigelow, who was addressing a crowd of journalists, well-wishers, and curiosity seekers. After Bigelow's arrest, Huntington rejoined the crew, and the "Golden Rule" snuck out of port. This time, they managed to get about three miles out from Honolulu before two Coast Guard vessels turned them around. All crew members except Peck (who had only violated the injunction once) were now given sixty-day jail sentences. One journalist quipped that jail was now the "Golden Rule's" home port.[11]

The "Golden Rule's" dramatic confrontations grabbed national headlines in 1958, much of it sympathetic to CNVA. *Newsweek* ran a long article on the protest in its religion section, and the *Boston Herald* referred to the crew's actions as "Thoreauesque." Protests in support of the action took place across the United States.[12] The generally favorable reporting of the action can be attributed in part to Bigelow's credentials as a patriot during World War II and to the middle-of-the-road statements made by Bigelow and Muste, which kept to the issues SANE had helped to make mainstream concerns, the health dangers of fallout and the fear of nuclear war. The crew members also garnered respect from some journalists and sections of the general public for their clear willingness to risk death at sea to convey their message.

To the surprise of everyone, including CNVA organizers, the "Golden Rule" action did not end with the imprisonment of its crew. The most dramatic event of the action occurred aboard another ship owned by Earle Reynolds, an anthropologist who had done fieldwork for the Atomic Energy Commission in Hiroshima after the war but who had no connection with CNVA whatsoever. Reynolds and his family were sailing around the world in 1858, when, by coincidence, they docked in Honolulu during the "Golden Rule" controversy. Attending the trial of the crew members, Reynolds became convinced that CNVA was right. Without prior announcement, he and his wife slipped out of Honolulu to complete the voyage of the "Golden Rule" aboard their own boat, the "Phoenix," an appropriate name from the perspective of those in CNVA who thought the "Golden Rule" action had ended with the imprisonment of Bigelow and his crew. The Reynolds family managed to sail several miles into the South Pacific zone marked for nuclear detonation before they were apprehended by the Coast Guard. The image of an entire family ("average" Americans, as opposed to "professional" activists) risking their lives in this way to complete the "Golden Rule's" mission was tailor-made for media consumption. Earle Reynolds went on a national speaking tour that included numerous radio and television appearances.

Despite their failure to effect military policy or even prevent the single detonation in the South Pacific that the action had targeted, CNVA's leaders considered the "Golden Rule" action, in its ability to command sympathetic publicity, a success beyond anything previously attempted by radical pacifists. As a result, there was considerable discussion within CNVA about what to do for an encore. These discussions exacerbated tensions that had already developed between an older, more cautious leadership and a younger, more combative group within CNVA. Scott and Bigelow argued that the "Golden Rule" action proved CNVA could reach more people on specific issues such as nuclear testing if the organization avoided jarring the political sensibilities of middle-class Americans. The younger group within CNVA advocated "upping the ante" with more militant action and rhetoric, which better expressed the urgency they felt about the nuclear arms race. These younger militants within CNVA coalesced around a "wildcat" project in Wyoming in 1958. This project drew sustenance from a new militancy that was emerging among American youth in the late 1950's.

The Cheyenne Project began in early 1958, when two young activists, Ted Olson and Art Springer, presented to the CNVA leadership a plan to disrupt the ongoing construction of ICBM missile silos in Cheyenne, Wyoming. Olson and Springer hoped to move CNVA beyond its focus on the public health dangers of above-ground nuclear testing to a more controversial challenging of the morality of possessing a nuclear arsenal. In the process, they hoped to shift CNVA's tactics from moral witness of the "Golden Rule" variety to a far more combative attempt to prevent construction of a nuclear installation. This tactical departure, termed "obstructionism," faced stiff opposition within CNVA. While it was harmonious with many radical pacifist pronouncements of the late 1940s, some radical pacifists in 1958, who were still savoring the invigorating tonic of favorable media treatment received by the "Golden Rule" after the arid years of the McCarthy period, opposed the Cheyenne Project. Others, such as Scott and Bigelow, felt that obstructionism was not in the best tradition of pacifism, insofar as it set up a confrontation based in part upon physical rather than moral coercion.

Wary of developments on the most militant wing of CNVA, Scott refused to back the Cheyenne Project, claiming that the organization's resources were already stretched too thin to take on such an action.[13] Undeterred, Olson and Springer proceeded to organize the action in CNVA's name without official organizational sanction. A flurry of letters went back and forth between Scott and the planners in Wyoming during the weeks prior to the action. Scott wrote to Ted Olson on July 22 that he was "very disturbed" by news that Olson and Springer were proceeding with plans for a project on a scale never approved by the organization's leaders. He pleaded with Olson to recognize "the serious nature of the mistake you are making." Scott argued that the American public would not support a civil disobedience campaign against the installation of ICBM silos, and he feared that "misuse" of civil disobedience might "discredit that method and leave a bitter fruit!"[14] Subsequent letters only confirmed how far Olson and Springer were from Scott in their perceptions about the amount of preparation and discipline required for nonviolent activism, about the need to consider the political sensibilities of the general public, and about the likelihood that the facility in Cheyenne could actually be shut down.[15] Olson and Springer raced ahead with their plans despite Scott's remonstrations.

In early August of 1958, participants in the Cheyenne Project began to prepare the local community for their action by passing out leaflets. Far from building goodwill with local residents, many of whom worked at the military base, the leaflets intensified animosity toward the project by questioning the humanity of those who worked on missile deployment. Demonstrators first attempted to obstruct the entrance to the base on August 18. They were easily removed, but they returned the next day even more determined to prevent trucks from entering the site. During the day, protesters were removed from the road-way dozens of times in tense confrontations. Trucks drove right up to the protesters before slamming on their brakes, behavior that many of the protesters believed was encouraged by military authorities. Then, late in the afternoon, Ken Calkins, a graduate student at the University of Chicago, suffered a fractured pelvis when he was hit by a truck at the entrance to the base. Calkins spent ten days in a hospital before beginning a jail term for trespassing. After the arrests of August 19 and the injury to Calkins, the Cheyenne Project faltered. Springer at this point negotiated a deal with Scott to have CNVA carry the financial and organizational burden of quickly wrapping up the project.[16]

Scott himself went to Cheyenne to oversee the project's end. He wrote back to Willoughby, Muste, and Rustin that his situation was difficult because young people continued to arrive on the scene from San Francisco intent upon continuing the confrontation at the base. Scott respected the intentions of these young men and women: "All of these people are solid, rational people with deep convictions," he noted. "The act of Ted [Olson] and Ken [Calkins] . . . spoke to their condition and they are ready to give their life if need be to make the same manner of witness." Yet Scott also felt that the young activists he con-fronted in Cheyenne "care little about whether this builds a peace movement or has any political relevance or communicative value."[17] As late as September 6, as young activists continued to arrive, Scott was still having difficulty preventing further obstructionist actions at the base in his organization's name. Scott was becoming deeply worried about the course this new activism was taking. "In the present situation at Cheyenne," he wrote, "I think that non-violent obstruction is immoral, ineffective and has the character of non-violent coersion [sic]. I am concerned because its use in Cheyenne may set a pattern for the peace movement in America, or split our efforts into holier-than-thou fragments."[18] Eventually, Scott was able to close out the Cheyenne Project. The action had received very little public attention and had even had negligible effect on construction of the missile installation, but the Cheyenne Project touched off an intense internal debate over obstructionism within CNVR.

Brad Lyttle, one of the participants in the action at Cheyenne, rapidly developed a reputation as the most influential apologist for the obstructionist camp within CNVA. Although he was only thirty years old at the time, Lyttle brought considerable knowledge of pacifist activism to his role as challenger to Scott's influence within the organization. Lyttle, whose father was a Unitarian minister and whose mother was a pacifist and Socialist, had been raised in a home where Socialist party leader Norman Thomas was a frequent dinner guest. He was, he recalls, "brought up in a pacifist atmosphere." In high school, he refused to stand for the national anthem, and, when he heard over the radio that Hiroshima had been destroyed by a single bomb, Lyttle, then eighteen, instantly felt certain that humanity now faced the stark, apocalyptic choice between continued war and survival. Lyttle enrolled at Earlham College, a Quaker school, in 1945. During his college years, he roomed with James Otsuka, whose studies had been interrupted by time in a CPS camp, and he developed a close friendship with Corbett Bishop. After graduation, Lyttle struggled to decide between pursuing a career in medicine and devoting his life to pacifism. He concluded that the presence of nuclear weapons made activism the more urgent vocation. When he was drafted for the Korean War in 1953 Lyttle refused to report for alternative service and was sentenced to a year and a day. After his release from prison, Lyttle spent eighteen months traveling the world to study peace movements, visiting Gandhian ashrams in India as well as peace groups in Europe and Southeast Asia. Lyttle joined the Cheyenne Project shortly after his return to the United States in 1958.[19] His considerable experience in pacifism and his fiery zeal to end the arms race soon catapulted him to the leadership of those within

CNVA who felt that the approach advocated by Scott and Bigelow was unnecessarily tame.

Lyttle's style was radical pacifism in a new key. Believing that nuclear Armageddon was imminent, he told other activists that they should sacrifice their personal lives to devote every ounce of energy and use every nonviolent tool at their disposal to prevent nuclear holocaust. Some radical pacifists who had themselves been castigated in the 1940s by traditional pacifists for being too urgent now leveled similar criticisms at Lyttle.

Lyttle wrote vigorous essays defending obstructionism as a method that had moral, religious, and political legitimacy.[20] He argued in *Liberation* that the hostility the activists encountered in Cheyenne was not a failing of the action but a sign of the "exceptional power of the educational technique of nonviolent obstruction." Lyttle, in other words, felt that obstructionism evoked hostility because it forced people to confront the disturbing possibility of nuclear war. He argued that pacifists should not be averse to upsetting the public, concluding: "Much of the weakness of the peace movement is due to anemia caused by too much middle-class prudence.... We must think and act on the assumption that we can bring about a nonviolent revolution against the tradition of military power."[21]

In the late summer of 1958, CNVA's future direction hung in the balance between Scott's supporters and the obstructionist contingent, increasingly led by Lyttle. Muste, who held enormous prestige in both camps, tipped the scales in Lyttle's favor. In September, he wrote to Scott: "My feeling about the debate between yourself and Ted Olson about 'obstruction' tactics is that you tend to see one important aspect of the problem but to emphasize it too strongly at times to the neglect of the other aspect.... Ted sees and feels the compulsion on himself and possibly others not to omit any act which places not only his words etc. but his body ... against the atrocity which is being perpetrated. If he were throwing himself in the way of a madman seeking to hurt a child no one would question that this was genuine nonviolent resistance and not obstruction in the derogatory sense of the term:" [22] Muste also circulated a memo within pacifist circles arguing that he was "quite unable to see" any "fundamental" moral difference between the "Golden Rule" and Cheyenne actions, even if the latter did involve a higher degree of confrontation.[23]

Muste's backing was enough to swing other radical pacifists--and, with them, CNVA--in line behind Lyttle. This change in direction eventually led Larry Scott, the founder of SANE and CNVA, and Albert Bigelow, CNVA's most famous member, to resign from the organization.

This was a shift of some moment for radical pacifism as well as for CNVA. In backing obstructionism, Muste and those who followed his lead reaffirmed the radicalism of their pacifism. They resisted the lure of respectability that had enticed CNVA after the "Golden Rule" action received such favorable and widespread coverage. In returning to their familiar prophetic stance, of course, they also returned in some sense to the desert of obscurity. For CNVA would never again command media attention even remotely as it had when it used more moderate tactics and ideologically cautious statements during the "Golden Rule" action. The shift in favor of obstructionism showed once again that radical pacifists privileged individual cathartic action over pragmatic efficacy. The eclipse of moderates such as Scott and Bigelow by obstructionists also exhibited radical pacifism's tendency to follow small victories with increased militancy, a tendency that would plague activism against the Vietnam War. On the other hand, Muste's decision to back Lyttle and his youthful followers placed the radical pacifist leadership at the end of the 1950s squarely on the side of the younger generation's confrontational militancy—a decision that would allow middle-aged radical pacifists to forge strong coalitions with youth movements during the 1960s.

Muste backed up his words in 1959 by participating in a CNVA action that included obstructionist methods organized by Lyttle, Homer Jack, and Muste himself at an ICBM installation outside Omaha. After weeks of leafleting and other activities by CNVA members in the Omaha area, the seventy-four-year-old Muste and two other men initiated civil disobedience at the missile site on the first of July by climbing over a fence onto military property. CNVA periodically sent small groups of two or three people onto the base to commit civil disobedience over the next several weeks, while supporters maintained a vigil outside. Muste violated his parole by returning to participate in the vigil. Brad Lyttle was arrested on July 8 and, like Muste, served a prison sentence for violating his parole after returning to the protest. On July 13, two of the younger participants attempted to obstruct the highway leading into the ICBM installation. All told, fifteen people committed civil disobedience in the Omaha Action between July 1 and August 10.[24] The Omaha Action had a negligible effect on the public debate about the arms race, but as an action with official CNVA sanction it did have the effect of solidifying CNVA in its support of obstructionist militancy.

Omaha Action's organizers, however, were surprised to see how much attention the media paid to Marj Swann, the long-time Peacemakers activist who, along with Lyttle, Muste, and others, served a prison term for violating her parole immediately after trespassing onto the base. What set Swann apart was the fact that she was the mother of four young children. Such behavior challenged assumptions about decent maternal behavior that were widely held in the late 1950's.[25] Swarm's treatment by the legal system and the media focused on whether she was a fit mother in choosing to go to jail despite what were perceived to be her domestic responsibilities. The judge who sentenced Swann lashed out at her during the proceedings in heavily gendered terms, calling her "an irresponsible, irrational, stubborn, foolish woman" and a "bad mother."[26]

Even articles sympathetic to Swann strove to reconcile her political radicalism with mainstream popular notions of maternal decorum. Jhan and June Robbins, freelance journalists who were experienced at conveying gender issues in the popular press (with such page turners to their credit as "129 Ways to Get a Husband" and "Forty-Nine Ways to Make Marriage More Exciting"),[27] wrote sympathetically of Swann's pacifism in an article in *Redbook*, but they hastened to portray her as a consummate mother and homemaker. Far from being hardened or otherwise defeminized after doing time in the penitentiary, for instance, the Robbinses assured readers that Swann "slipped back quickly into her normal household routine. A pile of mending awaited her. She went to P.T.A. meetings and pushed her basket at the supermarket, nodding to friends and neighbors." [28]

Swann herself employed traditional gender images to sup-port her radical agenda. The day after being sentenced, Swann wrote from prison that her concern for what the arms race meant for children motivated her actions: "And to children—all children—can we say we would not suffer that they might live? ... The children must know that we care enough." [29] She similarly called upon the language of maternal love as a justification for her activism when she explained to *Redbook* readers: "I love my children dearly. . . . I know that if there is another war—a nuclear, global war—they will die. So will millions of other children all over the world." Vividly connecting quaint images of child care in the home with public activism on global political issues, Swann added that for ensuring the safety and security of children "cod-liver oil and clean diapers and even good-night kisses are less important right now than stopping the H-bomb."[30] Swann's politicization of images of female domesticity was remarkably similar in style to Women Strike for Peace, an organization founded two years later.[31]

TOWARD A NEW LEFT

Throughout this period in the late 1950s, Muste was trying to foster dialogue and build coalitions in an effort to forge a new Left. Viewing CNVA as just one aspect of this broader venture, Muste became increasingly interested in harnessing the growing restiveness among students. Toward this end, Muste became particularly active in personally bridging the radical pacifism of the 1940S to the student activism of the late 1950s and 1960s.

In 1956 and 1957, Muste organized a series of meetings under FOR auspices to facilitate dialogue on the non-Communist Left, efforts historian Maurice Isserman considers "the first and most publicized attempt at regroupment" of the American Left after the McCarthy era.[32] In May of 1956, Muste organized a gathering in Carnegie Hall of several hundred representatives from a broad spectrum of the non-Communist Left. W. E. B. DuBois, Roger Baldwin, and Norman Thomas were among the speakers in what participants generally considered a fruitful exchange. Muste also organized a similar meeting in Chicago the following October. These meetings were then formalized in 1957 at Muste's initiative as the American Forum for Socialist Education. The forum sponsored gatherings throughout 1957 at which virtually every thinker of influence on the Left participated, including Max Schachtman, Irving Howe, C. Wright Mills, and I. F. Stone, as well as radical pacifists Muste, Rustin, and young Dave McReynolds. The forum broke down within two years under the weight of high-profile government investigation and due to internal sectarian strains, but during its short time of influence the forum managed to get disparate radical groups in America to consider new opportunities for cooperation on issues of peace and social justice, displaying yet again Muste's lifelong penchant for getting leaders with considerable defensiveness and egotism to talk together.[33]

One of the direct links between the radical pacifism of CNVA and the new student Left was the Student Peace Union, founded by Ken Calkins in 1959, a year after Calkins had fractured his pelvis at the Cheyenne Action. SPU spread rapidly to campuses. Its famous slogan, "No Tests, East or West," reflecting radical pacifists' critique of both belligerents in the Cold War, appealed to many students critical of the arms race. In one month during

1960, SPU was able to gather ten thousand signatures on a peace petition distributed at colleges.[34] During the first few years of the 1960s, SPU was the central organization for white student activism. As such, it became a vehicle by which the radical pacifist approach was disseminated to the next generation of student activists. By 1964, however, SPU was eclipsed by the Students for a Democratic Society (SDS), a group which had worked closely with SPU on peace issues in the early 1960s.[35]

In 1960, Brad Lyttle also built an important link between the radical pacifists in CNVA and student activists when he initiated the Polaris Action. Lyttle first conceived. of the project while in prison for his participation in Omaha Action. Reading an article in *Time* magazine about the destructive power of the new Polaris nuclear submarines, Lyttle quickly concluded that direct action against the centerpiece of the navy's nuclear program in the congested suburban area where the subs were being built would draw international attention. With Muste's support, Lyttle set up an office near the Groton, Connecticut, shipyard and organized a leafleting campaign. Lyttle himself was knocked unconscious by an angry shipyard worker while leafleting, and CNVA had to maintain an around-the-clock watch to protect the action's office, which had had every one of its windows broken within the first week of operation. This embattled action soon began to draw young activists, who engaged in daring acts of protest. Demonstrators, for instance, sailed a flotilla of skiffs out into the estuary in an attempt to obstruct a Polaris submarine's maiden voyage. One protester swam out and clambered aboard the sub's hull, generating a memorable picture of an individual at considerable personal risk placing his body against a black behemoth of the Cold War. Tom Cornell, a young member of the Catholic Worker whose great-grandfather had helped develop the first military submarine in the United States, remembers that in a related action his boat got caught in currents and unintentionally drifted into a submarine. Putting out his hand to prevent a crash into the sub's hull, Cornell felt strong emotions as he came "in physical contact

with a machine that could incinerate all of Europe in a flash." When he returned
to shore, Cornell burned his draft card as an act of "withdrawal from the
system." Although he had been classified as a conscientious objector, Cornell
no longer felt he could "recognize the legitimacy" of the government's
classification. Cornell would go through about a dozen draft cards by the end
of the decade.[36]

Lyttle recalls that the Polaris Action was marked by a full measure of
pacifist analysis, commitment, and action. It was, he feels, "the best pacifist
project I've ever participated in."[37] Tom Cornell, who credits Lyttle with
having "thought up or executed more than half of the project," concurs that
"there wasn't any departure from nonviolence" in the Polaris Action.
Cornell recalls that organizers would even welcome FBI agents at meetings
in the spirit of adherence to a principle of openness.[38]

At the same time CNVA was attracting student protesters to Lyttle's
Polaris Action, the organization's fraternal twin, SANE, was self-destructing
due to a failure to remain attuned to the changing tenor of the times.
SANE's troubles began when Senator Dodd of Connecticut attacked the
group, claiming that it harbored Communists among its leadership. Norman
Cousins promptly capitulated to Dodd's allegations by purging the
organization of any former or suspected Communists. Cousins, himself
vociferously anti-Communist, feared that Dodd's attack would alienate
SANE's moderate liberal membership if strong action to keep the
organization impregnable to red-baiting were not taken. Yet, in capitulating
to Dodd in 1960, Cousins unexpectedly appeared more as a relic of a bygone
phase of the Cold War than as a leader of a progressive antinuclear
organization. At the dawn of the 1960s, with the Communist party in the
United States moribund, liberals were inclined to agree with Leftists that the
excesses of anti-Communist campaigns represented a graver threat to
American democracy than did domestic communism. Cousins had expected

to preserve the support of moderates; to his astonishment, he watched helplessly as the liberal center of SANE melted and the organization became a pariah on the Left in the aftermath of his purges. Cousins would still have his moment in the sun--notably, when President Kennedy included him in the negotiations for the Atmospheric Test Ban Treaty in 1963--but by that point Cousins led a disemboweled organization.

The demise of SANE in 1960 was a clear signal that the tide in American politics was shifting to the left. There is every reason to believe that a principled resistance by Cousins to the Dodd inquiry would have significantly strengthened SANE. Muste, for one, lambasted Cousins for failing to take the pulse of the nation. "What has happened in SANE," he wrote in *Liberation*, "is tragic, partly because . . . it need not have happened. Everything in our political life shows that we are at a turning point and that Americans sense it.... [If SANE had stood up to Dodd], such an attitude might have called forth a tremendous response; might have put new heart into many people, especially young people fed up with conformism and apathy."[39]

This experience led Muste to become a strong and early advocate for a policy of nonexclusion in organizations of the Left during the 1960s. Nonexclusionists such as Muste frankly stated that Communists could participate in protest coalitions because they had become largely irrelevant on the Left. This policy cut through much of the red-baiting that had hamstrung organizations such as SANE and allowed for the building of coalitions that, as with Muste's American Forum, had usually broken down over sectarian questions of which stripes of Marxists to exclude.

Although they could not know it in 1960, Muste's nonexclusion policy later allowed radical pacifists to play a central role in organizing mass demonstrations against the Vietnam War. By building an inclusive tapestry of organizational alliances for specific actions, they would be able to periodically call into the streets a wide spectrum of groups that often agreed on little but their opposition to the war in the late 1960s.[40] Nonexclusion, however, would also prove to have a dark side, as many on the Old Left foretold. Nonexclusion made it nearly impossible for responsible leaders to control fringe insurgent forces within coalitions. When this danger was more fully actualized in 1968 and 1969, the consequences for the Left would be disastrous.

More than anyone else, Muste was able to mine the full potential for coalition building that nonexclusion offered. Freed to a degree from red-baiting and the full force of sectarianism in the early to mid-sixties, Muste was able to call upon a lifetime of personal relationships on the Left in bringing people together. Muste was a skilled negotiator who worked with stamina at meetings to find some common thread between groups highly suspicious of each other. Muste also had kept older radical pacifist groups attuned to the concerns of the new student Left by swinging CNVA behind Lyttle's obstructionist policies. Muste's New Left ethos made him a vital link between the Old Left and the student leadership of the New, who tended to dismiss the previous generation of activists. Writing in the *Nation* about the student leadership of the New Left in 1965, Jack Newfield commented that "the few older figures whom the new generation seems to respect come out of the radical pacifist tradition—men like ... the 80 year old A. J. Muste."[41]

The cross-fertilization these alliances facilitated was reflected in the pages of *Liberation* during the 1960s. Frequent contributors included Tom Hayden, Paul Booth, Carl Oglesby, and Todd Gitlin of the Students for a Democratic Society (SDS) as well as Jerry Rubin and Marty Jezer of the Yippies. *Liberation* also published a blueprint for society penned by the Diggers of the Haight-Ashbury counterculture and several early feminist and gay critiques and manifestoes, including a germinal feminist memo written by women in the Student Nonviolent Coordinating Committee. As the rapidly shifting shoals of activism demanded continual communication between contingents in the 1960s, *Liberation's* radical pacifist editors became central figures in the discourse on the Left. Also clear in the magazine's pages, however, is the fact that Muste, Dellinger, Lynd, and the other editors did not simply march to the tunes of young radicals but maintained their commitment to Gandhism, often gently remonstrating activists who seemed to be veering impatiently to-ward an advocacy of violent confrontation.[42]

FREEDOM RIDES AND PEACE WALKS

While Lyttle's Polaris Action, Day's air defense protests, and Muste's coalition building all strengthened ties between radical pacifists and students in 1960, what riveted the attention of activists that year was the sit-in movement begun by black students in the South. During 1958 and 1959, the Civil Rights movement had experienced a lull in activity after the promising mid-1950s. In the last two years of the decade, King's SCLC had struggled to keep the momentum of the racial revolution going; they knew the powder keg was there, but they couldn't strike the right spark. Then, unexpectedly, match was put to fuse in 1960 by a group of students in Greensboro, North Carolina, who decided to engage in a sit-in at a local dimestore lunch counter that did not serve blacks. Within weeks, the sit-in movement was rocking the South, with the rest of the country watching intently. Young activists like Tom Hayden were enthralled by the bravado of the student-led movement.

Media coverage at the time portrayed the students as acting with complete autonomy. There was some truth to this portrayal, insofar as the students were not part of a central organization and there was a strong element of spontaneity to the protests. Yet the influence of CORE certainly permeated the students' activities. Historians Meier and Rudwick point out that the Greensboro students were influenced by a sympathetic white businessman who had read Houser's *Erasing the Color Line*.[43] In that pamphlet, Houser outlined sit-ins at Woolworth's lunch counters conducted by CORE members in the late 1940s and early 1950s.

CORE soon did more than simply serve as a model for the sit-ins. The inexperienced student leaders of the ad hoc movement soon received consultative and institutional support from CORE as well.[44] CORE quickly dispatched two experienced organizers to Greensboro and, through its network of local cells, initiated a national boycott and picketing campaign against Woolworth's. CORE's close identification with the sudden up-surge of student activism redounded to a resurgence for CORE, which had felt sidelined during the most prominent racial struggles of the 1950s. Its linkage with the sit-in movement and with the student organization that would emerge in October of 1960 from that movement, the Student Nonviolent Coordinating Committee (SNCC), would catapult CORE into its period of greatest prominence.

CORE gave concrete aid to the sit-in movement. Jim Peck, who had been reared in New York mercantile society, took a prominent role in organizing white liberal support behind the boycott of Woolworth's in the North. Peck also represented CORE in the first negotiations with Woolworth executives to discuss desegregating their facilities in the South. CORE's leaders also called upon their local chapters to spread the sit-ins to as many southern cities as possible. Just twelve days after the initial sit-in at Greensboro, a CORE group sat in at a Woolworth's in Tallahassee. This chapter was not unprepared, for they had engaged in a similar sit-in at a local Sears in 1959.[45]

Rejuvenated from their mid-1950s stupor by their involvement with the determined young men and women leading the sit-in movement, CORE, led by Farmer and Peck, decided to reprise the 1947 " Journey of Reconciliation" in 1961, this time to be called the "Freedom Ride." On May 4, thirteen activists-- seven blacks, including Farmer and John Lewis of SNCC, and six whites, including Peck and Albert Bigelow--departed on a Trailways bus from

Washington, D.C., in a desegregated seating arrangement. Jim Peck was the only Freedom Rider who had participated in the Journey of Reconciliation.

Throughout Virginia and North Carolina, the group asserted itself as a desegregated cadre on buses, in terminals, and at lunch counters without serious incident. The first violent confrontation took place in South Carolina, where Lewis and Bigelow were beaten by a white mob. This was but a foretaste, however, of what awaited them farther along the road.

Despite warnings from the local black leader Fred Shuttlesworth that further violence awaited them in Alabama, the group continued on their prearranged itinerary, traveling on two buses toward Birmingham. The violence Shuttlesworth had feared met the riders at the Greyhound bus station in Anniston, Alabama. There, the Freedom Riders were confronted by a mob of over two hundred whites. One bus managed to pull out of the station after having all its windows broken, the driver not realizing that the tires had also been slashed. The driver managed to drive only six miles out of Anniston before he had to pull the bus off the road, where it was quickly surrounded by a portion of the mob that had followed in a convoy of cars. An incendiary bomb was hurled into the bus, gutting the interior with fire and forcing the Freedom Riders out to face their pursuers. Local police standing by refused to intervene. The situation would no doubt have rapidly worsened had not a group of cars presciently dispatched by Shuttlesworth arrived to rescue the besieged riders.

Meanwhile, before the second bus could leave the terminal, it was boarded by several men who severely beat Peck and fellow-rider Walter Bergman, a retired school administrator participating in the Freedom Ride with his wife. The driver of this second bus finally managed to drive from Anniston to the Birmingham station, where another dangerous mob awaited the group. Peck again took the brunt of this assault; he was beaten senseless with metal pipes and required fifty stitches. When no drivers could be found who were willing to drive the groups farther, CORE canceled the remainder of the Freedom Ride. Yet even in their attempt to call off their plans the group of riders was hampered by segregationists. They were delayed for several hours at the airport when bomb threats were phoned in against the plane they were waiting to take to New York. The group eventually did arrive in New York City, where Peck joined a picket line--on the same day he had been beaten.

At this point, the close ties CORE had forged with the student movement during the sit-ins of the previous year proved their mettle. Angry that CORE had been forced to abandon the ride, John Lewis and other SNCC members in Nashville courageously decided to continue the Freedom Riders' itinerary. After being turned away by Birmingham police, the SNCC group returned in greater numbers and eventually succeeded in continuing the Freedom Ride from Birmingham to Montgomery. They were so brutally attacked by a mob in Montgomery, however, that the Kennedy administration was finally embarrassed into sending six hundred federal marshals to protect the riders. At this point, King flew to Montgomery to participate in the reactivated ride. James Farmer (who had left the earlier incarnation of the Freedom Ride before the buses arrived in Anniston to attend his father's funeral) also flew down to Montgomery to reassert CORE's presence in the action. A coalition of CORE, SNCC, and SCLC then continued the Freedom Ride to Jackson, Mississippi. In Jackson, harassment arrests by local police led the protesters to initiate a policy of filling up the city's jails. Joined by hundreds of people, mostly students, who arrived in Jackson to be arrested, this tactic succeeded in keeping a national spotlight on the action throughout the summer and finally led to decisive federal action that enforced desegregated seating on interstate travel, the goal of the journey of Reconciliation fourteen years before.[46]

The Freedom Rides kept the momentum begun by the sit-ins moving forward, adding a greater sense of urgency to the Civil Rights agenda. The rides catapulted CORE into national prominence on a par with SCLC and SNCC, leading to a dramatic increase in membership. The rides also cemented CORE's close links with the militant leaders of SNCC, links that would keep CORE on the cutting edge of black militancy, but a militancy that would splinter the organization with the emergence of black power.

The black freedom struggles of the early 1960s captured far more national attention than did the antinuclear activities of pacifists during the same period. Nonetheless, the antinuclear actions of the early 1960s continued to build important links between radical pacifists and white student activists around an antiwar agenda. In these years, Brad Lyttle remained an important organizer.

Sitting in a coffeeshop after the Polaris Action had crested, Lyttle and a few others decided to initiate a walk from San Francisco to Washington, D.C., and then across Europe to Moscow, to protest the nuclear arms race. In 1961, Lyttle led this first transcontinental peace walk in American history, a tiny knot of marchers (only about forty people when the group briefly swelled after passing by Chicago) who straggled their way across the nation, speaking in towns along their route. In Washington, Arthur Schlesinger, Jr., politely but stiffly met them on behalf of the Kennedy administration. They traveled to England (where they participated in a joint rally with Bertrand Russell's Committee for Nuclear Disarmament) and then walked across Belgium and both Germanys into Russia (where Muste had flown to negotiate their entry). The marchers were welcomed warmly by the Soviet Peace Committee and even allowed to stage a rally in Red Square bearing signs with their own choice of words, because Khrushchev hoped to use the marchers in his propaganda campaign to convince the world that the Soviet Union was an open society. (The marchers, though, were shifted from a meeting with Khrushchev to a meeting with his wife when they refused to support the Soviet "peace" position that effectively portrayed the United States as the principal aggressor.)

The San Francisco to Moscow Walk took about eighteen months in 1961 and 1962. Lytle followed it up almost immediately with a Quebec to Guantanamo Walk, in 1963. While both walks enjoyed some media attention, however, they were far less effective at challenging the national conscience than the black freedom struggles of the same years. This was tacitly acknowledged by the marchers themselves when they diverted their march en route to Cuba to participate in the SNCC-led attempt to fill up the jails in Albany, Georgia. Even the pages of *Liberation* devoted far more attention to desegregation struggles in the South than to the peace marchers in 1962 and 1963. Indeed, many of the Quebec to Guantanamo marchers themselves seemed more interested in their Albany prison experience than in the other stages of their 1963 peace march.[47] Clearly, radical pacifists looked to the black movement for the nonviolent revolution for which they yearned in the early 1960s.

After the Quebec to Guantanamo Walk, which followed on the heels of the Omaha, Polaris, and San Francisco to Moscow actions, Brad Lyttle felt that he was emotionally exhausted. "I was unable to organize any major pacifist field projects after these," he recalls.[48]

Meanwhile, in 1963, the Civil Rights phase of the black freedom struggles reached perhaps its high-water mark when Randolph's dream of a March on Washington finally came to fruition. Rather than ten thousand blacks marching on the capital, as Randolph had envisioned in 1941, more than 250,000 people took part in August of 1963, making it the largest protest rally in American history up to that point. Bayard Rustin was given the primary responsibility for organizing the march, working as deputy director of the march committee under the nominal directorship of the venerable but aging Randolph. Again, Rustin's past Youth Communist ties and homosexuality plagued him, leading planners to make

Randolph the titular head of the committee in case opponents tried to discredit the rally by launching a character assassination of Rustin.

Rustin did a superb organizational job, planning the welter of logistics and ensuring widespread media coverage of the event. Determined to keep the event as mainstream as possible, he played a key role in pressuring SNCC leader John Lewis to excise passages of his speech that were critical of the Kennedy administration. King, too, struck a cautious note in his speech, which may be one reason why the first half of the famous "I Have a Dream" speech was so flat. King only hit his stride in that address when he shifted away from his prepared notes to soar into poetic eschatology in the best Baptist preaching tradition, but that second half alone was so inspiring as to enshrine the speech as an American icon—and contribute enormously to King's apotheosis.

By 1963, the Left had experienced a remarkable resurgence after its nadir in the mid-1950s. At least one movement of the Left, the Civil Rights component of the black freedom struggles, could now call upon masses of people to participate in its protests. In this movement, radical pacifists who had been active since World War II played critical roles. Glenn Smiley and Bayard Rustin, through their influence on King, helped establish nonviolent direct action as the orthodox Civil Rights methodology. With the March on Washington, Rustin synthesized his radical pacifist experience with Randolph's mass action techniques in a powerful alchemy that pricked the conscience of the American people. CORE, too, in its reprise as a militant vanguard, helped shift the center of the Civil Rights movement further in a radical, direct action course.

Much had happened in the late 1950s and early 1960s on the antiwar front as well. SANE and CNVA had in complementary ways galvanized dissent against Cold War nuclear policies. CNVA and Dorothy Day's Catholic Worker had applied direct action tactics to their opposition to the military-industrial complex in creative ways and, in so doing, had developed important links with a generation of student activists. Muste had done much to further these links by his efforts to foster dialogue and build coalitions on the Left. Most influential in this regard were his founding of *Liberation* and his support of Brad Lyttle and of nonexclusion, all of which kept the older radical pacifists fresh in the eyes of many younger radicals. In 1963, it appeared that the black freedom struggles would continue to absorb most of the attention of the Left. But events in Southeast Asia would soon become the focus of American protest. As antiwar sentiment became a groundswell in the mid-1960s, the peace efforts that radical pacifists had engaged in during the late 1950s and early 1960s would place them at the organizational center of the emerging antiwar coalitions.

NOTES

1. Unattributed first-hand account, probably Lawrence Scott, "The Nevada Witness," SCPC, Scott MSS, Box 2, Nevada folder.

2. James Peck, "Trespassing on the Bomb Site," *Liberation* 2, no. 6 (September 1957) 89.

3. On Bigelow's conversion to pacifism, see Albert S. Bigelow, "Why I Am Sailing into the Pacific Bomb-Test Area," *Liberation* 2, no. 11 (February 1958): 4-8.

4. Lawrence Scott, "Words Are Not Enough," *Liberation* 2, no. 3 (May 1957) 14-15.

5. For convenience, the organization will be referred to as CNVA in the text even during the period when it was still NVAANW.

6. On CNVA and SANE, see Winner, Rebels against War, pp. 242 ff.; Maurice Isserman, *If I Had a Hammer: The Death of the Old Left and the Birth of the New Left* (New York: Basic Books, 1987), pp. 147 ff.; and Neil H. Katz, "Radical Pacifism and the Contemporary American Peace Movement The Committee for Nonviolent Action, 1957-1967" (Ph.D. dissertation, University of Maryland, 1974)

7. See SANE press release, July 17, 1957, SCPC, Scott MSS, Box I, SANE folder.

8. Figures taken from Isserman, *If I Had a Hammer*, p. 149.

9. Albert S. Bigelow, "Why I Am Sailing into the Pacific Bomb-Test Area," *Liberation* 2, no. (February 1958): 4-8.

10. See statements to court given by Bigelow, Huntington, Willoughby, and Sherwood, May 7, 1958, SCPC, Albert Bigelow MSS, Box 1.

11. On the "Golden Rule" Action, see James Peck, "Jail Is Our Home Port"; William Huntington, "If You Feel Like It"; and A. J. Muste, "Follow the Golden Rule," all in *Liberation* 3, no. 4 (June 1958): 4-8.

12. On media coverage and the public response to the "Golden Rule" action, see Muste, "Follow the Golden Rule"; Wittner, *Rebels against War*, p. 249; and Isserman, *If I Had a Hammer*, p. 154.

13. See Lawrence Scott to Sam Tyson, et al., February 17, 1958, SCPC, Scott MSS, Box 2.

14. Lawrence Scott to Ted Olson, July 22, 1958, SCPC, Scott MSS, Box 5, Cheyenne folder.

15. See Ted Olson to Lawrence Scott, July 25, 1958; Scott to Olson, July 3o, 1958; Olson to Scott, August 1, 1958; Art Springer to Scott, August 4, 1958; and Scott to Springer, August 15, 1958, all at SCPC, Scott MSS, Box 5, Cheyenne folder.

16. On Cheyenne Project, see Bradford Lyttle, "Comments on the Use of Nonviolent Obstruction at Cheyenne," 1958, SCPC, Scott MSS, Box 5, Cheyenne folder; Neil H. Katz, "Radical Pacifism and the Contemporary American Peace Movement," pp. 72‒75; and Isserman, *If I Had a Hammer*, PP 156–58.

17. Lawrence Scott to George Willoughby, A. J. Muste, Bayard Rustin, and Robert Pickus, August 28, I958, SCPC, Scott MSS, Box 5, Cheyenne folder.

18. Lawrence Scott to George Willoughby, A. J. Muste, Robert Pickus, Lyle Tatum, and Bayard Rustin, September 6, 1958, SCPC, Scott MSS, Box 5, Cheyenne folder.

19. See author's interview with Brad Lyttle, 11/26/94.

20. While defending obstructionism, Lyttle was careful to draw the following distinction in his own position on its use at Cheyenne: "I believe nonviolent obstruction should be allowed at the Cheyenne demonstration, not that it should be a planned part of the program" [emphasis in original]. Bradford Lyttle, "Comments on the Use of Nonviolent Obstruction at Cheyenne," 1958, SCPC, Scott MSS, Box 5, Cheyenne folder.

21. Bradford Lyttle, "On Nonviolent Obstruction," *Liberation* 3, no. 8 (November 1958): 10-11.

22. A. J. Muste to Lawrence Scott, September 9, 1958, SCPC, Scott MSS, Box 5.

23.See A.J. Muste, "Reflections on Nonviolent Intervention," SCPC, Scott MSS, Box 5, Omaha folder.

24. See *Omaha Action Bulletin of July 1, 1959; July, 6 1959; July 8,1959: July 11, 1959; July 14, 1959; July 17, 1959;July 23, 1959; July28, 1959; August 5, 1959; November 3, 1959; and December 16, 1959*, all at SCPC, Scott MSS, Box 5, Omaha folder. See also Wilmer Young, "Visible Witness:" in Staughton Lynd, ed., *Nonviolence in America: A Documentary History* (New York: Bobbs-Merrill, 1966), pp. 347-60.

25. On expected female roles within the family in the 1950s, see Elaine Tyler May, *Homeward Bound: American Families in the Cold War Era* (New York: Basic Books, 1988).

26. Quoted in Jhan and June Robbins, "You Are a Bad Mother," reprinted from *Redbook* (August 1960 [?]), SCPC, Scott MSS, Box 5, See also author's interview with Marjorie Swann, 4/1/91.

27. Jhan and June Robbins, "129 Ways to Get a Husband," *McCall's 85* (January 1958): 28–29; and "Forty-Nine Ways to Make Marriage More Exciting," *Reader's Digest* 74 (January 1959) 113–14.

28. Jhan and June Robbins, "You Are a Bad Mother."

29. Marjorie Swann to Judge Robinson, July 28, 1959, reprinted in *Omaha Action Bulletin*, July 28,1959, SCPC, Scott MSS, Box 5, Omaha folder. In the *Bulletin*, Swann's letter appears below a photograph of her four children.

30. Jhan and June Robbins, "You Are a Bad Mother."

31. See Amy Swerdlow, *Women Strike for Peace: Traditional Motherhood and Radical Politics in the 1960s* (Chicago: University of Chicago Press, 1993).

32. Isserman, *If I Had a Hammer*, p. 174.

33. On the Forum, see Robinson, *Abraham Went Out*, pp. 100—102; and Isserman, *If I Had a Hammer*, pp. 174-80.

34. See Wittner, *Rebels against War*, p. 267; and Charles DeBenedetti, *An American Ordeal: The Antiwar Movement of the Vietnam Era* (Syracuse, NY: Syracuse University Press, 1990), p. 41.

35. See "What Is SDS?" Students for a Democratic Society pamphlet, 1962, Hoover Institution, Stanford University, SDS MSS, Microfilm reel 1.

36. Author's interview with Tom Cornell, 5/6/95. See also Nancy Zaroulis and Gerald Sullivan, *Who Spoke Up?: American Protest against the War in Vietnam, 1963—1975* (New York: Doubleday and Co., 1984), p. 57.

37. Author's interview with Bradford Lyttle, 11/26/94.

38. Author's interview with Tom Cornell, 5/6/95.

39. A. J. Muste, "The Crisis in SANE: Act II," *Liberation* 5, no. 9 (November 1960): 8.

40. A public statement by the pacifist-led National Mobilization Committee to End the War in Vietnam (Mobilization or just Mobe) shows that pacifist leaden understood this implication of nonexclusion by the late 1960s: "From its earliest conception in July 1966; the statement read, "one of the prime objectives of the Mobilization was the welding together of the widest possible grouping of people who are opposed to America's brutal and brutalizing war in Vietnam. This objective was carried out with unqualified success. Despite several attempts at red-baiting, 'black-power' baiting, and other attempts to split the movement, no political tendency was excluded either from planning or participating in the [1967] April 25th Spring Mobilization. The massive popular support given to the Mobilization confirmed the wisdom of this policy. . . . The Spring Mobilization is the widest coalition of political and social forces this country has seen." ("Statement of Purpose," National Mobilization Committee to End the War in Vietnam MSS, SCPC, Box 1.)

41. Jack Newfield, "Revolt without Dogma: The Student Left;" *Nation* 200, May 10, 1965:494.

182

42. See, for instance, Dave Dellinger, "Nonviolence and the Black Rebellion," *Liberation* 12, no. 4 (July 1967): 3-5; and Henry Anderson, "A Case against the Drug Culture," *Liberation* 1 2 , no. 2 (April 1967) 34-39.

43. See Meier and Rudwick, CORE, p. 102.

44. See *ibid.*

45. See "Sit-Ins: The Students Report," CORE pamphlet, May, 1960, SCPC, CORE, MSS.

46. See 1961 CORE pamphlet, "Violence Follows the Freedom Riders in Alabama," SCPC, CORE MSS; and Meier and Rudwick, *CORE*, pp. 135-44.

47. Barbara Deming, a marcher who had recently joined CNVA, was moved by her experience in Albany to write a powerful book of poetry, *Prison Notes,* incorporated with other material into *Prisons That Could Not Hold* (San Francisco: Spinsters Ink, 1985).

48. Author's interview with Brad Lyttle, 11/26/94; and Brad Lyttle letter to author, 5/18/95.

CHAPTER SEVEN

FROM CIVIL RIGHTS TO THE SECOND WAVE OF THE FEMINIST MOVEMENT, 1960-1975

Harriet Hyman Alonso

Along with labor history, peace history, African-American history, and ethnic studies, women's history came into prominence during the political and social upheavals of the turbulent sixties. Alonso, Professor of History at City College, City University of New York, is one of the authorities on U.S. women's peace history. This excerpt from her book, *Peace as a Women's Issue*, charters the emergence of women's rights peace organizations as part of the larger feminist movement that appeared in the 1960s. In looking at the Vietnam Anti-War Movement, Alonso notes how that protest contributed to a growing sophistication of feminist peace activism. She examines various women's responses to the war, including the influence of new female peace groups such as Women Strike for Peace and Another Mother for Peace. The author details the role of feminist ideology within the women's peace movement and its impact on traditional female peace organizations like the Women's International League for Peace and Freedom. Her study raises a number of important questions readers should look at. How did feminism present a challenge to the older and more traditional leadership within women's peace groups? What distinguished the new movement from the old? What links can be drawn between institutionalized violence and violence against women? How has the idea that women, as the child bearers of society, endowed them with a particular vested interest in world peace? How has this notion also afforded women "a socially acceptable cover for their highly political work? Lastly, how have their actions in the cause of peace help strengthen their convictions that women must also be responsible citizens?

From PEACE AS A WOMEN'S ISSUE: A HISTORY OF THE U.S. MOVEMENT FOR WORLD PEACE AND WOMEN'S RIGHTS by Harriet Hyman Alonso. Copyright 1993 by Syracuse University Press. Used by permission of Syracuse University Press.

The 1950s set the stage for the political activism of the 1960s. The various movements that took root ever so tentatively during the fifties finally burst forth, attracting many people to their causes--especially students, women, workers, and people of color. At first, racial injustice, the expanding nuclear arms race, and the growing U.S. military involvement in Vietnam were the three most urgent issues behind this new activism. As the decade progressed, however, questions about women's equality also rose to the forefront. The "second wave" of the feminist movement germinated throughout the 1960s. (It was so designated because at the time many historians felt that the "first wave," which began in 1848, had ended once women had gained the vote.) By 1965 student activists Mary King and Casey Hayden were expressing discontent with the way women and their issues were being treated in such civil rights organizations as SNCC (Student Non-Violent Coordinating Committee) and New Left groups such as SDS (Students for a Democratic Society). From this discontent rose the grassroots women's liberation movement based on community-organized consciousness-raising and self-help groups. Around the same time, in 1966, Betty Friedan and a few other middle-aged professional women organized the National Organization for Women (NOW), a pressure group intent on improving women's lot through legislation and other structural changes within government and business. Emphasizing different populations but often embracing similar issues, the two prongs of the women's movement secured sweeping changes within U.S. society. With the slogan "The personal is political," women moved from their homes into the streets to demand equal wages, equal rights, reproductive freedom, personal opportunity, and respect.[1] For the peace movement as a whole, the women's movement was like a vitamin shot. Spurred on by rage at how they were oppressed by society, women once again pointed an accusing finger at the war machine and the "military-industrial complex." They blamed the men in power for tying the nation's economic prosperity to the production of weapons, thereby militarizing the society. In such a climate, racism, poverty, and sexism had ample opportunity to abound. Even worse, people were made to live their daily lives under the constant threat of a nuclear holocaust.

During the early sixties women fostering this new spurt of interest in feminism focused their efforts largely on the civil rights movement or in trying to understand their discontent with their affluent, but generally boring, suburban lives. Until the escalation of military involvement in Vietnam during the Johnson administration from 1965 on, antiwar work among women still rested primarily with WILPF. That organization, however, was still reeling from the effects of the McCarthy era, even though McCarthy himself had long before fallen into disgrace with the U.S. Senate. In 1960 the U.S. national office of WILPF, in its efforts to attract new members, was still trying to explain its position on communism and the Cold War. In a widely disseminated memo entitled "W.I.L.P.F. and the Cold War," the national leaders once again stressed their position of opposing all wars by non-violent and "democratic" means: "The WILPF has opposed every war, hot or cold, and has supported negotiation, mediation or arbitration of all international disputes, world disarmament, world organization to insure peace and raise the economic status of vast areas of the world, self determination of peoples, and insurance of basic human rights to every individual man."[2]

In addition, the women felt the need to reiterate their disdain for the "totalitarianism" they perceived in a communist system. Yet they still acknowledged that while they continued to define the Soviet Union as "totalitarian," they also shared goals and phraseology with communists that

WILPF would not give up, "If the USSR sings the praises of 'peace' and 'freedom,'" the memo continued, "pleads for disarmament, the meeting of mankind's material needs, or the ending of colonialism, WILPF does not, therefore, feel compelled to demonstrate its anticommunism by dropping 'peace' and 'freedom' from its vocabulary: or declaring itself in favor of the arms race, poverty, or imperialism!"[3]

To avoid harassment from HUAC and to keep its "peace and freedom" position clear, the national WILPF organization took the unofficial position that local branch development should be discouraged in countries that were believed to limit freedom of speech. As a result, neither the international WILPF organization nor the U.S. section would collaborate with the Women's International Democratic Federation, and the WIDF was left without a strong U.S. ally until 1975, when Women for Racial and Economic Equality (WREE) was formed by a group of New York City women. The furthest WILPF would go in its relationship with the WIDF was to allow nonparticipating observers to attend each other's international conferences. WILPF also refused to cosponsor conferences "in which Communist organizations [took] the initiative." This included the widely attended Youth Congresses in Moscow and Vienna.[4]

Despite the national organization's problems during the 1950s and the unstated narrowing of its definition of membership, WILPF members continued to involve themselves in a broad range of issues.[5] From the 1950s on, the major efforts of the national organization were directed against the proliferation of nuclear weapons and against U.S. military intervention wherever and whenever it occurred, and for a strong international community through the United Nations. During the early sixties the organization campaigned for the cessation of nuclear tests, emphasizing the importance of having a test ban treaty that would apply to all nations--but especially the United States and the Soviet Union. Also of great importance was WILPF's work towards an agreement among the military powers not to sell arms to tension-filled underdeveloped areas such as the

Middle East, Africa, Latin America, or Central Europe. Understanding the dynamics of the military-industrial complex dad not deter the women from this work. Indeed, it spurred them on to create broad international pressure on the big powers to stop both aboveground and underground testing of nuclear weapons.

To develop this pressure, WILPF continued its efforts, begun in 1915, to build international peace links. In 1961 the national WILPF organization sponsored its first seminar intended to establish a network with Soviet women. This meeting at Bryn Mawr College in Pennsylvania opened the door to many other such interchanges held in both the United States and the Soviet Union. Needless to say, these conferences produced a certain amount of criticism from those who saw the Soviets as a threat and any contact with them as treasonous.

Although the national board of WILPF also took a strong stand on the seating of delegates from the People's Republic of China in the UN's Security Council, they did not reach their goal until 1971, just before President Richard Nixon opened the door for detente with that communist nation. WILPF's position on the inclusion of "Red" China in the UN, as stated in 1954, paralleled their previous stands on the Soviet Union. The organizers felt that the 450 million people of China could only "benefit" from their government's exposure to the workings of the international body. As long as the People's Republic was kept isolated from the world community, it was not possible to observe its actions, much less to criticize them. Once a member of the UN, China would be "subject to all its restraints" should it take an aggressive action against another country. In addition, if China were not included, its government, out of a sense of "antagonism rather than cooperation," might come "more completely under the influence of the U.S.S.R."[6] Little did the leaders realize that, even though the Soviet Union and China had the potential to form an enormous united communist front, the two nations would remain on basically unfriendly terms, bickering over borders and taking vastly different stands on international issues--at times worrying that each was conspiring with the U.S. government against the other.

More frustrating to the women than the issue of seating the People's Republic of China on the Security Council was their recognition of the UN's impotence to prevent U.S. military intervention or arms sales in developing countries. Because international WILPF policy continued to allow for the criticism of each nation's government only by the WILPF members of that country, the national organizers in the United States had a big job on their hands. U.S. businesses--and hence the government--had emerged from World War II with enormous profits, prestige, and power. As a result, U.S. interests exerted themselves in every part of the globe, and the U.S. section of WILPF found itself addressing worldwide issues. By the mid-1960s, for example, concerns in Asia had shifted from the occupation of Japan and the incursion into Korea to U.S. involvement in Vietnam. As early as 1962, when President John Kennedy was deploying military advisors to South Vietnam, WILPF leader Annalee Stewart acknowledged that the United States was carrying on "an undeclared war" there.[7] In 1965 the women had already announced their support for negotiations that would result in an independent South Vietnam, responsible for determining its own future. By the late sixties, much of the organization's time and effort centered around the Vietnam War, including cosponsorship of and participation in almost every national antiwar demonstration, from Washington, D.C., New York, and San Francisco to hundreds of other cities and towns. Besides protesting the war in Vietnam, the women continued to emphasize that the United States needed to recognize the People's Republic of China and that U.S. military personnel in Asia should cease supporting the counterrevolution of Chiang Kai-shek (Jiang Jieshi).

In the Middle East, where the United States was heavily involved, first in supporting Israel and then also in selling arms to the Arab nations, WILPF took a stand against arms sales and for negotiated settlement in the area. In addition, the women took a strong stand in favor of maintaining the Jewish homeland. The organization consistently spoke out against apartheid in South Africa. The women lobbied the U.S. leaders, who sanctioned extensive trade with the minority-controlled white South African government, to exert pressure on South Africa to abolish apartheid, just as the U.S. was attempting to eliminate racial oppression at home. The women also stressed the importance of allocating U.S. aid to help all the developing African nations. In such an effort, the women preferred that the money be dispersed through such UN organizations as UNICEF, UNESCO, and the World Health Organization. Because the U.S. economy was experiencing such great expansion, WILPFers saw it as the nation's responsibility to share its good fortune with the international community, especially as U.S. companies not only often exploited foreign labor but also obtained raw materials largely from other nations.

In the 1960s, as always, WILPF was greatly concerned about U.S. relations with Latin America. In much of the world, U.S. policy was conditioned by competition with the Soviet Union and China, but Latin America had long been seen as part of the U.S. domain. The terms of the Monroe Doctrine of 1823 stated that foreign nations were unwelcome in the area, and in 1904 the Roosevelt Corollary to the Doctrine provided for U.S. military intervention if those nations south of the border seemed unsettled or in danger of foreign interference. These two policies gave the United States unilateral power to make decisions and take actions that determined the fate of Central and South Americans and all of the peoples of the Caribbean. Exactly as it had done as the Woman's Peace Party in 1915, WILPF spoke out against U.S. military presence in the area and particularly against the U.S. colonization of Puerto Rico. To the women of WILPF, the 1954 invasion of Guatemala, the 1965 invasion of the Dominican Republic, and U.S. troop placement in Puerto Rico, Cuba, and Central America seemed foreboding.

The greatest affront to peace in the Americas during this period was the Bay of Pigs invasion in 1961. The success of the Cuban Revolution in January 1959 had caused great consternation for U.S. government leaders. Fidel Castro, the leader of the new government, established the first communist nation in the Americas. With the Monroe Doctrine as justification, first President Eisenhower and then President Kennedy planned a secret invasion of the island, alleging that Fidel Castro was being controlled by Moscow and thus Cuba was under foreign domination. The two presidents authorized the CIA to train a volunteer force of Cuban exiles to return to Cuba to overthrow the new government. Much to everyone's surprise, when the invaders landed at Playa Giron (the Bay of Pigs), they met with organized resistance and total failure. The entire episode was an embarrassment for the Kennedy administration, which nonetheless continued its trade embargo against Cuba.

Immediately after the Bay of Pigs fiasco, the national board of WILPF issued a statement demanding that Cuban exiles not be encouraged to continue in their vendetta against Castro and that under no circumstances should they be supplied with weapons or trained for the military. In addition, the women favored an end to the economic boycott, stressing that friendly relations with Cuba were desirable and historically natural and that to continue the present policy would only encourage the island's reliance on trade and support from the Soviet Union. A year later they were proved correct when Cuba's request for placement of Soviet-made missiles to deter further U.S. aggression precipitated the Cuban missile crisis. Although people worldwide were frightened by how close the confrontation came to nuclear war, when it was over, the United States continued its economic boycott and political harassment of Cuba. The WILPF members continued to protest. Their position on Cuba, consistent with the organization's stand against U.S. intervention in Latin America, also reflected their point of view that communist nations should be integrated into the "democratic" world so that they might benefit from its openness.

During the sixties WILPF also paid close attention to domestic issues. Of primary concern was continued support of the civil rights movement. WILPFers lobbied tirelessly for the passage of the Civil Rights Act. Members also participated in many demonstrations demanding an end to racial discrimination, including the March for Jobs and Freedom in 1963 and the Selma to Montgomery voting rights march in 1965. WILPFers demanded federal action in the case of the three civil rights workers murdered in Mississippi in 1964. The following year they organized a boycott of products and investments in that southern state; among the companies targeted were Armstrong Tire, International Paper, International Telephone and Telegraph, Kraft Foods, Procter and Gamble, Wurlitzer, Pet Milk, Borden, Sw Dairy Products, and Hunt's Foods. In conjunction with this effort, the organizers once again pressed for U.S. economic sanctions against South Africa until it ended apartheid.

By this time, the Metropolitan New York branch of WILPF was supporting all of the national board's stands on international and domes-tic issues.[8] They had been able to resolve most of their differences be-cause of UN work, a link resulting in constant communication and greater participation of the local women in the national structure. The local Metropolitan New York branch board was still in the hands of a few dedicated women, often the same ones involved at the UN. The branch, however, continued to attract a more diverse group of members than many other branches. Although recruiting younger women and women of color remained a challenge, Metropolitan New York WILPF members came from both the working and middle classes and represented many ethnic groups, but especially Jews. Indeed, the Metropolitan New York group was still ethnically unique in WILPF. In addition, because New York City was traditionally a home for political dissenters, the branch maintained its attraction for moral pacifists as well as socialists, Communist party members, and labor organizers.

In the early sixties, the Metropolitan New York branch continued to grow and to pursue its own programming. In 1961, under the presidency of Dr. Rose

Mukerji, the branch won the WILPF membership award for having enrolled the largest number of new volunteers. Like the national board, the local women concentrated much effort upon the civil rights movement. Their presence in marches and participation in educational activities reflected a particular concern for their own city as well. Starting in 1964 and continuing for several years thereafter, these women spoke out against the lack of satisfactory results from efforts to integrate the New York City public schools.

At least one of the Metropolitan New York branch's leaders had come to the organization with a history of civil rights activism. Bess Cameron, whose parents had marched in favor of woman suffrage, had become involved in civil rights in the late 1930s when she was a student at the University of Chicago. From her French tutor, an African-American, Cameron learned that they could not eat in the same restaurants; moreover, the tutor could not live in the dorms, and she could join Cameron for a swim only on Friday afternoons (the school's pool was cleaned on Saturday mornings). Cameron, the daughter of a Ku Klux Klan member who had encouraged her to carry a banner in a Klan parade in the 1920s, soon came to know most of the African-American students at the university. Years later, as a faculty member at Indiana University, she became actively involved with the Congress of Racial Equality (CORE) and the National Association for the Advancement of Colored People (NAACP). There she also learned about WILPF and helped a group of women obtain a branch charter. When she moved to New York City a short while later, Cameron joined the local branch. Naturally, she became a great supporter of their civil rights activities.[9]

Both nationally and locally, WILPF had apparently survived the fifties and reemerged in the sixties as a leading force for peace and justice. Yet this was not entirely true. Although the organization did make a comeback, many members were left with a bad taste in their mouths from the incidents of the 1950s. In 1964, Mildred Scott Olmsted, executive director of the U.S. section, remarked in her report at the annual meeting: "It is a mystery to me why an organization with the courage and the standards, the services it provides and the record of accomplishment of the WILPF does not increase in numbers more rapidly than it does."[10] She and most other WILPF leaders had not understood the dynamics of the McCarthy era or their role in it. As a result, there were prospective peace activists who looked for alter-natives to WILPF. Some felt the organization was too wishy-washy, while others continued to view it as part of the "Communist front."

Either way, WILPF was losing out. In terms of the reemergence of feminist peace activism as a whole, however, WILPF's fall into disfavor was not an entirely bad thing, for out of the organization's internal convulsions sprang a fresh movement with new ideas, new blood, and, as in the 1920s, a diversity of ideologies.

The initial resurgence of activity, begun in 1961, centered around the nuclear arms race. By the mid-sixties the activities revolved around the Vietnam War. Voice of Women (VOW) became the first alternative to WILPF. Founded in July 1960 in Canada, the organization was adopted by U.S. women on June 25, 1961, in Cleveland, Ohio. In its rhetoric, VOW retained much from the feminist peace movement. Women, as the "givers" of life were "particularly concerned" about their children's survival. Moreover, women worldwide shared not only maternal interests but also an "abhorrence" of nuclear, biological, and chemical warfare. It was thus important, VOW stressed, to utilize "the tremendous creative power" of women in finding a way of easing world tensions and "the turning of men's minds from war."[11] The U.S. branches of VOW existed throughout the 1960s; the Canadian organization is still a large pressure group.

More powerful than VOW was Women Strike for Peace (WSP) (pronounced "wisp") organized in the fall of 1961. WSP was not simply an alternative to WILPF; indeed, it was born directly out of the discontent with WILPF's hierarchical structure and anti-Communist stance, as well as from a concern that red-baiting had harmed the organization's credibility and effectiveness. Women Strike for Peace also grew out of the concern over radiation fallout caused by aboveground nuclear bomb tests.[12] (The organization is also known as WISP, from an alternate name, Women's International Strike for Peace, adopted in 1961. It has also been called Women for Peace.) WSP was founded when Dagmar Wilson, a book illustrator based in Washington, D.C., who claimed "wife and mother" as her primary identities, called together a group of women to plan some action around the bomb tests. The women were particularly apprehensive because a three-year Soviet moratorium on nuclear tests had come to an end, and they feared that tensions over the Berlin Wall would set off a nuclear confrontation between the Soviet Union and the United States. Most of the original organizers of WSP—including Wilson, Eleanor Garst, Folly Fodor, Margaret Russell, and Jeanne Bagby—were members of the Washington branch of SANE (National Committee for a Sane Nuclear Policy), but WILPF members also became actively involved in the project.

In September the women began their work by picketing in front of the White House. Within a month they had organized a major demonstration. On November 1, 1961, Women Strike for Peace had its first major success: marches taking place in sixty cities across the nation that involved more than 50,000 women. Taking their babies with them, the marchers headed for their local city halls and federal buildings. The rationale behind the action was that women would call a one-day "strike" in order to illustrate their collective power. On that day women walked off their jobs and out of their kitchens in order to take to the streets. The resounding success of the event inspired Wilson and her friends to establish Women Strike for Peace as a permanent organization.[13] However, as a reaction to the internal red-baiting which had taken place within both SANE and WILPF, they decided not to establish a national hierarchy, not to require or even encourage official membership, not to charge dues, and not even to have any boards of any kind. Rather, WSP would operate as a loosely tied network of women working together to protest the nuclear arms race.

According to historian Amy Swerdlow, who has done a comprehensive study of the organization (she was also an active member), the great appeal of WSP to numbers of women was that it projected an image of "respectable middle-class, middle-aged peace ladies in white gloves and flowered hats."[14] In addition, the organizers exploited the age-old myth of mothers as the protectors of life and the peace movement's portrayal of women as angry citizens. As Swerdlow notes, WSP publicity emphasized that men in power undermined "the ability of American mothers to carry out their assigned role of life-preservation and moral guardianship."[15] Unlike WILPF, the Women's Peace Union, the National Committee on the Cause and Cure of War, and the Woman's Peace Party, whose average member was fifty or older, at first Women Strike for Peace attracted women from their mid-thirties to their late forties. By the late 1960s, WSP was appealing to women in their twenties. The leadership consisted of the usual mixture of pacifists, Quakers, Communists, and socialists, giving the group the variety of liberal to radical participants also characteristic of WILPF. In their public stance, however, the women in WSP generally denied or played down their political backgrounds, relying on their middle-class veneer to produce favorable public reaction.

Unlike WILPF, which managed to avoid a direct hit from HUAC, in December 1962, the WSP found a number of its activists, largely from the New York metropolitan area, called before the committee. The subpoenas arrived after the organization had been at work only one full year. Within that time the leaders had sparked the creation of numerous educational programs, demonstrations, and civil disobedience actions. Their immediate goal was to pressure for a treaty that would put an end to atmospheric nuclear testing. Their long-term goal was clearly stated in their motto: "End the Arms Race—Not the Human Race." In June, 1962,

a few months before the summons from HUAC, the leading activists had held
WSP's first national conference in Ann Arbor, Michigan. The women in
attendance adopted a statement to unify their informal membership network:

> We are women of all races, creeds and political persuasions.
> We are dedicated to the purpose of general and complete disarmament.
> We demand that nuclear tests be banned forever, that the arms race
> end and the world abolish all weapons of destruction under United
> Nations safeguards. We cherish the right and accept the
> responsibility to act to influence the course of government for
> peace.... We join with women throughout the world to challenge
> the right of any nation or group of nations to hold the power of life and
> death over the world.[16]

Women Strike for Peace, which appeared mild in its program, was
charged by HUAC with harboring Communists. Because at least two of the
specific women subpoenaed were known Communist party members, WSP
leaders worried over HUAC's intentions. Accordingly, the main decision-makers
took a united stand--much as the WILPF leaders had done--that any woman could
join WSP, no matter what her political, religious, or other ideology. All that the
organization desired of a prospective member was that she oppose the testing of
nuclear weapons by both the United States and the Soviet Union and that she
support UN control over a universal disarmament program. In addition, WSP
leaders decided to take the initiative in their own defense. In a letter to their
membership, they pointed out that HUAC was out to "tarnish" their "image" in
order "to intimidate women who might become active" and "to stifle public
debate," concluding in the classic suffragist-pacifist style that "more and more
it's obvious that it has to be 'the women' who speak for mankind."[17]

Once again in a style echoing earlier years, the leading organizers
proclaimed that peace work was "the highest form of patriotism" and proceeded
to the hearings.[18] There, HUAC officials attempted to question WSP members
about their "united front" activities, especially in its section consisting of
Metropolitan New York, New Jersey, and Connecticut.[19] As each woman was

called for questioning, the other WSP members broke into applause; Dagmar Wilson was presented with a bouquet of white roses when she took the stand. Furthermore, the women attempted to make the all-male government panel look foolish by hinting that their "masculine minds" could not grasp the concepts supported by WSP.[20] The press had a field day, using such headlines as "Peace Gals Make Red Hunters Look Silly," "Redhunters Decapitated" and "It's Ladies' Day at the Capitol: Hoots, Howls and Charm" to describe the hearings. Certainly, the press no longer took HUAC as seriously as they had during the McCarthy years.

Many of the New York women involved in WSP came from the local branch of WILPF. Minna Kashins, one of the first women to cross over to the Metropolitan New York, New Jersey, and Connecticut section, recalled: "See, we gave birth to Women Strike for Peace. . . . I remember when Bess Cameron, one of our members, came to me one day, and she says, Minna, we're going to start a new organization named Women Strike for Peace."[21] The New York WILPFers, just like several members in Philadelphia and Washington, D.C., were seeking an alter-native to their mother organization. In the end, however, they remained active in both. One Metropolitan New York branch member was attracted to WSP because of the anti-Communist stance of the WILPF leadership. She complained that Orlie Pell, president of the local branch, was "violently anti-Communist" and therefore made it close to impossible for New York Communist members to move freely within the group. At one point during the 1950s, Pell had actually recommended that the branch cease having meetings and simply use its efforts to raise money for the national board; that would be one way of limiting the activities of Communist members.[22] Also, in 1961, she voted against WILPF's attending a conference in the Soviet Union and cautioned the organization against cooperating with the Fair Play for Cuba Committee, which she believed was "extremely pro-Castro and anti–United States, if not actually Communist-oriented."[23] WSP was also appealing to some

New York WILPF members because its meetings often took place in women's homes rather than in an office or rented hall, thereby giving the participants, as one woman put it, "a communal relationship, whereas with WILPF it's a little impersonal."[24] Nonetheless, there was for many years a core of women, particularly in New York City, who worked for both WILPF and WSP.

The most important "victory" for Women Strike for Peace during the 1960s was its influence on the passage of the 1963 Test-Ban Treaty. This agreement between the Soviet Union and the United States ensured the termination of the aboveground testing of nuclear weapons, a phenomenon which had resulted in over two hundred U.S. and USSR nuclear bomb tests by 1960. The signing of the treaty was partly the result of effective lobbying and protesting on the part of WSP and other peace organizations. As in the HUAC hearings, the organization utilized its unique interpretation of its members' "femaleness." Playing once again on the theme of motherhood, the WSP organizers created their "Mother's Campaign for a Test Ban Treaty." With slogans such as "Let the Children Grow" and "Milk Not Poison," the women emphasized the fact that after each aboveground nuclear explosion, the level of radiation in milk rose dramatically. To bring the point home, WSP leaders encouraged women to have their children's lost baby teeth tested for the radioactive isotope strontium 90, present in nuclear fallout, which is deposited in place of calcium in bone. The teeth, with the lab results, were then forwarded to each woman's senator. In addition, many women organized boycotts of their local dairies and milk delivery services, insisting that their patronage depended upon the installation of equipment capable of removing strontium 90 from the milk.[25]

The signing of the Test-Ban Treaty did not mean the end of WSP protests against the nuclear arms race. Rather, it signaled further commitment and international cooperation. In May 1964, for example, thousands of U.S. and European women joined together at The Hague to voice their anger at NATO for equipping its multilateral naval fleet with nuclear weapons. In addition, WSP members continued WILPF's longtime campaign against the sales, advertising, and production of war toys. Most important to the WSP's program, as for WILPF, was the formation of an international women's network. The woman most influential in this work for the WSP was Ruth Gage-Colby, a member of the Metropolitan New York branch of WILPF and, as of 1963, also the coordinator of worldwide activity for the WSP.

Gage-Colby came to Women Strike for Peace with much experience in international work.[26] Because of her own opposition to World War I, she was drawn to WILPF as early as 1920, soon after the founding of the international organization. At that time, she was residing with her husband in Vienna, where he was completing his medical studies. During World War II, Gage-Colby joined WILPF's protest against the internment of the Japanese in the U.S., criticizing the policy for its racism. At the end of the war, she took an active interest in the organization's support of the founding of the United Nations and was one of WILPF's representatives at the founding meetings in San Francisco. Soon after, Gage-Colby worked for UNICEF in both Egypt and China. Through her UN efforts she became personally acquainted with Secretary-General U Thant. This friendship, combined with her extensive experience in WILPF and WSP work at the UN made her an ideal choice for WSP's international coordinator. In addition, from 1966 to 1970 she took on the presidency of the Metropolitan New York branch of WILPF, a striking indication of the spillover from that group to WSP.

The Women's International Strike for Peace appealed to the women of both Eastern and Western Europe, Canada, and Japan, but much of the antinuclear activity centered around Geneva, where the UN often held its disarmament discussions. One of the most successful Geneva protests took place in March 1962, when fifty-one WSP members from the United States, including Dagmar Wilson and Coretta Scott King, flew to Europe to join women from sixteen other nations to lobby for nuclear disarmament. Dagmar Wilson's explanation for their action, as the New York Times reported on March 9, was that the nuclear threat had made it impossible for the women to carry on their usual domestic chores. "When women's normal work becomes meaningless in the face of annihilation, international affairs become our direct concern, affecting every hour of our lives."[27]

Soon after the Geneva action, the WSP leaders in the United States voted to send a delegation, headed by Dagmar Wilson, to the Soviet Union. Because of the HUAC activity, the decision was not an easy one. In 1961, WILPF had met with Soviet women at a conference held at Bryn Mawr College, but now WSP was proposing a visit to the Soviet Union. To gain the approval of the U.S. government and media, the women accepted the argument recommended to them by Arthur Dean, the U.S. delegate to the Geneva disarmament discussions: that the U.S. women's mission was to convince the Russian people that the United States was sincere in its desire for peace. With this rationale, the WSP paid its visit, thereby establishing contact with Soviet women, which Gage-Colby would later develop.[28]

Women Strike for Peace also used a strategy originated by the international WILPF organization. Just as in 1919 when the leaders of WILPF had decided to hold a women's peace conference in Zurich while the major powers were meeting in Versailles, so the WSP leaders decided to hold an alternative conference in May 1964 in the Netherlands at the same time and place as NATO's general meeting at The Hague. Women from all the NATO nations except Turkey attended the conference. U.S. delegate Eleanor Garst was much encouraged. "In two years, we have succeeded in changing the image of the 'ugly American' abroad.... we have told the world that there are women on this smug and fat continent who are aware of their existence and determined to fight for their right to exist--but to fight non-violently and nonpartisanly, as Gandhi, the American Negro and the peace people ... have so aptly demonstrated."[29]

The overriding issue for both WILPF and Women Strike for Peace--as for all other peace organizations--from the early 1960s through April 1975, was the U.S. military involvement in Vietnam. Although the United States had become embroiled in the small Southeast Asian country after the French had been defeated in 1954, the use of U.S. troops there did not become a main concern until President Johnson increased the U.S. military presence in 1965. From then until 1972, when the majority of the U.S. soldiers left Vietnam, over 57,000 U.S. military personnel and over two million Vietnamese lost their lives. The Vietnam War ripped the United States apart. Antiwar organizations proliferated to protest the conflict, and super-patriotic groups rose to confront them.

Both WILPF and Women Strike for Peace played key roles in propagandizing against the war; in working with coalitions like the Fifth Avenue Vietnam Peace Parade Committee to plan massive demonstrations in Washington, D.C., New York, and San Francisco; in supporting draft-counseling centers and other sources of aid to conscientious objectors; and in lobbying Congress and working for the election of peace candidates. The election of Richard Nixon to the presidency in 1968 added fuel to the peace activities. Nixon promised to bring an end to the conflict but, instead, increased the bombing of North Vietnam and Cambodia. As a result, antiwar activity increased. WILPF members worked ceaselessly to bring an end to the war, for the sakes of both the U.S. personnel and for the countless Vietnamese being terrorized, maimed, or killed. One of the most successful coalition efforts the women supported was the Vietnam Moratorium Day, October 15, 1969, which involved millions of U.S. citizens in protest activities throughout the nation. The Moratorium, cited as the largest peace protest up to that day in all U.S. history, involved the expertise of all the local WILPF organizers. At the same time, the national board instituted "Tuesdays in Washington," which included a variety of events to dramatize the war. The nature of these demonstrations pointed the way to the more spectacular theatrics used during the Women's Pentagon Actions in the early 1980s. On one Tuesday, for example, WILPF members formed a procession and carried coffins, each marked with the name of an actual victim of the war, around the Capitol. On another Tuesday, before the White House fence, women acted out what author Catherine Foster described as the "chaining of industry to the U.S. military."[30]

Overall, for many organizations the Vietnam War produced renewed interest in peace work. Young men eligible for the draft sought out help from the War Resisters League, the Fellowship of Reconciliation, and other traditional groups, whose memberships grew each year. In addition, many new organizations, such as SDS, which supported draft resistance, emerged out of the counterculture and student movements of the New Left. Next to these groups, the older women of WILPF seemed staid. Women Strike for peace, however, held some appeal for younger, budding feminists who wanted to protest the war within a female context.

According to economist Nan Wiegersma, who joined WSP around1967, younger women, especially those with children, found some attraction in the organization's structure and method of decision-making. Like WILPF, WSP relied on reaching a consensus, but unlike WILPF, it was not bogged down in a hierarchy on the local level. Wiegersma contends that even though WSP was commonly viewed as a group for middle-class mothers, in fact, many of the organization's Vietnam-era members were "more of the 60s." They eagerly joined older WS Persin protesting the war as well as the nuclear arms race. In 1969, Wiegersma herself joined a WSP delegation to Cuba. There, she and the other women met with visiting members of the National Liberation Front and became more convinced than ever that the war in Vietnam was wrong.[31]

In the fall of 1969, Memo, the national bulletin of Women Strike for Peace, reported on the trip to Cuba. From this one issue, it becomes clear what Wiegersma meant by WSP being "more of the 60s." The issue was dedicated not only to Ho Chi Minh, the leader of the North Vietnamese and a national hero, but also "to all the Vietnamese in that magnificent land who have fought and died, been burned and mutilated" and to those U.S. citizens "who have worked desperately to end our nation's crime: to WSPs and all others who are struggling to change America's direction; students, blacks, third-world, poverty mothers, G.I.'s, deserters, draft resisters, political exiles, burners of draft cards, all those in civil and military prisons."[32] Obviously, the WSP of 1968 reflected a New Left approach. The younger women coming into the group, like Nan Wiegersma, were particularly influenced by the student movement and its new interest in Marxism. By 1968, however, some of these women had woken up to the sexism within their student organizations and had sought out separate female groups in order to have a say in decision making and to be part of the power structure. Furthermore, they discovered that men involved in antiwar, draft resistance, civil rights, and student movements were generally not very interested in women's equality. Often crude and condescending in their reactions to the women's assertiveness, the younger men of the New Left unintentionally fostered the formation of the women's liberation movement. By the early 1970s, more and more women were choosing to work within a female environment. The new feminists were walking in the paths of their women's rights foremothers, but, at the time, they were unaware of it.

As the war progressed, WILPF concentrated its efforts more and more in the nation's capital, the seat of the warmakers. In June 1970 the national board called a Women's Emergency Conference on Vietnam. Held in Washington, D.C., the meeting attracted leaders from many organizations. There, the organizers formulated plans on how best to put pressure on Congress to end appropriations for the war. Besides supporting antiwar candidates for local, state, and federal offices and campaigning against those who supported the war, WILPF stressed the importance of maintaining a public presence in Washington. If the public were constantly reminded that large numbers of people opposed the war, then they could feel comfortable about adding their own voices to the outcry. Public demonstrations offered an outlet for those who were indignant about the war after watching television news reports showing actual battles and seeing magazine and newspaper photos of never-ending lines of flag-draped coffins returning to the United States.

Many of WILPF's efforts "to bring the war home" were aimed at U.S. women. On International Women's Day, March 8, 1971, for example, WILPF members once again picketed in front of the White House. Demanding that Richard Nixon abide by his promise to withdraw U.S. troops from Vietnam, the women carried multilingual posters with such messages as "Set the Date" and "Out Now." They also delivered to the president 8,000 handwritten postcards from WILPF members demanding an end to the conflict; the cards, which included eight hundred from women then residing in South Vietnam, represented the international community of the organization.[33]

The Metropolitan New York branch, with its office so close to the United Nations, maintained constant antiwar activity. As early as 1964--before Johnson's troop escalation--the women maintained a weekly vigil in Times Square. Every Saturday afternoon from 12:30 to 2:30, while thousands of people scurried to lunch before theater and movie matinees, branch members and sympathizers stood silently in the triangle between Broadway and Seventh Avenue where the Armed Forces recruiting stations were located. That same year, under the leadership of Ruth Gage-Colby, the women held a protest in front of the U.S. Pavilion at the World's Fair, which was then taking place in Queens, a borough where many branch members lived. From 1967 into the 1970s, the Metropolitan New York branch of WILPF also mobilized its members to participate in massive antiwar demonstrations held each spring and fall in their city.

The New York women, like many other antiwar organizers, were pushed into further action by Nixon's escalation of the war in North Vietnam and into

Cambodia.[34] After Helen Kusman became president in 1970, the local board instituted a "Never on Tuesdays Shoppers' Stop-page," one small effort in trying to reach the millions of women who shopped in Manhattan stores every day. As residents of a large urban area, the New York women continuously tried to appeal to the consumer side of a very material-oriented but not heartless city. For one such event, the women handed out a leaflet to guests and onlookers outside a reception being given for Nixon. The leaflet, headed with a black bordered box and the hand-written title "We Mourn The Death of 300 Vietnamese Each Day," contained this message: "Tonight at $500. a plate dinners, people are listening to Pres. Nixon and enjoying fine food while in Vietnam, people do not have enough to eat—Because our planes have destroyed food crops—HAVE WE NO SHAME?"[35] If anger, as exemplified by the "Evict Nixon" campaign, and a sense of simple human compassion, as emphasized in such activities as the 1971 "Rice and Tea for Peace" event intended to raise money for WILPF's support of a Maternal Child Health Center in Hanoi, did not grab people's hearts, then perhaps guilt would.

Women Strike for Peace also utilized several different methods to protest the war. Soon after the Kennedy administration became entangled in the near-nuclear confrontation with the Soviets during the Cuban missile crisis, the organization had also begun addressing the issue of "conventional" wars. The women realized that a small hot spot could lead the nation into a prolonged conventional war, such as the one in Korea. At its June 1963 national meeting in Champaign-Urbana, Illinois, therefore, the WSP leaders attempted to show that the Cuban crisis was not an isolated incident but rather a link in a long chain of U.S. involvement in the affairs of Third World nations. Although the organization took no concrete actions at that time, the discussion set the stage for future work concerning Vietnam.[36]

These talks came to fruition on July 8, 1965, when ten representatives from WSP flew to Indonesia to meet with women delegates of both the National

Liberation Front from South Vietnam and the communist government of North Vietnam. At this meeting both groups of women signed a statement expressing their opposition to the U.S. military presence in Vietnam. Throughout the war WSP members consistently opposed the drafting of young men and supported the rights of conscientious objectors. This concern increased as many of the younger, less traditional women joining WSP chapters worked through the National WSP Draft Counseling Service. Traditional WSPers also continued to use their role as mothers and their "feminine" image to attack the "masculine" war machine. In 1967 they employed this tactic in Washington, D.C., when approximately 2,500 of them appeared before the home of the military, the Pentagon, and removed their shoes to bang them on the building's doors.[37]

Younger women contributed greatly to WSP's work. Besides radicalizing the organization in new ways, they also contributed to the group's already contagious sense of humor. One example of this humor invoked a sense of longing for an end to the Vietnam War. In a cartoon appearing in Peace de Resistance Cookbook #1, issued by the Los Angeles section of WSP, a mother complete with lacy apron was shown carrying a sign which read, "Bring the Boys Home for Dinner."[38] Also relying on a woman's heart but devoid of all humor was a WSP flier produced by the New York office during Johnson's escalation of troops. On top of the handout in large black block letters were the words "WHAT FOR?" and under them, bordered in black, was the photograph of a soldier's corpse wrapped in a tarpaulin and tied up with rope. The major text, which reflected the Old and New Left elements in WSP, emphasized that the business of running Vietnam belonged to the Vietnamese. The emotional feeling reflected in the text was dramatic:

HE LIES DEAD IN VIETNAM-WHAT FOR?

For corrupt and power-hungry South Vietnamese "leaders," whose own people do not support them.

HIS PARENTS WEEP.

But the war goes on and the Vietnamese people are no closer to freedom,

HIS WIDOW GRIEVES. WHAT FOR?

For an American policy that sent her man, and continues to send more men, half way round the world to barge into a civil war between Vietnamese. The G.I. casualty toll in Vietnam is *now* over 22,303.[39]

The young age of eighteen of the average U.S. soldier in Vietnam as op-posed to the twenty-four or twenty-five year average for World War II was one factor which accounted for the involvement of two generations of women in WSP. The older women feared for their sons. Young men barely out of high school were being drafted into a war very few people understood. The younger women feared for their friends and lovers.

The motherhood theme was also adopted by an organization composed of younger and older women. In March 1967 this group of fifteen "close friends" created Another Mother for Peace.[40] By 1972 this small but effective group of women from the Hollywood film industry had accumulated a mailing list of over a quarter of a million people and had utilized the talents of such stars as Debbie Reynolds, Patty Duke, Mercedes McCambridge, Barbara Rush, Joanne Woodward, and Paul Newman to promote their cause. The founder of Another Mother, Barbara Avedon, an Academy Award–winning screenwriter, became concerned about the war after she had given birth to a son: "Before I know it, he will be old enough to go to war. I wonder which one will be his and where it will be and what it will be about. . . . We are the ones who create life, and we should be the ones to preserve it; yet, here we are, accepting the idea that war is inevitable."[41]

In an attempt to reach out to mothers and to touch their hearts, Avedon and her friends printed one thousand Mother's Day cards to send to congressional representatives. The message on the card read:

> For my Mothers' [sic] Day gift this year
>
> I don't want candy or flowers.
> I want an end to killing.
> We who have given life
> Must be dedicated to preserving it.
> Please, talk peace![42]

Popular response to the card was so enthusiastic that the women kept printing more and more of them. By the end of May, they had sold 200,000 cards. Opening an "Invest in Peace Fund," they used the money to support legislators who would vote against war appropriations. The fact that Donna Reed, the quintessential mother in her television sitcom, was one of the co-chairs of the organization probably reinforced its image.[43]

Another Mother for Peace was not organized by experienced activists. Its bylaws, written in 1967, indicated that there would be no chapters, no endorsements of political candidates, and no political concerns except peace. Intending "to educate women to take an active role in eliminating war as a means of solving disputes between nations, people and ideologies," Another Mother took the position that war was "obsolete—that civilized methods must be creatively sought and implemented to resolve international differences in Vietnam and elsewhere,"[44] To promote its educational goals, Another Mother for Peace held its first annual Mother's Day Assembly in Los Angeles in May 1969. At this meeting the organizers introduced their vision of Pax Materna, "a permanent irrevocable condition of amnesty and understanding among mothers of the world" and unveiled their new logo. Created by Lorraine Schneider, the logo consisted of a large flower around which was written in big letters, "War is not healthy for children or other living things."[45] This logo, with its inscription eventually translated into more than twenty languages, retains its popularity today. The assembly was also the beginning of the women's efforts to pass on information about the nuclear arms race, chemical and biological warfare, the environmental effects of the nuclear arms race, and the military budget. Another Mother for Peace extended its efforts beyond the Vietnam War era. Although it announced its intention to disband after January 1979, it continued producing a newsletter and other peace literature until 1985.

Although the Vietnam War sparked the creation of innumerable antiwar organizations, it also produced a sense of disunity in the older, more established groups. After the election of Nixon in 1968, antiwar organizing became more difficult. Nixon's order to cut back the number of troops in Vietnam anesthetized part of the society into believing the war was ending, while his escalation of the bombing of North Vietnam and the incursions into Cambodia infuriated others. Those whose self-appointed spokesmen styled themselves the "Silent Majority," expressing support for Nixon and such traditional U.S. values as patriotic fervor, came into conflict with the counterculture, represented by hippies, Yippies, and peace activists. As the war moved into the 1970s, the antiwar movement, which had produced a national feeling of disgust for the war, no longer had much momentum, and many younger women opted to move into women's liberation organizations. By January 1973, when the United States and Vietnam signed a cease-fire agreement, the antiwar movement had lost its cohesiveness. Harriet Barron of the Metropolitan New York branch of WILPF had already expressed this feeling very clearly in the summer of 1970. After several years of dedicated activism in protest of the war, Barron still felt a lack of accomplishment. To a fellow WILPFer, Ruth Sillman, who was also feeling disheartened, she wrote, "I know pretty much how you feel because I'm feeling the same way. We've done so many things (not enough I know) and made so little actual headway in ending the war; and the peace movement is splintered."[46]

Nevertheless, WILPF had done a great deal to contribute to the demise of popular support for the war. In fact, membership actually rose during that period. As the effects of McCarthyism became a part of history and the Vietnam War itself became a symbol of the toll of war, the organization once again attracted new members. By the 1980s, it averaged between ten and fifteen thousand members each year. Women Strike for Peace, on the other hand, saw a decline in membership after the war. In 1974 the organization's leaders decided to redirect their attention back to their original concern over nuclear disarmament and to address the issue of amnesty for Vietnam era draft evaders.[47] WILPF, always a multi-issue organization, in the meantime maintained its interest in Vietnam. After the North Vietnamese swept through South Vietnam in April 1975, driving the remaining U.S. military and governmental personnel from the country, WILPF joined many other voices urging the normalization of relations between the two nations, an end to the U.S. economic blockade, and the establishment of U.S. assistance in the rebuilding of a united Vietnam.

The great assortment of people and organizations that participated in the antiwar movement of the Vietnam era bore a surface resemblance to the pro-peace movement of the interwar era. As a popular cause they had indeed affected U.S. government policy in Vietnam and contributed to the termination of the war. For women, however, the significance of the Vietnam-era movement was very different from that of the earlier movement. During the 1920s and 1930s, the former suffragists played a dominant role in the creation of all-female peace organizations. In a feminist voice, they often linked the effects of war with violence against women. By the mid-thirties, this voice had become one of panic, in reaction to the expansion of fascism and the apparently inevitable approach of another world war. The feminist tone was lost, at least in the rhetoric, though not in the women's method of organizing. When World War II began, this voice was drowned out.

The antiwar movement of the mid-1960s had quite the opposite fate. Not only did it influence the end of the war, but it also gave impetus to the rebirth of feminist expression within the peace movement, especially in Women Strike for Peace. This reawakening was part of the emergence of what was then called the "Women's Liberation" movement, an outgrowth of white female discontent within the civil rights, New Left, and antidraft organizations, all of which tended to highlight the importance of male leadership and men's issues. The female exodus from SDS was especially important to the renewal of feminism in the peace movement. In turn, the peace movement was a natural place to cultivate this new feminism. After all, there were already existing organizations of women keeping the issue alive, and, traditionally, feminists had played a central part in peace organizing.

Although younger women were changing the face of Women Strike for Peace and tentatively approaching WILPF, the new feminism officially burst onto the peace movement scene in January 1968, when a coalition of women's organizations, including WILPF and WSP, joined together under the name of the Jeannette Rankin Brigade in order "to confront Congress on its opening day, January 15, 1968, with a strong show of female opposition to the Vietnam War."[48] Jeannette Rankin as a member of the House of Representatives had voted against U.S. participation in World War I and had been the only member of Congress to vote against a U.S. declaration of war in 1941. In 1967, Rankin, still committed to a peaceful world, had stated that if, 10,000 women would be willing to risk imprisonment to end the war, then the fighting would cease.

Thousands of women responded to Rankin's suggestion, resulting in a WILPF member's proposal that Rankin lead a march on Washington. Between 3,000 and 5,000 women turned out for the occasion. After the women reached the Capitol, Jeannette Rankin and Coretta Scott King entered the building to present the petition to the Speaker of the House and the Senate Majority leader. Beginning "We, the United States women, who are outraged by the ruthless slaughter in Vietnam, and the persistent neglect of human needs at home ... ," the document demanded the end of the Asian war and the beginning of the healing process at home.[49]

What was most important about the event, however, was not its traditional aspect of presenting a statement to the men in power, but rather its break with tradition. In a ritual organized by a recently formed women's liberation group calling itself New York Radical Women, various members of the Jeannette Rankin Brigade who were disturbed by the nature of the presentation to Congress, marched to Arlington Cemetery carrying the dummy of a rather staid-looking woman to bury as "Traditional Womanhood." Before the event the women distributed the black-bordered invitation, created by Shulamith Firestone, which challenged feminist peace activists to break from their older conservative strategies and to venture into new waters.

> Don't bring flowers ... Do be prepared to sacrifice your traditional female roles. You have refused to hanky-wave boys off to war with admonitions to save the American Mom and Apple Pie. You have resisted your roles of supportive girl friends and tearful widows, . . . And now you must resist approaching Congress and playing these same roles that are synonymous with powerlessness. We must not come as passive suppliants begging for favors, for power cooperates only with power. We must learn to fight the warmongers on their own terms, though they believe us capable only of rolling bandages.... Until we have unified into a force to be reckoned with, we will be patronized and ridiculed into total political ineffectiveness.[50]

At Arlington, the New York Radical Women performed a ceremony accompanied by a "Liturgy for the Burial of Traditional Womanhood" written by Peggy Dobbins. The "Liturgy," although intended to break new ground in the way women were to perceive war, actually reflected the sentiments prevalent in feminist peace activism as far back as the early 1800s. Just as in 1836, when William Ladd had admonished women for teaching their children to sing war songs and to play military games and for going themselves to military balls, so the Radical Women blamed their sisters for glorifying the military spirit:

> Oh women
> YOUNG WOMEN (response)
> Civilized women, we have sinned.
> We have sinned to the trill of martial trumpets
> And patriotic hymns
> For the thrill of pride and power
> And to glory in lusty men
> We cheered and waved and goaded
> Our men to murder and maim
> For heroic virility in our eyes.[51]

The ritual also expressed the same sentiments of World War I and interwar activists, who believed that women needed to gain the vote and equal participation in government in order to prevent the scourge of war. During both eras, women actively organized and lobbied, supporting only those political candidates who promised to work for peace legislation, although they were aware that their views on government were more often than not disparaged as being feminine, not masculine ones. The Radical Women promised the same action:

> Women unabashed of feelings
> Loving peace
> And lively bodies
> More than efficiency
> And exigencies

Of war.

We also *[sic]*

We have sinned

Acquiescing *[sic]* to an order

That indulges peaceful pleas

And writes them off as female logic

Saying peace is womanly.

We sin with brimming hearts conceding

Our arguments are filled with feeling

And feeling must give way to legalese.

We sinned today

If we indulge our hearts

And leave thought and action to men.

We sin tomorrow

If cool computators act out their parts

Blameless, if we cannot find our minds and courage

To force rediscovery of heart.[52]

The Radical Women appeared to assume full blame for the male power structure's lust for blood. Women had made a tradeoff. In exchange for the privileged position of housewife and mother, as exemplified by the suburban dream of the 1950s and the first half of the 1960s, women had allowed the "destruction of our intellect and courage."[53] But times were about to change.

According to Kathie Sarachild (at the time, Kathie Amatniek), one of the spokeswomen for the New York Radical Women, the drafting of large numbers of young men for service in Vietnam indirectly worked against women's desire to gain equality within the antiwar movement and within the larger society.[54] Indeed, the exclusion of women from the draft emphasized all the more that they were second-class citizens. Whereas young men could exert some semblance of power over their own lives by refusing to be drafted, all that the women could do was to support that effort. Women as a group had no concrete way to exert real pressure on governmental leaders.

In "A Call for Women's Liberation," published in the January 1968 issue of *The Resistance,* Sue Munaker observed: "Men are drafted; women can counsel them not to go. Men return their draft cards; women sign complicity statements. That is, men take the stand, women support there."[55] Munaker pointed out that "a new consciousness" was developing among women. "Out of the frustration of trying to find our place in the anti-draft movement, we have come to realize that our total lives have been spent defining ourselves in relation to men."[56] In an address to the Jeannette Rankin Brigade, Kathie Sarachild drew upon the lingering sense of frustration also felt by earlier generations of feminist peace activists as she described a broader vision of equality. Although it was evident that women were "powerless and ineffective over the issues of war and peace," it was also true that women were powerless over their own lives as well. In order to gain power, it was necessary for all women to join together so that men were no longer offered the alternative of the "other woman" when the one they lived with began "acting politically," insisting on such personal equality as shared housework and childcare, "fully and equally, so that we can have independent lives as well." With the insistence that women be allowed their freedom, "as full human beings," Sarachild pointed the way towards a more egalitarian society than even her foremothers had envisioned.[57]

The women of WILPF, in particular, were no strangers to the idea that gender and war were intimately related. Therefore, while some WILPFers may have been taken aback by the new use of women's traditional roles as a form of protest art, others welcomed the revival of feminism into the organization. The Metropolitan New York branch, with its long history of adventurous stands, issued a recruitment flier in 1968 directly acknowledging that autumn's women's liberation demonstration in Atlantic City criticizing the annual Miss America pageant. At this demonstration, women allegedly burned their bras.

The flier--headed "All Women are Victims in this Man's War!"--emphasized that until the war in Vietnam was ended, "other important issues," such as the "liberalization of abortion laws, Federal funding for child care, real equality under the law, equal employment opportunities for women and a strong women's political voice" could not be addressed. WILPF, the flier continued, had a "long history in the struggle for peace and women's rights," and, indeed, "women's liberation" had been one of the organization's goals since 1915 when Jane Addams was its president. As the flier pointed out, "She never burned her bra that we know of but she knew how to get things done."[58]

The national WILPF organization also moved towards reaffirming its commitment to feminism. In February 1967, the U.S. section of WILPF sponsored a conference whose theme was "Women's Response to the Rising Tide of Violence." At this meeting, the organization once again drew connections between the violence of war and violence against women, especially through rape and battering. By 1970 the national board *was* taking up a theme and its attendant rhetoric from WILPF's earlier days: women were superior to men, and women's liberation proponents should not "Equate equality and similarity—the idealization of masculine attributes."[59] WILPF's national board, however, continued its balancing act as it had on the declarations of the two world wars, on neutrality, on the conscription of women and on Communism. Feminism and equality should be respected, the board emphasized, but so should women's traditional values and roles within the home and family for their moral contribution to society.

With the Vietnam War had come a resurgence of feminism within the peace movement. When the war ended, the women's liberation movement did not evaporate as many antiwar organizations did. That movement continued to thrive, and feminist peace sentiment was one of its beneficiaries. Feminists in the new era would have to continue reaching out to other women. In 1972, on her ninety-first birthday, Jeannette Rankin offered the new generation this advice: "It never did any good for all the suffragettes to come together and talk to each other. There will be no revolution unless we go out into the precincts. You have to be stubborn. Stubborn and ornery." She added, "And when the men make fun of you, that's when you know you're getting on well."[60] As the years after 1975 would show, the younger women took her advice to heart.

NOTES

1. For a good summary of the development of the women's movement of the 1960s, see Sara Evans, *Personal Politics: The Roots of Women's Liberation In the Civil Rights Movement and the New Left* (New York: Vintage, 1979); Myra Marx Ferree and Beth B. Hess, *Controversy and Coalition: The New Feminist Movement* (Boston Twayne, 1985).

2. *"W.I.L.P.F AND THE COLD WAR,"* statement, Aug. 23, 1960, courtesy of JAPA.

3. *Ibid.*

4. *Ibid.*

5. The summary of WILPFs activities was derived from Eleanor Fowler, "The WILPF Story . . . Then and Now," booklet, 1986, WILPF/US: SCPC and a scanning of the Reports of National Board Meetings from 1960-1975, WILPF/US: SCPC.

6. *Ibid.*

7. Annalee Stewart to Beatrice Pearson, Dec. 13, 1962, OP: RU.

8. The summary of the activities of the Metropolitan New York Branch of WILPF reflect a scanning of the branch's reports to the national board, 1960-1975, WILPF/US: SCPC.

9. Bess Cameron, interview by Brenda Parnes, Dec. 30, 1987, NYHP.

10. Olmsted, quoted in Margaret Hope Bacon, *One Woman's Passion for Peace and Freedom*, 306.

11. Voice of Women, USA leaflet, n.d., CDGA, VOW: SCPC.

12. Details about Women Strike for Peace were derived from both primary sources as indicated in the following notes and from the work of historian Amy Swerdlow, *"The Politics of Motherhood."*

13. Swerdlow, 1-3, Swerdlow, 2-3.

14. *Ibid.*, 3.

15. "Historical Background," box 1, series 1, DG115, WSP: SCPC.

16. "Dear WISPs," Dec. 16, 1962, quoted in Swerdlow, 308.

17. "Women Strike for Peace Statement on 'House Un-American Activities Subpoenas' to WSP"

18. "Participants in New York," quoted in Swerdlow, 309.

19. Swerdlow, 329-330.

20. U.S. Congress, House Committee on Un-American Activities, Communist Activities in the Peace Movement, quoted in Swerdlow, 346.

21. Minna Kashins, interview by Brenda Parnes, Oct. 7, 1986, NYHP.

22. Bess Cameron, interview by Brenda Parnes, Dec. 30, 1987, NYHP.

23. Orlie Pell to Savina Weisman, Apr. 3, 1961, OP: RU.

24. S.B., interview by Harriet Alonso, Nov. 20, 1987, NYHP. (The interviewee requested that initials be used in place of her full name.)

25. Swerdlow, 379-429.

26. Biographical information about Gage-Colby is drawn from Swerdlow, 245-251.

27. Swerdlow; 256.

28. Swerdlow, 274.

29. Eleanor Garst, "NICH Issues for Discussion, #4," Oct. 11, 1963, quoted in Swerdlow, 294.

30. Catherine Foster, *Women for All Seasons: The Story of the Women's International League for Peace and Freedom* (Athens: Univ. of Georgia Press, 1989), 51-52.

31. Nan Wiegersma, interview with author, Fitchburg, Mass., May 1, 1991.

32. Memo (Fall 1969), 2, personal collection of Nan Wiegersma.

33. Catherine Foster, *Women for All Seasons*, 66–70.

34. Metropolitan New York branch activities derived from branch minutes, 1960–1975, WILPF/US: SCPC.

35. "We Mourn the Death" flier, n.d. [c. 1970], NYHP.

36. Swerdlow, 211–214,

37. "Historical Background," DG115, series 1, box 1, WSP:SCPC.

38. Kathie Sarachild, "Taking in the Images: A Record in Graphics of the Vietnam Era Soil for Feminism," *Vietnam Generation* 1, nos. 3–4 (Summer–Fall, 1989): 235.

39. "What For?" flier, n.d. [c. 1968] subj. file I6, S/L: NYPL.

40. "Historical Background," AMP: SCPC.

41. Martin Hall, "Another Mother for Peace," *New Perspectives: Journal of the World Peace Council* 2, no. 5 (Sept: Dec. 1972): 79–82.

42. *Ibid.*

43. "Historical Background," AMP: SCPC.

44. "By-Laws," 1967, series 1, box 1, folder 2, AMP: SCPC.

45. "Historical Background," AMP: SCPC.

46. Harriet Barron to Ruth Sillman, Aug, 19, 1970, series B,6 box 27, WILPF/ US: SCPC.

47. "Historical Background," WSP: SCPC.

48. Shulamith Firestone, quoted in Jenny Brown, "Women for Peace or Women's Liberation? Signposts from the Feminist Archives" *Vietnam Generation* 1, nos. 3–4 (Summer-Fall 1989): 248. For a good analysis of this event, see Ruth Rosen, "The Day They Buried 'Traditional Womanhood': Women and the Politics of Peace Protest," *Vietnam Generation* 1 nos. 3–4 (Summer–Fall, 1989): 208–234.

49. *Congressional Record* 90th Cong., 2d sess., vol. 114, no. 4, Thursday, Jan. 18, 1968.

50. "Invitation to 'Burial of Traditional Womanhood,'" Jan. 15, 1968, quoted in Brown, 248.

51. Peggy Dobbins, "Liturgy for the Burial of Traditional Womanhood," Jan. 15, 1968, quoted in Sarachild, 239.

52. *Ibid.*

53. *Ibid.*

54. *Ibid.*, 241.

55. Sue Munaker, quoted in Brown, 251.

56. *Ibid.*

57. Sarachild, 249.

58. "All Women are Victims in This Man's War" flier, n.d. [c. 1968], NYHP:

59. Kay Camp, "Up With Women," *Peace and Freedom*, March 1970, quoted in Catherine Foster, 56.

60. Elizabeth Frappollo, "At 91, Jeannette Rankin is the Feminists' New Heroine," *Life*, Mar. 3, 1972, 65.

CHAPTER EIGHT

THE CLAMSHELL ALLIANCE: CONSENSUS AND UTOPIAN DEMOCRACY

Barbara Epstein

Barbara Epstein, Professor of History at the University of California, Santa Cruz, an activist in the movement herself, offers an engaging history of the nonviolent direct action movement from the mid-1970s to the mid-1980s. As part of the larger "modern" American peace movement's heritage, Epstein concentrates her work on the efforts of citizen activists in their attempts to control and regulate the construction of nuclear power plants. This essay, from her book, emphasizes that peace and justice are not simply defined by war. Like their predecessors after World War One, these reformers sought to build communities based on shared beliefs and values. Beginning with the Clamshell Alliance in New England shortly after the end of the Vietnam War, these activists presented a new style of politics shaped by "a vision of a ecologically balance, nonviolent, egalitarian society." In practicing mass civil disobedience in opposition to the spread of nuclear power, these groups also expanded their efforts to protest the arms race of the early 1980s. Their attempts did lead to a popular referendum in the early 1980s calling upon the United States Government to abandon its development of nuclear weapons. How did political action through affinity groups inspire the notion of grass roots democracy as well as a feeling of spirituality? With regard to these issue-based movements -- peace, ecology, feminism, nonintervention (especially in Latin America), and gay and lesbian rights -- how did nonviolent direct action influence the notion of community building? How did does direct action equate itself to a particular social vision? In which respects did the dissolution of the Clamshell Alliance offer instructive examples of how to avoid bitter internal disputes? Despite its breakup, how did its formation inspire the use of consensus and effectiveness of nonviolent direct action employed by later action groups such as the Abalone Alliance and the Livermore Action Group?

****

Editor's Note: One of the more remarkable developments within the "modern" twentieth century American peace movement has been its expanding parameters to meet the new challenges posed by an increasingly complex and technologically-driven society. While much of the discipline of peace history has focused efforts on examining the causes and cures of warfare, more recent innovations have taken the movement in new directions. This is not meant to imply that working to abolish war is no longer the main objective. Quite the contrary, I might add. However, since the Vietnam War, citizen activists in the United States and in other parts of the world have called upon governments to ensure their well being as part of a patriotic obligation. In particular, asking government leaders to protect the environment against those elements brought about by industrial and technological development has been linked to the peace movement's quest for a world all inhabitants can share and enjoy.

More to the point. While government leaders proclaim the need to protect and ensure national security, citizen activists are encouraging local and national leaders to examine more carefully the consequences of developing technologies, especially those linked with military needs. Certainly, nuclear technologies have been a major component for both energy needs and military capabilities. But citizen activists are concerned about the impact of such needs when weighed against the health and safety of local inhabitants.

In the past, Messianic proclamations have called for an end to all wars. Today, however, such calls have been tempered by a more calculated and reasoned approach to human welfare. The present chapter looks at how the movement views technological development and what is in the best interests of society and its inhabitants. Indeed, peace is more than the absence of war.

FROM POLITICAL PROTEST AND CULTURAL REVOLUTION: NONVIOLENT DIRECT ACTION IN THE 1970S AND 1980S by Barbara Epstein. Copyright 1991 by the Regents of the University of California. Used by permission of the University of California Press.

The nonviolent direct action movement of the late 1970s and the 1980s began in 1976 with the formation of the Clamshell Alliance to oppose the construction of a nuclear energy plant near the town of Seabrook, on the New Hampshire coast, through massive civil disobedience. The Clamshell arose from a coalition of local environmentalists who turned to civil disobedience after legal efforts to block the construction of the plant failed and activists who moved to New England in the late sixties and early seventies, disappointed by the antiwar movement and hoping to build a movement in the countryside more in line with the values of the countercultural left. Antinuclear civil disobedience drew massive support from young activists throughout New England and beyond. The Clamshell combined small-group structure and consensus process with nonviolent civil disobedience on a large scale. The Clamshell's mass occupation of the proposed plant site in 1977 led to 1,401 arrests, a euphoric experience of community at the site and in the armories that served as jails, and the creation of alliances around the country modeled on the Clamshell.[1]

Though the Clamshell was unable to stop the construction of the plant at Seabrook through direct action, the nuclear power industry was nevertheless stalled by the early seventies, partly by intra industry problems: growing evidence that nuclear power was costly, inefficient, and dangerous, as dramatically demonstrated by the accident at Three Mile Island in 1981, and partly by growing popular opposition. The Clamshell, along with other, more conventional antinuclear and environmental organizations, played an important role in generating that opposition.

The greatest contribution of the Clamshell, however, lay not in containing the growth of the nuclear power industry, but in the creation of a mass movement based on nonviolent direct action and infused with a vision of a better world, which it at-tempted to prefigure in its own practice. Other than the early civil rights movement, on which it was modeled to some degree, the Clamshell represented the first effort in American history to base a mass movement on nonviolent direct action. It continued the New Left impulse toward a politics of living out one's values and rejected the antiwar movement's machismo and authoritarianism. For many of its members the Clamshell was a realization of the hope that had seemed to fade in the late sixties for a movement based on shared commitments and mutual trust. Many younger people who had not been directly involved in the anti-war movement came out of their experience in the Clamshell determined to be part of radical politics for the rest of their lives.

Participation in the Clamshell was, for many people, a trans-formative experience; but the way the Clamshell ended was shattering. The euphoria did not last. Plans for a second occupation that promised to be much larger than the first were highly publicized, and it seemed likely that this time the gate would be locked. A small group of Clams argued that occupiers should he pre-pared to cut through the fences, regardless of the police response. Clamshell founders and local seacoast activists argued for strict adherence to nonviolence on principled and practical grounds. With both groups determined to stand fast, there could be no resolution through consensus process. State intervention led the informal leadership of Clamshell founders and others to circumvent consensus process, violating the Clamshell's basic principles. The organization fell apart, leaving deep hostilities and raising the question of whether the radical egalitarianism of consensus process and the ecstatic experience of direct action were viable bases for a political movement.

Years later Anna Gyorgy, a founder of the Clamshell, told me that she would never again become part of an organization that was open to anyone who wanted to join and gave every member power to block the decisions of the majority.[2] Cathy Wolff. Clam media representative and seacoast activist, blamed the deterioration of the Clamshell on the turn toward pursuit of community for its own sake. "We started out wanting to stop Seabrook," she said.

The sense of community was a side benefit. We were all working in unison, we were all motivated. The primary motivation was stopping the nukes, the secondary one, how good it felt. That secondary motivation became primary for a lot of people. Happiness has to be a side benefit. For a lot of people, the process became more important than the product, the means became an end. People said, "I just want to lay my body on the line." They got involved as an opportunity for community, for self-expression, for a sense of purpose--and especially as an opportunity to stay in jail for two weeks.[3] Cindy Leerer, another seacoast activist, added, "It was magic. Magic doesn't last."[4]

The environmental activists on the New Hampshire seacoast, at least, turned to civil disobedience only after extensive efforts to stop the plant by more conventional means. Since the early seventies there had been talk that the Public Service Corporation (abbreviated PSCo, and pronounced "Pisco") might establish a nuclear power plant in Seabrook, on a piece of land jutting out into the ocean. Preventing this had been a principal concern of the environmental organizations in the seacoast towns. A nuclear power plant, recycling water into the ocean, would have polluted the seacoast and destroyed the ecology of the area. The possibility of a nuclear accident placed residents of the seacoast area in particular jeopardy.

The Seacoast Anti-Pollution League had taken the lead in opposing PSCo's plans for a nuclear plant. Later, the Granite State Alliance brought together environmental and antinuclear activists from around the state. In 1975, Guy Chichester, a staff worker for the Seacoast Anti-Pollution League (and soon to be a founder of the Clamshell Alliance), initiated a referendum on the question in Seabrook, which ran against the plant, 767 to 432. Referenda were then held in about a dozen nearby towns. Voters were asked whether or not they supported the people of Seabrook in their vote against the PSCo plant. All but a few towns that tabled the issue endorsed the Seabrook vote.

Local votes against the plant were not enough to stop its construction, and when the license for the plant was granted by the New Hampshire Nuclear Regulatory Commission in June 1976, many local activists felt it was time to move from electoral and legal activity to direct action. Antinuclear activists were inspired by the example of Wyhl, Germany, where in 1975 a site proposed by the government for a nuclear plant was occupied by 28,000 people. That occupation was begun by several hundred from the local farming community and joined by thousands of antinuclear activists from Germany, France, and Switzerland.[5] It was maintained for a year, halting and finally canceling construction of the plant. The occupation at Wyhl, and others like it elsewhere in Europe, reinforced the belief of radicals in the antinuclear movement that it was time to turn from electoral to direct action.

A Signal to the Movement

By 1976, when the Clamshell was formed, there was already considerable interest in rural New England circles of countercultural leftists in civil disobedience as the focal point of a new kind of politics. In February 1974, Sam Lovejoy, a member of the Montague Farm, outside the town of Montague in northwestern Massachusetts, took a crowbar and knocked down a tower erected by Northeast Utilities as part of a projected nuclear power plant. Lovejoy then hitchhiked to the Montague police station and handed the police a written statement explaining and taking responsibility for the action. Lovejoy was charged with "malicious destruction of personal property" and went on trial in September. He presented expert witnesses who testified to the dangers posed by nuclear power and to the legitimacy of civil disobedience as a form of protest. After a nine-day trial before a packed courthouse, Lovejoy was acquitted by the judge on grounds that the charge was erroneous: it should have been "destruction of real [rather than personal] property," which would have been a misdemeanor, not a felony. Later interviews with the jurors made it clear that even if Lovejoy had not been acquitted on a technicality, they would have found him innocent on the ground that they did not regard his action as malicious.[6]

Sam Lovejoy's action became something of a legend in New England, especially among activists and the counterculture. Montague Farm had been established after a split in the Boston-based Liberation News Service (LNS) in the early 1970s. One group moved to Montague and had established an organic farm, supporting themselves mostly by writing until the farm was producing to capacity. The fact that the Montague group had taken the LNS press, which sat in the barn unused, provoked some skepticism among other rural New England activists, but Lovejoy's action and the local political work of other Montague Farm people nevertheless placed them in the leadership of the emerging New England antinuclear movement.

Lovejoy's action had, in fact, been intended to encourage that movement and to give it some direction. Lovejoy argued that through the issue of nuclear power, the antiwar movement would be able to establish itself in local communities and find a strength that the student base and the national focus of the antiwar movement had not allowed.

To dump the tower was to send a signal to the politicians, and also to the movement. Not just the upper-middle-class antinuclear power movement but also to the New Left, which I was a member of, that the war was ending, there were other issues. The single biggest failure of the New Left was that it never had a home base. It had a student base. But movements don't last unless they have home base, a population base, not just an age-segment base. To the antinuclear power movement I was saying, there are other tactics. If you lose every legal fight, there are other tactics. Civil disobedience is one way to invigorate, empower younger people.[7]

Other strains of nonviolent civil disobedience contributed to the formation of an antinuclear movement in rural New England. Ware, New Hampshire, was the home of the Greenleaf Harvesters' Guild, a farming collective organized on pacifist principles by Arthur Harvey, a Gandhi scholar. Harvey and others from the Guild participated in the activities of the People's Energy Project, one of the environmentalist groups on the seacoast. In January 1976, Ron Rieck, one of the Guild's apple pickers, erected a sleeping platform on top of a pole on the site designated for the nuclear plant. To bear witness against the projected plant, Rieck climbed up to the platform and stayed there two days and nights, with supporters bringing food and comfort, until he was arrested. His supporters included not only local activists but also a few people from the Cambridge office of the American Friends Service Committee, which had, since the mid-sixties, been more willing than any other to involve itself in active protest. The AFSC members who went to New Hampshire to encourage Ron Rieck hoped that his action might be one more step toward a nonviolent antinuclear movement. Two staff members from the Cambridge AFSC, Elizabeth Boardman and Suki Rice, were invited back to the seacoast by local activists to give training in non-violent direct action.

The Creation of the Clamshell Alliance

In June 1976, when PSCo was granted a license to begin construction of the plant, the networks already existed for the formation of an antinuclear movement that would focus on the use of nonviolent direct action. A small meeting was held at Guy Chichester's house in the seacoast town of Rye. Soon after, a somewhat larger meeting of about fifty people was held to ratify and expand the decisions made at the first meeting. Seacoast activists made up most participants in those early meetings, joined by Sam Lovejoy from the Montague Farm. Two other Montague people, Anna Gyorgy and Harvey Wasserman, were to become members of the Clamshell steering committee, but neither was present at the initial meetings. Anna was coordinating antinuclear efforts in Western Massachusetts, and Harvey Wasserman was in Europe; he became involved in the Clamshell on his re-turn, nearly a year later. Two staff members from the Cambridge office of the AFSC, Elizabeth Boardman and Suki Rice, drove up to New Hampshire to participate in forming the organization. Boardman and Rice had the support of Cambridge AFSC but were not representing it: the AFSC cannot join a coalition or officially lend its support to another organization without a decision of the board of directors, which had been neither requested nor given. Nevertheless, Boardman and Rice continued to be among the most active of the inner circle. All of the founding members of the Clamshell were in their twenties or early thirties, with the exception of Elizabeth Boardman, a long-time Quaker and peace activist a generation older than most of her fellow Clams.

The name Clamshell Alliance (often shortened to "the Clam") referred to the clams living in sand and mud flats along the seacoast, which would have been destroyed by nuclear wastewater. The Clamshell's adherence to nonviolent direct action, semiautonomous local groups, and decision making by consensus emerged more or less spontaneously at its first meetings. The organization had been formed out of a shared sense that the limits of electoral and legal action had been reached; and nonviolence made sense to everyone, for various reasons. "I was not a pacifist, but I was a committed nonviolentist when it came to nuclear power," Sam Lovejoy remembered. "Elizabeth [Boardman] is a committed nonviolentist; they believe in it as a religion. The principle of nonviolence was laid out at our first meeting, ratified at the second. As for consensus, it went from 'it's operating this way' to 'there's got to be a word for it,' so Elizabeth said, 'it's consensus.' She laid out how it was used in the AFSC and earlier movements. It was legitimized at our second, large meeting."[8]

Although nonviolence and consensus decision making were articulated by the Quakers, they were also identified with the early civil rights movement, in which some founding members of the Clamshell had participated, and which many, including the Quakers, regarded as a model for political action. Guy Chichester recalled that "nonviolence came [into the Clamshell] because of the trainings [conducted by the Quakers]. We knew that the AFSC people knew about nonviolence. Also, I had grown up through the civil rights marches in the South, and I saw nonviolence as a way for people to come together." [9]

The First Occupation

The focus of the Clamshell's activity was a series of occupations of the site of the proposed Seabrook plant, leading up to the massive occupation of the spring of 1977. These occupations combined dramatic political action with an intense experience of community; they attracted public attention to the issue of nuclear power, and they drew to the Clamshell a constituency in search of a morally charged experiential politics. At the first meetings of the Clamshell, it was decided that the first occupation should be small and made up only of New Hampshire residents. The second should be larger and should include people from other states as well, and the third should be a mass occupation. One local activist, Rennie Cushing, proposed a "power of ten" rule: the first occupation should be limited to 18 people, the second to 180, and the third, it was hoped, would draw 1,800 willing to be arrested. The reality turned out to be surprisingly close to this projection. On August 1, 1976, 18 people walked down the abandoned railway tracks leading into the site and were arrested. On August 22, in pouring rain, 180 people, some of them from Boston and Western Massachusetts, were arrested. Suki Rice provided non-violence training before each action.

After the August 22 occupation, planning began for the mass occupation, originally scheduled for October but put off to the following spring because of the possibility of bad weather, and because it had become clear that the occupation would draw a large number of people and more time was needed for preparation. In the meantime, an Alternative Energy Fair was held to introduce local residents to the idea of safe energy as opposed to nuclear energy. Through the winter, intensive nonviolence trainings were held. On April 30 and May 1, 1977, some 2,400 people, mostly from New England, gathered at Seabrook. Only members of affinity groups were allowed to participate; this rule ensured that the action would be restricted to people who had been introduced to the ideas of nonviolence and were part of a collective structure. Elizabeth Boardman remembered that one man, "roaring drunk," tried to join at the last minute but was turned away by marshals trained for the event on the ground that he was not attached to an affinity group. When he tried to push the marshals away they "hugged him out of the way."[10]

The protesters walked onto the site, which, because it was Saturday, was empty of workers. The occupation was set up on a village model, with several affinity groups in each space marked out as a camping area, and with "roads" laid out between the encampments. Each "village" of affinity groups chose a representative to attend a "spokes council," which would attempt to arrive at consensus on any issues that arose and would convey those decisions to the police when they arrived. Saturday afternoon was spent digging latrines and setting up camp. The next morning the occupiers awoke to find the National Guard on the other side of the fence that surrounded the site. Around noon a helicopter arrived bringing New Hampshire governor Meldrim Thompson. The occupiers were told that anyone not off the site within twenty minutes would be arrested. About a thousand left, while 1,401 remained to be arrested. The protesters were taken by bus to be arraigned at the Portsmouth armory. Some were kept there, but the majority were again placed in buses and distributed among six other armories throughout New Hampshire, where they stayed until they were released two weeks later.

A Community of Protest

The occupation and the armory experience built a strong sense of community among the protesters, an important source of which was the affinity group. The Clamshell Alliance was made up of local groups that might be of any size; it had been agreed that civil disobedience actions should be based on affinity groups made up of roughly eight to fifteen people who already knew one another and could work well together and rely on one another. Those who participated in the first small action did so as individuals; the second, larger action was based on affinity groups. The concept of an affinity group had been introduced to the New Left in the mid-sixties by the philosopher Murray Bookchin, who found it in his studies of Spanish anarchism. Though Bookchin was to become involved with the Clamshell

Alliance, along with others at his Institute for Social Ecology in Burlington, Vermont, it was in fact the Quakers who introduced the idea of affinity groups to the Clamshell. Guy Chichester remembered, "Before I met Elizabeth and Suki I never in my life had heard of any such thing as an affinity group, and I was a fairly well read person. They showed us the special protections afforded by an affinity group in times of stress, when there might be violence by the police. The affinity group evolved into something that included that part, and also the part that Bookchin described [in his account of Spanish anarchism], the spirit of community."[11]

The bonds among members of affinity groups helped many people through the frightening aspects of arrest. Some groups waited for hours to be arrested and then were kept in the buses for sixteen or twenty hours before being arraigned. In some cases the police confiscated the food the protesters had brought with them. After arraignment, the protesters endured long bus rides to the armories where they were to stay. People from the Movement for a New Society (MNS), a Philadelphia-based group with Quaker origins that had for many years brought nonviolent training and a Quaker process to various protest groups, participated in the occupation and played an important role in bringing a sense of community to the armories.

Meg Simonds, a member of Boston Clam, was separated from her affinity group and without sleep for thirty-six hours before she was deposited at the Manchester armory, where the rest of her affinity group had been brought earlier. "There were seven hundred people," she remembered. "It looked like a mass of bodies. I didn't see one person that I knew. I began to lose it. A man came over and welcomed me to the Manchester armory; he was from MNS. He took me around; "We'll find your affinity group," he said. I don't know if I would have made it without that. I was on the verge of hysteria. Once I found my affinity group I was okay."[12]

The experience in the armories quickly created a sense of community among protesters. In the Manchester armory, the MNS people called a meeting of facilitators from the various affinity groups to discuss whether to accept bail or demand release on "own recognizance" (OR). Each affinity group was asked to decide this question separately. When the affinity groups came together for a mass meeting, spokespersons (spokes) from the various affinity groups were asked to stand up to indicate their groups' decisions. No one stood up when asked which groups wanted to go out on bail. When asked which groups would demand OR, all the spokes stood up. "Once we got that done, we were united as a group," Meg Simonds said. "You need a unifying decision that you can make quickly and easily at the beginning."

This demonstration of the capacity of the consensus process to affirm solidarity strengthened the protesters' determination to insist on their right to use it. "The authorities were always coming in and saying we had to make some decision now," Meg Simonds recalled. "We would say, that's not enough time. We're going to use our process. They had to allow us to do what we wanted. The officers said, 'We want to talk to your leader.' We said no, we have a committee of two men and two women, which will rotate daily; that's who will speak with you. The first time we said it the officers walked out. But several hours later they came back and said okay."

For several days the protesters had no beds, but slept on the concrete floors. Finally someone remembered that the state of New Hampshire had cots stored away for civil defense, and these were brought in. In spite of relatively difficult physical conditions, a spirit of euphoric community developed quickly. Workshops were organized. Elizabeth Boardman, who was also being held in the Manchester armory, recalled that "one group led singing, another gave lessons in journal writing. We were as busy and organized as you please, running around and taking our lessons." Boardman was on the liaison committee when the authorities raised the issue of "immorality" in the armory. If it did not stop, the officers said, men and women would be separated. "It was evidently supposed to be my role as an older woman to be shocked about this," Boardman said. "I said to the lieutenant, 'If you break up our arrangement of affinity groups, if you separate us from our affinity groups, we are not going to be responsible for what hell breaks loose.' "[13] The protesters eventually found a solution in the cardboard boxes in which the cots had been delivered. Two structures of cardboard boxes were erected, each with a little curtained door. One was for privacy for women, the other was for couples. There were no more complaints about immorality.

The protesters were released after two weeks, pending their trials. A few trials were held during the winter but most were put off; finally, in most cases, the charges were dismissed. The occupation and the experience in the armories put the Clamshell on the front page of newspapers, especially in New England. Dick Bell, at the time managing editor of the Boston Real Paper, and beginning to get involved in the Clam, points out that the reporting of those events did not highlight the issue of nuclear power. "There was likely to be one paragraph about nuclear power in thousands of inches of coverage. Nevertheless, it was a tremendous spectacle, the people moving onto the site, digging the la-trines, being taken to the armories, the legal process. It could not have been a better media event." [14]

Soft and Hard Clams

The occupation and the armory experience showed that the Clamshell represented a new kind of politics, one that many people, especially young people, found attractive. Over the summer and fall of 1977 the Clamshell was flooded with new members. The occupation had been extremely successful, but of course it had not stopped PSCo's plans to construct a nuclear plant at Seabrook. The Clamshell decided to hold another mass occupation in June 1978, with the hope that this one would be two or three times as large as the last. By December, conflicts about what form the occupation should take were breaking out in Boston Clam, which was an important group because of the large number of occupiers from Boston in the April occupation and because of the numbers of people joining the Clam in Boston. A committee had been set up by Boston Clam, called the Occupation/Restoration Task Force, to plan the upcoming occupation (and the subsequent "restoration" of the site); the committee drew a number of Clams who called themselves anarchists.

The term "anarchist" was a slippery one in the Clamshell, because many--probably most--Clams regarded themselves as anarchists. The rejection of hierarchy, the espousal of the consensus process, the affinity group structure, spokes and spokes councils, were all regarded as coming directly or indirectly out of an anarchist tradition. But the Boston anarchists brought a new element into the Clamshell. Associated with groups such as the Black Rose, which ran an anarchist lecture series at MIT, and Hard Rain, a Boston affinity group, they put themselves forward as representing militancy against what. they regarded as the prevailing timidity. Some argued later that the Boston anarchists never believed in nonviolence. Whether or not this was true, they were willing to stretch the limits of nonviolence considerably further than the Quakers and other founding members of the Clamshell.

The terms "soft Clams" and "hard Clams" began to be used to distinguish the two approaches. As the Hard Rain affinity group moved to the center of debate, its name came to be identified with the hard Clam position, even though not all hard Clams were members of Hard Rain. The debate focused on the question of what the Clamshell should do if, as seemed likely, the gate to the Seabrook site were locked when the next occupation was attempted. In April, the demonstrators had been permitted onto the site on Saturday as long as they were prepared to leave on Sunday, to allow the workers to enter. The demonstrators' refusal to leave had been the signal for the arrests. After the success of the first action, PSCo was unlikely to leave the gate open on the date of a planned Clamshell occupation. And it seemed very likely that the New Hampshire police, under the direction of Governor Thompson, a vociferous supporter of nuclear power, would back up PSCo.

The Hard Rain people argued that the demonstrators should take wire cutters and be prepared to cut through the fence. Others objected that to do so was contrary to their principles, because it was more or less guaranteed to provoke police violence for which the Clamshell could be regarded as responsible. The Hard Rain people argued that the American working class would never take an organization seriously that was not willing to confront the police. The opposition feared that the prospect of violence would severely limit the numbers of people who would be willing to take part in the occupation.[15]

Guidelines for the June 24 action required nonviolence training and adherence to a code of nonviolence by all participants:

> Everyone must receive preparation in nonviolent direct action before taking part in the action—either in support or as an occupier.
>
> No weapons of any kind.
>
> No damage or destruction of PSCo or Seabrook property.
>
> No running at any time.
>
> No strategic or tactical movement after dark.
>
> No breaking through police lines.
>
> No dogs.
>
> No drugs or alcohol.
>
> In case of confrontation, we will sit down.
>
> We will not block workers' personal access to the site.[16]

In a further elaboration of nonviolence, occupiers were asked to adopt an "attitude towards officials and others who may oppose us ... of sympathetic understanding of the burdens and responsibilities that they carry" and to "speak to the best in all people, rather than seeking to exploit their weakness to what we may believe is our advantage.... No matter what the circumstances or provocation, we should not respond with violence to acts directed against us." [17]

The most controversial item in the guidelines was the proscription against destruction of property. It was argued in favor of cutting fences that an assault on property rather than on people was acceptable and that anyway the fences would be repaired as soon as the demonstrators were on the other side. Some Clams suggested other ways of getting in, such as digging under the fences or using large ladders to climb over them. But there were practical problems with each of these proposals. Ultimately the debate about fence cutting was a debate about the relationship between militance and nonviolence, about whether the Clam should adopt the confrontational style that had been the measure of commitment for many in the antiwar movement or attempt to construct a different kind of politics.

Conflicts about Leadership and Decision Making

The debate about fence cutting raised the questions how decisions should be made in an organization that described itself as leaderless and what the content of those decisions should be. Through the winter and spring of 1978 the organization grew rapidly. Week-to-week direction was provided by a coordinating committee centered on the Portsmouth office staff and other seacoast and Western Massachusetts activists, most of whom had been part of the Clamshell since its earliest days. As the debate about fence cutting proceeded, the Hard Rain people argued that it was the old guard, especially the "Montague Farm gang" (or, less affectionately, the "Montague Farm mafia") that was holding back militancy. This argument hit home in many quarters because there were others, many with no sympathy for fence cutting, who for other reasons had doubts about the role of Montague Farm in the Clamshell. By that time Sam Lovejoy of the Montague group was spending most of his time traveling around the country, speaking about nuclear power and encouraging resistance to it, in the effort to start a national movement. Lovejoy's efforts, although instrumental in organizing a number of other antinuclear alliances, did little to endear him to critics in the Clamshell who regarded him as "star-tripping." Harvey Wasserman and Anna Gyorgy, also of Montague Farm, were traveling frequently for the antinuclear movement at that time.

The Montague people's assumption of what amounted to leadership roles in a movement that purported to have no leadership caused resentment. The fact that neither Lovejoy nor Wasserman nor Gyorgy had taken part in any of the Clamshell's occupations provided further rationale for animosity toward them. The Montague Farm people, along with many of the founders of the Clamshell, regarded civil disobedience as only one of a number of tactics that should be used to oppose nuclear power. But most of those who joined the Clamshell after the 1977 occupation were inspired by civil disobedience and regarded it as central to what the organization was about.

Tensions over leadership were heightened by the media's seeming to choose leaders. Sam Lovejoy drew the attention of the press after he knocked over the tower. Lovejoy, Gyorgy, and Wasserman all had forceful, charismatic personalities that attracted media attention. After the Montague gang, the media focused on a few activists on the seacoast, Guy Chichester and Rennie Cushing in particular, whose self-confidence and flair for public speaking made them good subjects. It was easy for rank-and-file Clams in other parts of New England to feel that their organization was being dominated by leaders they had never chosen.

If not for the leadership question, and if it had not been seen as a challenge to the "old guard," the Hard Rain call for cutting fences probably would have made less headway. The conflict was fed by confusion over the Clamshell's decision-making process. The founding group had agreed that the Clamshell should be run by consensus, with Quaker process as a working model. In the Clamshell's first year, when it was still relatively small and there was a great deal of good will and agreement on basic aims, consensus had worked wonderfully. It had also worked well in the armories, even when large numbers of people tried to make decisions together. Relatively brief but intense experiences of community building, such as the occupation and the time spent in the armories, can generate either sharp conflict or a euphoric spirit of cooperation. In the armories, consensus process worked well because everyone wanted it to work and because there was plenty of time to work out every question.

There were, however, structural problems in the decision-making process, which went unnoticed as long as it worked well, no factions arose in the organization, and power struggles were not prominent. If someone could not agree on a particular point, it was possible to "stand aside" and allow a decision to be made without giving assent but also without impeding the will of the group. When, in the fall of 1978, the Clamshell began to expand rapidly and nonviolence training began to take place on a large scale, the concept of the "block" was introduced: a person with strong principled objections could stand in the way of a group decision. The block was a departure from the Quaker practice of putting aside a seemingly unresolvable conflict for a time and allowing the disputants to rethink it. During the fall of 1977 and the spring of 1978, the MNS was heavily involved in nonviolence training. The block was included as an element of consensus process in MNS sessions, and no one seems to have given much thought to the problems that could arise if every individual had the power to halt the whole organization.

In the context of the debate over fence cutting, blocking consensus assumed an important role within the Clamshell. Hard Rain and the people who came together around them had no stake in arriving at consensus. They saw their differences with the old guard as fundamental and based on principle. As Harvey Halpern, not a member of Hard Rain but one of the leading proponents of fence cutting, told me, the question was whether to sit down and be arrested or to "physically stop the nuke, to act in concert with others to stop the nuke ourselves."[18] The question was whether to "appeal to the authorities" through a symbolic action or to pull down the fences, get onto the site, and build villages, as the Germans had done at Wyhi. Halpern told rue that this could have been done if fifty or seventy thousand people had come to Seabrook to occupy the site. Others recall that in the debates that took place at the time, the Hard Rain people had also argued that part of the question was how to draw working-class people into the antinuclear movement. The working class, they claimed, had no patience with merely symbolic protest or with middle-class protesters who were afraid to confront police violence.[19]

The fence-cutting proposal was an attempt to revive the confrontational style of the antiwar movement in an organization that had been formed in the hope of finding a different approach to protest. Faced with sharp disagreements, the Hard Rain people did not hesitate to block any consensus that would. exclude fence cutting from the occupation. There were perhaps ten or fifteen people actively arguing for the Hard Rain approach. Within Boston Clam a roughly equal number of people argued strongly against it, primarily on the ground that a threat of violence would deter many people who might otherwise join the occupation. These two groups contained the most vocal people in Boston Clam; between them were those who were reluctant to come down firmly on either side.

The middle group, whose allegiance was sought by both sides, consisted of people who did not especially like the idea of fence cutting but sympathized with Hard Rain's hostility to the Clamshell's unofficial leadership on the seacoast and in Western Massachusetts, and tended to see the Hard Rain group as a minority trying to make themselves heard. In Boston, the anti-fence-cutting group began to regard Hard Rain as troublemakers, turned to heavy-handed tactics against them, and became increasingly impatient with the middle group and its continued sympathy for Hard Rain. Out of frustration, the anti-fence-cutting group pro-posed that the Clamshell's process should be revised. When consensus could not be reached, the vote should be resorted to, with an 80 percent majority required for a decision to stand.

The middle group opposed this modification on the ground that it would disempower the 20 percent whose votes were not necessary to arrive at a decision. In proposing that consensus process be modified, the anti-fence-cutting group managed to cast itself as the opponents of what the Clamshell stood for, namely, a political process in which everyone's voice would be heard. Dick Bell, a leading opponent of fence cutting, argues that resistance was based on a general identification with that remaining 20 per-cent as a disenfranchised minority (and by implication with the fence cutters, who would undoubtedly have found themselves in that percentage). There was a widespread feeling, Bell said, that to overrule a minority would not be nice. Feelings would be hurt. "What we had was the politics of niceness. For a significant group, being nice was more important than being right. To argue for a position was not nice. It was difficult, under these conditions, to have a simple principled argument. People who argued strongly would be condemned for not being nice, not for whether their argument was right or not."[20]

The Rath Proposal: State Intervention

The debate over fence cutting raised three crucial issues for the Clamshell: where the line between violence and nonviolence should be drawn, what to do when consensus could not be reached on a major issue, and whether there was any legitimate role for leadership. Any one of these questions had the potential to divide the organization; the three combined led to an explosion that destroyed the organization. If the organization as a whole had seriously addressed these issues as soon as they arose there might have been some chance of resolving them. But conflicts were al-lowed to simmer within Boston Clam for a very long time before the rest of the organization paid any attention.

The anti-fence-cutting group in Boston appealed to the unofficial leadership on the seacoast and at Montague Farm to come to Boston and help resolve the debate. But the coordinating committee and the people in the Portsmouth office were busy trying to pull together a rapidly growing regional movement. Furthermore, in an organization that officially had no leadership, in which the coordinating committee was regarded as simply expressing the accumulated will of the various local groups, no one had the authority to intervene. Many people at the center of the Clamshell had been doing little but Clamshell work for a year and a half or more and were tired of being told that they were dominating the organization. They had no desire to travel to Boston and subject themselves to a barrage of such criticisms. Furthermore, many of the Clamshell activists in northern New England believed that the rural roots of the movement mattered most, that what went on in Boston should not be given undue weight. The view circulated among the rural people (most of whom had recently fled the cities themselves) that the behavior of the Hard Rain people could be put down to urban stress: city life drives people crazy.

As the estimated number of those who would join the occupation grew and the debate about fence cutting continued unabated, the activists on the seacoast grew uneasy. The seacoast communities had voted their opposition to nuclear power, and those towns contained a reservoir of good feeling for the Clamshell because of its prominence in the effort to keep the plant from being constructed. But the Clamshell had never had a strong local base of support for civil disobedience. Many of the seacoast activists had themselves either grown up in the area or lived there for many years. But the majority even of the local activists were young people who had led relatively mobile lives and were not integrated into the older, more stable seacoast communities. Some older residents gave active support to the Clamshell: a number had made their houses available to organizers and had allowed protesters to camp on their land before the occupation of 1977. But there were few such people. The Clamshell could count on the support of the rural countercultural left, but the more tenuous support of the indigenous communities could easily be destroyed by the threat of a violent action.

In the late spring of 1978, signs of trouble appeared. Supporters of the Clamshell along the seacoast who had volunteered their land as staging grounds for the occupation were warned by the state that their property might be reassessed for increased taxes. A few reported fires on their property. At this point New Hampshire attorney general Tom Rath publicly proposed that the Clamshell hold a demonstration on the site over an agreed-upon weekend, with the stipulation that the demonstrators would leave at the end of that time. The Governor's council endorsed this proposal. The Clamshell coordinating committee was in touch with Rath and other state officials, and began to discuss how to respond to Rath's proposal.

Pressures for a rapid decision were created by the fact that Rath announced his proposal through the media rather than going to the Clamshell first, and the fact that the proposal came in May, close to the planned occupation of the site. Members of the coordinating committee canvassed Clamshell supporters on the seacoast and reported that few remained willing to let occupiers use their land. Critics of the coordinating committee later claimed that some of these canvassers were not merely polling Clamshell supporters but trying also to convince them that it would be unwise to allow their land to be used for an occupation. It is possible that some members of the coordinating committee, having concluded that the occupation should not take place, wanted to make their position as strong as possible. But it is hard to believe that the seacoast communities were very enthusiastic about an occupation that was likely to lead to violence.

The core members of the coordinating committee felt that it would be a bad idea to go ahead with the occupation; they were afraid that the Hard Rain people would do something to cost the Clamshell its local support. The problem was not so much that the coordinating committee decided to abandon the action that had been the focus of Clamshell organizing for a year (though that in itself would have been very difficult for the organization to have absorbed) but that their lack of confidence in the possibility of resolving the issue led them to violate Clamshell procedures. An expanded coordinating committee meeting was held with spokes from Clamshell groups throughout the region. Consensus was reached to accept the attorney general's proposal. As soon as the meeting was over, before the decision could be relayed back to the local groups and discussed there, the media were informed that the occupation had been canceled.

In both form and spirit, Clamshell procedure had been violated. Some spokes were genuinely persuaded to support the Rath proposal, but others had agreed only under pressure. The decision was reached, according to one seacoast activist, by "an arm-twisting type of consensus." Many spokes went against the instructions of local groups in giving their support. The failure to relay the decision back to the local groups presumed that the coordinating committee had the authority to make final decisions, contrary to the idea that power should be decentralized and that the purpose of the coordinating committee was to facilitate decision making by the organization as a whole, not to make decisions itself. The fact that the decision had been announced in the press made it irreversible. For local groups to reject the decision of the coordinating committee would have been meaningless, because there was no time to revive the occupation.

Many members of the coordinating committee and other activists on the seacoast and in Western Massachusetts believed that Clamshell groups in the seacoast communities had a special right to veto Clam actions. The local people, the argument went, had special concerns about a nuclear plant because of the damage it would do to their area and because they would be most vulnerable. Furthermore, a badly planned action would have more impact on the local activists than anyone else. According to this line of thinking, the coordinating committee was within its rights to stop the occupation, since local Clamshell groups and supporters were against it.

The founders of the Clamshell understood that people living near the Seabrook site had a privileged place in Clamshell decision making, but this understanding had never been formally endorsed by the Clamshell as a whole. Many newer Clams in other areas of New England were unaware of it and assumed, during the months of preparation for the occupation, that the action belonged as much to them as to the seacoast people. Murray Bookchin, who played an important role in organizing the Clamshell in Vermont, pointed out that an accident would have endangered everyone in the region and beyond. In that sense, the local communities had no special claim to a veto over actions.[21] In fact the idea of the special veto came partly from a commitment to local autonomy and partly from the understanding that to retain its legitimacy and political clout, the Clamshell must maintain support in the communities close to the site.

The decision not to hold an occupation effectively destroyed the Clamshell. Members of the coordinating committee, along with seacoast activists, went to local groups throughout the region to try to explain the decision. Angry meetings were followed by de-moralization. Throughout New England, people began to leave the Clamshell. In Vermont, Murray Bookchin recalls, a meeting was addressed by two activists from the seacoast who had been involved in the decision to call off the occupation. Making a personal appeal for trust, they called for unity and tried to revive commitment to the aims of the movement, but their arguments fell on deaf ears. People drifted out of the meeting and then out of the movement entirely.

Division and Collapse of the Clamshell

The shift from occupation to a legal demonstration was the signal for the Hard Rain people, and others who had become disillusioned with the existing informal leadership of the Clamshell, to form their own organization, Clams for Direct Action at Seabrook (CDAS), committed to continuing militant occupations of the Seabrook site. But the constituency for such actions was in fact considerably more limited than when the original Clamshell mobilized, with its clear commitment to nonviolence and its attempt to find a nonconfrontational style of protest. The Hard Rain people had said that they were committed to physically preventing the construction of the plant while the old guard was only interested in symbolic politics. But the first occupation they mobilized was much too small to have any effect on the plant and the second was smaller than the first.

CDAS was unable to sustain a return to the militant style of the late sixties: the people who came to occupy the plant site could not bring themselves to engage in such confrontational politics. The new series of actions slipped into the style of politics the Clamshell had originally embraced, without being able to articulate the process or acknowledge that it was happening. In fact the appeal of CDAS had more to do with the opportunity to occupy the site, and disaffection with the regular Clamshell for its violation of democratic process, than with enthusiasm for late-sixties style militancy. The founders of CDAS, and much of its constituency, identified themselves as anarchist much more vehemently than had the founders of the Clamshell, for most of whom non-violence had been the central term. But anarchism and nonviolence were nevertheless linked in many people's minds as components of a new kind of democratic politics. The CDAS actions were shaped by the same new spirit of radicalism as the earlier Clamshell.

In accordance with the Rath proposal, a legal demonstration was held at the site in place of an occupation. Twenty thousand people came. It was the largest demonstration the Clamshell had ever held and on that ground alone could be considered a success. Meanwhile, local groups were dwindling. Clamshell held an action in Washington, D.C., in which several hundred people camped out in front of the Nuclear Regulatory Commission for several days, demanding that the plant at Seabrook not be constructed. The sit-in culminated in the announcement of a temporary halt in construction, which overjoyed the demonstrators and led to what one described as "the most incredible street party."[22] But the Clamshell as a whole was crumbling, and no single demonstration could revive it.

At the legal demonstration at Seabrook in June, the Hard Rain/Black Rose people passed out a leaflet calling for occupation and signed "Clams for Democracy." A month later, activists were unhappy enough about the direction being taken by the Clamshell to meet and set up what amounted to a rival organization. Out of this meeting came CDAS and a call for an occupation in October. The publicity did not make the distinction between CDAS and the Clamshell clear. The Clamshell office in Portsmouth, fearing that there would be violence at the CDAS occupation, sent a letter to peace groups around the country denying any connection with that action. This denial caused further hard feelings between the Clamshell leadership and CDAS.

In October, the first CDAS occupation of Seabrook took place. About two thousand people came, many from outside New England. Some wore helmets and other military-style protective gear. Many brought fence-cutting tools. The demonstrators stood outside the fence; the police stood on the site, inside the fence. A number of demonstrators began cutting into the fence. As sections of the fence fell to the ground, removing the barrier between them, the police were standing directly in front of the demonstrators. Aikos Barton, a demonstrator from Boston, recalls that the results were not what the organizers of the action had expected.

> Now the police were standing in front of us. So everyone stepped back. That summarizes the whole year-long debate. If there had been thirty thousand people there, or more German-style alienation [of the sort that characterized the German antinuclear movement of the time], maybe there would have been a confrontation. But people never walked through the fence. We decided to circle the site, walking around the fence. That's not a Hard Rain thing to do. The police inside didn't really know what was going on. But they didn't want to arrest people, they wanted to disperse us. When we finished circling the site, we went back to camp.[23]

CDAS attempted a second occupation of the site in the spring, and some five hundred people came. Having failed to mobilize effective direct action at Seabrook, CDAS disbanded. The Clamshell office continued to exist and to mount local efforts against nuclear power, at Seabrook and elsewhere. Many Clamshell activists on the seacoast returned to electorally oriented activities, similar to those in which they had been involved before the formation of the Clamshell. Clams played a major role in mobilizing public opinion to defeat a state ballot initiative, "Construction Work in

Progress," which would have allowed PSCo to charge consumers for the cost of construction while a nuclear energy plant was being built. The initiative's failure was a prime factor in the deferral of the Seabrook plant to the indefinite future. A number of the Clams who took part in that campaign had been involved in electoral struggles against nuclear energy before the Clamshell emerged. Their return to electoral activity reflected some degree of disillusionment with civil disobedience.

Nonviolent Direct Action: Democracy and a Better World

The Clamshell was the first important political expression of an anarchist/countercultural tendency that emerged from the movements of the sixties and flowered in the seventies. It drew on a philosophy and tradition that had been pushed aside by much of the antiwar movement: the nonviolent direct action of Gandhi and of Christian pacifism, the Quaker devotion to consensus and community, and the example of civil rights in creating a mass movement based on these principles. The Quakers in the founding Clamshell group, especially Elizabeth Boardman, played a key role in articulating nonviolence and consensus and in pointing to their historical roots.

The fundamental reason nonviolence and consensus were adopted by the Clamshell was that the culture of which it was a part was already imbued with those values. The Clamshell's commitment to feminism deepened the democratic component of nonviolence, and opened up more space for female leadership than had been present in the movements that had preceded it. That commitment was particularly important for a movement that relied on the support of local constituencies: in the seacoast communities, women were at the center of the opposition to the plant and played a larger role than men in holding the movement together. The Clamshell's commitment to environmentalism was an important addition to the tradition of nonviolence. Feminism and environmentalism were both elements in the better world the Clamshell envisioned. The broad appeal of the

Clamshell had a great deal to do with its ability to bring together values that were held by many people, and to associate them with the specific and seemingly winnable issue of nuclear power.

The concept of democracy was at the heart of the Clamshell's vision, and its rapid growth and public appeal were based to a large extent on the fact that it spoke directly to people's ability to make the decisions that would shape their environment. The postwar era has seen the emergence of a national security state that has shielded U.S. foreign policy from democratic intervention to a greater degree than ever before. The atom bomb has been the rationale for this shift, and questions involving nuclear power have in particular been made the province of the national security community. To the founders of the Clamshell, nuclear weapons seemed too large and too abstract to be a promising basis for building a mass movement. Nuclear power, on the other hand, was concrete and local. Unlike nuclear weapons, which threaten everyone more or less equally, nuclear power plants pose special dangers for those living near them. Furthermore, victories seemed more easily attainable in the arena of nuclear power. It is easier to halt the construction of a particular plant than to take on the arms race.

Protest against nuclear power tapped emotions engendered by the larger nuclear issue and the public's lack of control over it. The Clamshell attempted to be an embryonic grass roots democracy, accepting everyone who pledged nonviolence and open to the press, the state, or anyone else who asked about its plans. The question of democracy was highlighted by the contrast between an organization of this sort and a nuclear energy corporation with a great deal of power over the lives of people living in the vicinity of the plant and little if any accountability to them. Unlike the more electorally oriented antinuclear organizations, the Clamshell was thoroughly aware of the larger implications of its work. The committee planning the June 1978 occupation of the site tried to express the relation between these two goals:

> The reason why we face the problem of nuclear power is
> because a small group of people are in control of, amongst other

aspects of people's lives, their energy policy. To try all on our own to force the ruling class to stop nukes through the actions of our presently small and unrepresentative group of members and supporters would be elitist and would probably prove counter-productive to our effort to stop nukes and furthermore to our effort to create a better world. The best and most effective way to fight the problem of nukes in such a way that the world does get better is to help the vast majority of the country to take control over the energy aspect of their lives.[24]

In addition to giving expression to anger about the infringement of democratic rights, the Clamshell did a great deal to give its members a sense of having some control over their own lives--in the language of the movement, to empower them. It gave them a way of making themselves heard on an issue ordinarily restricted to those claiming scientific expertise. It gave them the hope that if they could be heard on this issue, they could be heard on other issues as well. As the movement grew, it gave them hope that their views might make a difference.

The movement was also prefigurative of a community in which one could construct a life based on one's highest values. The occupations of the site seemed to be opportunities to put ideas about a better society into practice. The handbook for the June 1978 action urged each affinity group to develop an alternative energy project to bring to the site. "Returning the land to its former condition will be difficult and in some cases impossible, but we can make a start. We can plant trees and grain and vegetable crops and fish the river to demonstrate that the land has other uses. Instead of just taking things away from the earth and marshland, we can build a model of a sane, energy independent society on a restored and venerated land." The handbook suggested that occupiers might want to bring solar cookers and ovens, small windmills, or compost toilets. A supplement to the handbook further suggested that each occupier might want to bring a packet of sunflower or other hardy seeds to spread around the site, that kites could be used to demonstrate wind power, and that "theater, music, dance, painting, all have a place in the restoration. These, in conjunction with signs and banners, can help clusters to begin to establish a genuine sense of community."[25]

The Clamshell attracted a sympathetic audience that, although mainly white and of middle-class origin, included people of all ages. But the largest numbers of those who became Clamshell activists were in their twenties or early thirties; the distinctive character of the Clamshell came from the particular outlook of this group, who were in a broad sense the younger brothers and sisters of the antiwar protesters. They had been infected by the idealism of the sixties, but they had also seen the weaknesses of the antiwar movement, its tendency to resort to internal hierarchy and violent rhetoric, its sexism. Many of them had come to the Clamshell from the women's movement or the environmental/ecology movement, or had been deeply influenced by them.

Many of the young people drawn to the Clamshell expected that their life's work would be to create a better world. But in the late seventies the nation was moving toward the right, and the professional and academic jobs that often attract people with such aspirations were not as available as they had been. The Clamshell provided community in a society from which many of these people felt alienated and an arena in which people could, however indirectly, begin to address what they would do with their lives. Many Clams, especially those who became central activists, gained skills that enabled them to go on to jobs in alternative energy or to do other kinds of organizing or political work. Even those who went on to more conventional work in many cases carried with them a strong belief in social change and a determination to mold their jobs so as to allow them to contribute to it.

Experience of a movement dedicated to egalitarian democracy had at least a temporary effect on the personal lives of those involved. The movement's commitment to feminism undermined patterns of male dominance and mitigated assumptions that the nuclear family was superior to other forms of personal life. If any social form was privileged in the movement, it was the collective. The influence of the Montague Farm people was enhanced by the fact that they represented a rural commune in which family merged with community and manual labor was interspersed with political work. Anna Gyorgy expressed an ideal widely held in the Clamshell community when she admiringly described Sam Lovejoy, a fellow member of the Montague Farm, as one who "believe[d] that the struggle against nukes begins at home."[26]

The Limits of Consensus: Efficacy Versus Community

In view of the many strengths of the Clamshell, why did it break apart so dramatically and so rapidly? One answer is that in certain respects it recapitulated the history of the antiwar movement on which it was hoping to improve. The Clamshell's spontaneity, its lack of firm organization, made it unable to absorb rapid growth easily or to ride out sharp internal divisions. Like the New Left, the Clamshell was most harmonious in its early phase, when its members were more aware of what drew them together than of their differences and the organization was suffused with the generosity of people working in harmony, who value each other's contributions and want to protect the movement they have constructed.

The almost ecstatic sense of community the Clamshell enjoyed in its first year or so led Clams to believe that internal harmony was the automatic result of consensus process and a philosophy of nonviolence. But in fact consensus probably worked best among people who were more or less like-minded, as the original group was, or in the special circumstances of incarceration in which power struggles were not at issue and there was both the time and the desire to work out differences. The Hard Rain people brought the sectarian style of the late sixties into the Clamshell. The Clamshell decision-making process could not absorb a group who were more interested in shifting the organization toward their point of view, and in gaining power themselves, than in arriving at consensus.

The Clamshell's process made it vulnerable to disruption. Many of the people who joined the Clamshell after the spring 1977 occupation regarded the Clamshell as being fundamentally about organizing another occupation. They viewed the coordinating committee's decision to call off the projected occupation as, at the very least, a huge mistake--and at most, a sign of an overly cautious and conciliatory approach to politics. Nonviolence, many would point out, did not mean vacillation or compromise. Aikos Barton, for instance, believed that the old guard made a serious error in agreeing to the Rath proposal and substituting a legal demonstration for the planned occupation. "They failed to see that we needed a dramatic action," he said. But he argued that it was Hard Rain, and the contentious spirit they brought to the Clamshell, that was most destructive. "People came in to be a community of resistance, to see if nonviolence would work. They left once the Clamshell stopped being a community. After October 1979, we were no longer seen as sincere antinuclear people. When we lost that friendly nonviolent spirit, in the CDAS action, we lost a lot of our capital. Hard Rain was crucial in destroying that spirit of good will." [27]

The Clamshell might have withstood the conflict over fence cutting (and the issue of the limits of nonviolence more generally) if it had not already been somewhat fragile. In the wake of the successful occupation of May 1978, a number of issues emerged in the Clamshell that were not addressed in any systematic way, partly because so much energy was going into the occupation planned for June of 1978, and partly because the issues were difficult, possibly unresolvable. One was the existence of an informal, unelected leading group in an organization that claimed to be leaderless. Another was the place of local autonomy within a regional organization--whether groups near the plant site should have a veto over actions of the organization as a whole and, if not, how their relationship with the local community could be protected. Many of the newer people were unhappy with the informal leadership because they had played no role in choosing it, because those leaders claimed special rights for the seacoast people (especially suspect because the two groups were seen as allied), and perhaps most substantively because both the informal leadership and the seacoast activists seemed reluctant to go beyond the issue of safe energy, content to leave the larger implications of their critique implicit.

The tensions over the questions of leadership and local autonomy reflected a deeper division over the Clamshell's political orientation- -the balance between a focus on nuclear energy and a broader attack on the system of power relations in which nuclear energy is embedded. Hard Rain gained the sympathy of many of the newer activists not only because it challenged a firmly entrenched (though unacknowledged) leadership but also because it seemed willing to go beyond the critique of nuclear power to a larger critique of power relations in the United States.

Many of the seacoast activists joined the Clamshell because conventional challenges to nuclear power were not working and it seemed that it was time to try direct action. For those from other parts of New England, especially those inspired to join the Clamshell by the 1977 occupation, the Seabrook plant was an example of what was wrong with American society and the appeal of the Clamshell lay in its radical environmental and social vision. Among the newer Clams were some who were dissatisfied with both the narrowness of the concerns of the old Clams and Hard Rain's confrontational style and failure to understand the concept of nonviolent revolution. According to Crystal Gray, a member of an anarcha-feminist group from the West Coast that attended the CDAS action in 1979 (and that used the spelling "anarcha-feminist" intentionally to underline its rejection of the masculine universal), many anarcha-feminists were attracted to CDAS initially because of its anarchism but were disappointed to find how little the group had been influenced by the feminist critique of the macho style.[28] The appeal of the Clamshell to local environmentalists and to activists from the radical counterculture lay in its novel approach to political action--its use of civil disobedience and the consensus process. But both elements of the Clamshell's politics raised problems that were never resolved. The founders of the Clamshell intended to create an organization that would engage in a variety of nonelectoral forms of action against nuclear power. But occupations were much more dramatic and compelling than the other activities the Clamshell engaged in. Civil disobedience on the site quickly came to define what the Clamshell was about. The focus on civil disobedience created a confrontational atmosphere in which commitment was measured by one's determination to occupy the site regardless of the potential for the destruction of property or of police violence.

The Clamshell's emphasis on civil disobedience made it difficult to answer the Hard Rain challenge and committed the organization to the notion that nuclear power could be defeated by occupation. Some Clams in fact believed that an ongoing, massive occupation could force PSCo to abandon its plans. That most Clams probably did not believe it was ultimately beside the point. The intoxicating, almost addictive nature of civil disobedience made it difficult for the organization to engage deeply in any other form of political activity. Thus it would have been virtually impossible for the organization to survive the cancellation of a major occupation, regardless of the reasons for it or the process by which the decision was made.

Many people came out of their experience in the Clamshell believing that the consensus process was partly responsible for its demise, that consensus might work in small groups but needed modification to be effective in large organizations. The Clamshell's rigid commitment to its process, its unwillingness to consider such alternatives as the 80 percent majority when consensus could not be reached, froze the tensions within the organization.

The Clamshell wanted both political efficacy and community. In its early history these aims reinforced one another easily; after the first large occupation, continuing to build community seemed to require putting aside practical political considerations. Hard Rain's maximalist position was based on the argument that occupation was not symbolic politics but a real threat to nuclear energy, that if the Clamshell took a sufficiently militant approach, enough people would stay on the site long enough to make construction of the plant impossible, just as thousands of Germans had prevented the building of a nuclear plant at Wyhl. In fact, a repeat of the Wyhl experience in the United States was highly unlikely. The American antinuclear movement was not nearly as large as its German counterpart.

Nevertheless, Hard Rain's argument that no obstacles should be allowed to prevent occupation of the site resonated in the Clamshell because it legitimized the Clam's focus on civil disobedience, and it was in the experience of civil disobedience that community was most vividly realized. Dick Bell, a Boston Clam and a leading opponent of the Hard Rain group, argued that the Clamshell's emphasis on civil disobedience laid it open to these problems. There is an important difference, he argued, between civil disobedience (CD) as a tactic to be used when political analysis suggests that it is appropriate and CD as a life-style.

> If you say, this is a CD organization, people come in because they want to do CD; the organization is very limited in what it can do. You have this internal double bind that's sitting there waiting for you when you have a successful action. People come in based on what you already did, not what you might want to do next. New people are hooked on your past. Now you have three clumps of people, people who went through the last action and liked it, want to do it again, new people who think it was nifty and want to do it. And a small group of people who want to discuss what to do next. That's when debate gets sticky, even if you don't have a group of anarchists around.[29]

Cathy Wolff, part of the Clam's informal leadership and much more sympathetic to the organization's anarchist/countercultural ambiance than Bell, nevertheless believed that that ambiance caused serious problems, some of which could not be attributed to the influence of Hard Rain. In the context of the Clamshell's claim that it had no leaders and that decisions were made by consensus, it was irresponsible for the leadership to step into the breach and make decisions before consensus was reached. It was in the same vein, she said, "as people saying we would stop Seabrook by sitting there. There was magic in the Clam, but the magic was not that we would stop Seabrook by sitting there. People believing that made the magic stronger, but then the magic doubled back on us." [30]

The promise of community had much to do with the Clamshell's magic. Like the focus on CD, it caused problems, in particular a reluctance to confront potentially divisive issues or firmly to reject a minority position. Even in Boston, where Hard Rain was based, most Clams did not think that cutting fences or other actions that might provoke police violence were a good idea. Nevertheless, Bell argued, the majority of Boston Clams were unwilling to take a stand on the issue, because Hard Rain was perceived as the underdog, a beleaguered minority, and because they feared that sharp debate would disrupt the Clamshell.

> One of the messages that the Clam put out, and the armory experience fed into, was here is a way for you to find the community you have always longed for. If you are isolated, lonely, living in an apartment in Boston, come to this meeting and it'll be better; here are people who care about you. Then you come to the meeting and discover conflict. The debate was threatening on two levels. It threatened the concept of community that a significant minority had come to the Clam to find. Also, to the extent that people felt unable to participate [in the debate] themselves, it was threatening. Clamshell clearly was perceived as a dialectical response to the failures of the New Left. This is one of the reasons consensus decision-making was such a sacred cow. If you put out the message that this is a

community, sharp debate is jarring, alarming, people say this isn't what they want.[31]

One of the strengths of the Clamshell was that it linked the specific, immediate issue of nuclear energy with a vision of a society in which policy would be democratically decided, people would treat the environment and one another with respect, and technology would be appropriately scaled to its tasks. But the Clamshell never developed a strategy for achieving such a society. Instead it remained content with the assumption that the values it espoused would be adopted by more and more people and would somehow lead to the transformation of society. The fact that the Clamshell's constituency was almost entirely white and middle-class, and that it was dominated by the counterculture, made it unlikely that its values would spread to the rest of the population easily or straightforwardly. Many Clams were aware of the problem but unable to solve it.[32]

At the heart of the Clamshell's difficulties was the tension between moral witness and political efficacy. Moral witness and civil disobedience have always had a place in American protest: the American Revolution, for instance, rested in large part on the tactics of civil disobedience. In the late twentieth century, the centralization of power in the state and the corporate elite, and the often sharp contrast between human needs and the official policies, give the politics of moral witness a special resonance. As Noel Sturgeon argues in her discussion of the political theory of non-violent direct action, there is something about placing one's body in the way of "progress" that expresses a truth about our relation to the state and to corporate power. In the late twentieth century, as we confront the large issues of the fates of the environment and of the human race, moral witness is an important ground for political action. But by itself, moral witness is a fragile basis for a lasting movement. It does not recognize the question of political efficacy or the fact that movements need victories to survive.

The Clamshell wanted efficacy, but it relied largely on the politics of morality. Some Clams recognized the contradiction. Activist Marty Jezer wrote, at the height of Clamshell activity,

Historically, moral witness has proven itself an effective way of starting a movement, but inadequate in sustaining or building a movement already in existence. During the 1950s, for instance, when there was no radical movement, individual actions (like sailing small ships into nuclear testing zones) had a profound effect in making people aware of the nuclear issue and inspiring them into action. But once people are mobilized to act in a political way, individual witness loses its effect.[33]

Jezer's point of reference was individual moral witness. Collective moral witness, especially when it involves thousands of people, is more likely to get results. It can produce a movement with staying power, especially if it is combined with other approaches and forms of action. But the Clamshell was unable to solve the problem to which Jezer pointed. The Clamshell had a brilliant beginning but a short history and an end that left much bitterness. Antinuclear alliances around the country inspired in part by the Clamshell, and following its philosophy and organization, dealt more successfully with similar issues. The largest and most prominent of the Clamshell's immediate successors was the Abalone Alliance, which emerged from the struggle against the Diablo nuclear plant near San Luis Obispo, California.

NOTES

1. Little has been written about the antinuclear movement of the late seventies, and most of what has appeared is descriptive rather than analytical. See Marty Jezer, "Who's on First? What's on Second? A Grassroots Political Perspective on the Anti-Nuclear Movement," *WIN*, October 12, 1978, 5–12; Stephen Vogel, "'The Limits of Pro-test': A Critique of the Anti-Nuclear Movement," *Socialist Review* 54 (November–December 1980): 125–134; and Jim O'Brien, "Environmentalism as a Mass Movement: Historical Notes," *Radical America* 17, nos. 1, 2 (May June 1983): 7–27. The June 16–23, 1977, issue of *WIN*, entitled "Seabrook 2," was devoted to the Clamshell Alliance and similar organizing efforts around the country; see in particular Murray

262

Rosenblith, "Surrounded by Acres of Clams," 4–10, and Marty Jezer, "Learning from the Past to Meet the Future," 17–23.

2. Interview with Anna Gyorgy, January 26, 1985.

3. Interview with Cathy Wolff, August 25, 1985.

4. Interview with Cindy Leerer, August 25, 1985.

5. For an account of the Wyhl occupation and other European antinuclear actions, see, Anna Gyorgy and friends, *No Nukes: Everyone's Guide to Nuclear Power* (Boston: South End Press, 1979), 347.

6. Interview with Sam Lovejoy, January 26, 1985. See the account in Gyorgy, *No Nukes*, 393–402; and also the film *Lovejoy's Nuclear War*, distributed by Green Mountain Films.

7. Interview with Sam Lovejoy.

8. *Ibid.*

9. Interview with Guy Chichester, August 24, 1985.

10. Interview with Elizabeth Boardman, June 8, 1985.

11. Interview with Guy Chichester.

12. These and quoted remarks in next two paragraphs from an interview with Meg Simonds, November 13, 1984.

13. Interview with Elizabeth Boardman.

14. Interview with Richard Bell, June 7, 1985.

15. My account of this debate is drawn from interviews with many former Clams, including Harvey Halpern, who was a leader of the hard Clam group (August 25, 1985); Richard Bell, a leader of the opposition within Boston Clams (June 7, 1985); Anna Gyorgy and Sam Lovejoy (January 26, 1985), who were members of Montague Farm; and seacoast activists Cathy Wolff (August 25, 1985) and Sharon Tracy (August 24, 1985). Former Clams disagree sharply among themselves about why the organization was destroyed. The interpretation that I give here, and elsewhere in this chapter, is my own.

16. *Seabrook '78: A Handbook for the Occupation/Restoration Beginning June 24*, Clamshell Alliance, 1978, 9.

17. *Seabrook '78*, 14.

18. Interview with Harvey Halpern.

19. Interview with Richard Bell.

20. *Ibid.*

21. Interview with Murray Bookchin, May26, 1986.

22. Interview with Cathy Wolff.

23. Interview with Aikos Barton, January 17, 1986.

24. "Goal of Clamshell: Stopping Nukes and Creating a Better World" (mimeographed paper in Anna Gyorgy's archives).

25. *Seabrook '78, 10.*

26. Interview with Anna Gyorgy.

27. Interview with Aikos Barton.

28. Interview with Crystal Gray, October 3, 1985.

29. Interview with Richard Bell.

30. Interview with Cathy Wolff.

31. Interview with Richard Bell.

32. Marty Jezer discusses this problem in his article "Learning from the Past." The limited nature of the Clamshell constituency is also the subject of a pamphlet produced by a Clamshell group, "Strange Victories: The Anti-Nuclear Movement in the U.S. and Europe" (Boston: Midnight Notes Collective, 1979). The pamphlet argues (as I do here) that the social base of the antinuclear movement was mainly the middle-class youth counterculture, transplanted from the cities to the countryside, strongest in northern New England and California. The pamphlet points to the difficulties in maintaining a coalition between this group and local inhabitants uneasy about nuclear plants in their backyards, and the political cost to the Clamshell of its restricted constituency.

33. Jezer, "Learning from the Past," 21.

CONCLUSION

A PERSPECTIVE ON THE HISTORY OF AMERICAN PEACE MOVEMENTS

Charles F. Howlett

This essay details the rich and expanding historiography of the American peace movement. Howlett traces the history of peace writing from its religious-pacifist beginnings in the early nineteenth century to its professionalization and proliferation during the Vietnam War era. The author also discusses the emerging role of citizen activism, interdisciplinary approaches to the field, and the growing emphasis on transnational studies with respect to nuclear disarmament. How has the sub-field of peace history played a major role in examining American foreign policy? What led historians to promote the study of peace history? How was the discipline first greeted by practicing historians? Who were the major figures in the field and how did they influence the research of younger scholars? What accounts for the rapid expansion of peace history and its allied disciplines such as women's history and civil rights? In what ways are peace history and peace education advancing the field? Is it possible for historians and other social activists to tap the rich archival sources now available in order to draw parallels between various movements calling for change? This is a revised version of a much larger discussion that first appeared as "Studying America's Struggle Against War: An Historical Perspective." THE HISTORY TEACHER Vol. 36, no. 3 (May 2003), pp. 297-330.

A BRIEF DEFINITION AND PERSPECTIVE ON THE
DISCIPLINE OF PEACE HISTORY

American history surveys and monographs have been dominated by discourses on war.[1] The vocabulary itself -- the interwar period, postwar planning, the prewar economy, the revolutionary war generation, the irrepressible conflict strongly suggests that the United States has been in a virtual state of war throughout its history. Ironically, this emphasis on war is out of proportion to the actual amount of time Americans have spent fighting wars. The basic question educators should ask is why do historians and social studies teachers devote so much of their scholarship and teaching to war and, conversely, so little to peace studies? Why is it that peace has been the reform sought most vocally by Americans, yet remains the most elusive?[2]

The heightened passions surrounding the Vietnam War led some historians to integrate peace research into scholarship as a legitimate alternative perspective on the past. Previously, to the extent that pacifists, peace advocates, and peace movements were even included in historical monographs and textbooks, they were usually treated negatively -- denounced as misguided idealists or even traitorous. But the 1960s and decades following witnessed a significant increase in the number of peace history scholars and courses. The field itself -- defined as the historical study of nonviolent efforts for peace and social justice --became widely recognized, accepted as a sub-field of the discipline of history, and as part of a larger multidisciplinary approach known as peace studies.

The study of peace history can be classified into three categories. First, conflict management, which involves achieving peace through negotiation, mediation, arbitration, international law, and arms control and disarmament. Second, social reform, which involves changing political and economic structures and traditional ways of thinking. Third, a world order transformation, which incorporates world federation, better economic and environmental relationships, and a common feeling of security. Specifically, the discipline's basic focus has been historical analysis of peace and antiwar movements and individuals, international relations, and the causes of war and peace.[3]

SCHOLARLY BEGINNINGS

Initially, the earliest forms of peace writing were undertaken by the activists themselves--religious and sectarian pacifists who were organizing the movement from the eighteenth century and throughout the nineteenth century. Among the more representative works of this period were *The Journal of John Woolman* (ed., Frederick Tolles, 1961), Anthony Benezet, *Thoughts on the Nature of War* (1776), Noah Worcester, *A Solemn Review of the Custom of War* (1815), David Low Dodge, *War Inconsistent with the Religion of Jesus Christ* (1812), William Ladd, *The Essays of Philanthropos on Peace and War* (1827), and the letters and journals of Elihu Burritt, edited by Merle Curti as *The Learned Blacksmith: The Letters and Journals of Elihu Burritt* (1937). For the most part, this literature was didactic, personal, and geared for general audiences with Christian proclivities. There were also a few peace leaders from the Civil War to World War I who stressed the virtues of pacifism and nonresistance, notably Alfred Love of the Universal Peace Union and Benjamin Trueblood of the American Peace Society (and author of *The Federation of the World* [1899]). Additionally, Rufus Jones recounted earlier Quaker efforts for peace in *The Quakers in the American Colonies* (1911), and Margaret Hirst continued the story up to 1913 in *The Quakers in Peace and War*.[4]

It was not until the period between the two world wars when, for the first time, peace history writing came under the purview of scholarly analysis. Reflecting postwar disillusionment were William F. Galpin's *Pioneering for Peace: A Study of American Peace Efforts to 1846* (1933), Devere Allen's *The Fight For Peace* (1930), and A.F.C. Beales' *The History of Peace: A Short Account of the Organized Movements for International Peace* (1931). Each of these studies produced a critique of war influenced by economic and religious considerations. Their narratives were solid and sympathies clearly defined.[5] Yet no one approached the productivity and historical acumen of Merle Curti. Curti was the first historian to capture the rich tradition of peace efforts in the American past and bring to light the contributions of individuals and movements in the struggle against war.

In the 1920s, Curti began examining pacifist ideas and peace movements. Although not a pacifist, he was influenced by the postwar disillusionment characteristic of the writings of progressive historians Charles Beard and Carl Becker. His studies of the American peace movement took up the better part of two decades. In 1929, his Harvard University doctoral thesis was published as *The American Peace Crusade, 1815-1860*. In 1931, *Bryan and World Peace* appeared. Five years later his work culminated in the classic *Peace or War: The American Struggle, 1636-1936*, the first serious scholarly study of the American peace movement. Although, by the end of the decade, Curti supported the war against fascism, his postwar views on the development of American patriotism and its effects on the war mentality was published in 1946 as *The Roots of American Loyalty*. From the 1920s to the early Cold War years, Curti "stressed the need for open and active channels of democratic communication during wartime."[6]

Curti's historical work reflected three general assumptions about pacifist ideals and peace movements that would eventually shape the parameters of the field: an instrumentalist view that the history of pacifist ideals could help change the world; a subjective belief that the story of peace movements can be just as exciting and rewarding as accounts of battles and wars; and a rational belief in the public value of assessing the true meaning of patriotism and nationalism. "The history of this crusade," he claimed in his classic study, "is a stirring one. The struggle could be waged only at the cost of great toil and devotion and sacrifice." The movement for peace was also part and parcel of a larger development in social change: "What Americans did to limit or uproot the war system was at every point affected by the traditions and ideals of American life which were dominant in varying degrees at different times."[7] Throughout all his writings, Curti emphasized that the study of history must not dwell on the glories of war, which is only temporary and terribly destructive, but on the efforts of "rational," "intelligent," and "concerned" human beings who recognize the true value of human relationships and their enduring importance to society.[8]

Unfortunately, the conservative temper of the 1950s and early 1960s produced meager results, despite Curti's groundbreaking efforts. There were, however, some works carrying on the tradition. Prompted by the threat of atomic war and McCarthyism, Curti's former Columbia University student, Arthur A. Ekirch, Jr., examined the origins of antimilitarist thought in *The Civilian and the Military* (1956). H.C. Peterson and Gilbert Fite's *Opponents of War, 1917-1918* (1957) narrated the effects of antiwar protest and government suppression during the Great War, while Mulford Q. Sibley and Philip Jacob's *Conscription of Conscience* (1952) provided a comprehensive study of conscientious objection during World War II. These works relied heavily on primary sources and were scholarly in tone and substance.[9]

PROFESSIONALIZATION AND PROLIFERATION

The study of modern peace history resulted from two developments in professional scholarship. One was "the tremendous expansion in size and the associated drive toward increased specialization that overtook the American historical profession after 1960, at the same time as a host of change-making forces--from the civil rights to the women's movement--worked their transforming effect upon American life and the nation's historical consciousness." The other cause was the "peace research movement that emerged in the United States in the mid-1950s with the aim of applying social scientific techniques toward the resolution of the global war problem." The second development, in particular, originating at places like the University of Michigan and "boasting such figures as the economist Kenneth Boulding and the psychologist Charles Osgood," managed to bring together "a constellation of scholars who anticipated important contributions from historians in what was envisioned as a necessarily inter-disciplinary undertaking." The creation of the *Journal of Conflict Resolution* promoted the collaboration between historians and social scientific peace researchers.[10]

Immediate results were not forthcoming, however. Cold War consensus mitigated the professional historians' reception to the proposal. Yet, by the early 1960s things started to change. The call for a community of scholars from history and the social sciences prompted some members of the historical profession to promote peace history as a distinctive realm of inquiry. At the December 1963 American Historical Association meetings, radical intellectual and former Curti student at the University of Wisconsin, Arthur Waskow, along with respected scholars like Curti and Quaker historian, Edwin Bronner, formed an affiliated society, the Conference on Peace Research in History - today, the Peace History Society - to "communicate its findings to the public at large in the hope of broadening the understanding and possibilities of world peace." In 1972, the organization inaugurated its official journal, *Peace and Change*.[11]

After 1965, inspired by peace consciousness on campus, the efforts of reputable historians within professional organizations, and a growing number of mature historians disillusioned with the war, newer scholars receiving their doctorates in history thus began legitimizing the field of peace history as a professional endeavor. Opposition to an ever expanding American military presence in Southeast Asia provided a windfall for scholars anxious to examine the role of peace and antiwar activism in America's past. Peace history proliferated rapidly from the Vietnam War era to the 1980s. A considerable portion of the literature written during this period of rapid social and political change focused on issues of peace and justice and the emergence of activist-oriented peace organizations and leaders after World War I. More specialized studies began supplementing the earlier broad surveys provided by Curti, Allen, and Ekirch.

In particular, these specialized studies were most effective in their examinations of the composition of each antiwar coalition that developed. The new research showed that membership in each group is bonded by a distinct viewpoint (e.g., pacifism, world court, international government), together with social characteristics (e.g., Christianity, socialism, feminism, environmentalism) or functional programs (e.g., dramatizing issues, lobbying, educating). An antiwar constituency, therefore, attracted groups with inconsistent interests, much as opposition to World War I aligned socialists with some moderate liberals, as the position of strict neutrality in the 1930s captured both isolationists and pacifists, and as condemnation of the Vietnam War enjoined New Left radicals and conservative business leaders, as well as cold war political warriors. Complementing these new studies, moreover, was a growing interest in historic feminist peace activism.

Basically, the peace history literature of this period can be classified into six primary categories: specialized works on the story of the U.S. peace movement; peace biographies; works on the Vietnam War; insider accounts; women and peace; and anti-nuclear activism. Nicely complementing the specialized studies are surveys such as Peter Brock's massive work, *Pacifism in the United States: From the Colonial Period to the First World War* (1968), and Charles DeBenedetti's *The Peace Reform in America* (1980). DeBenedetti's contribution was designed as a classroom survey text updating both Curti's *Peace or War* and Charles Chatfield's useful anthology, *Peace Movements in America* (1972).[12]

First, the achievement of specialized works is their thorough use of primary sources. Adding both texture and context to the narrative, these studies have provided new understanding and meaning to the peace crusade as well as important criticisms regarding its successes and failures. Although the cadre of younger scholars writing about the historic aspects of the peace movement began making names for themselves, there were four studies which stood out: Lawrence Wittner's *Rebels Against War: The American Peace Movement, 1933-1983* (1969, rev. 1983), Charles Chatfield's, *For Peace and Justice: Pacifism in America, 1914-1941*(1971), C. Roland Marchand's, *The American Peace Movement and Social Reform, 1898-1918* (1972), and David S. Patterson's, *Towards a Warless World: The Travail of the American Peace Movement, 1887-1914* (1976).[13]

Rebels Against War's contribution is its extensive examination of the principles and methods, successes and failures of the active peace organizations, as well as delving into the personal papers of the various leaders of nonviolent movements. Wittner's interest in peace history was a result of his own distrust of U.S. foreign policies. As a Master's student at the University of Wisconsin, he was encouraged by Curti to update the historic role of the peace crusade. He did so by completing his studies under the direction of William Leuchtenberg at Columbia. In his efforts to link the peace movement's moral influence with political relevance, *Rebels Against War* provided new leads in peace history research: particularly, the role of organized labor movements; human rights; and the relationship in America between race relations and its international ramifications.[14] Chatfield's *For Peace and Justice* shows the transformation of pacifism from mere opposition to war to a greater concern for social reform. Chatfield's own religious pacifism was channeled into historical research by Henry Lee Swint at Vanderbilt University. He argues that "Peace was built on social justice," while dispelling many of the myths surrounding the pacifist's lack of political realism - a point Wittner also emphasizes. "Contrary to prevailing thought," Chatfield writes, "the pacifist leaders were essentially internationalist, politically active, and influential." His point: scholars and students should not dismiss so easily the role of the peace movement as a subject worthy of further examination.[15] Marchand's *The American Peace Movement and Social Reform*, studies various reform groups that joined and then dominated the movement for peace. As a graduate student at Stanford University, Marchand was encouraged to research "possibilities in the history of the peace movement" by George Harmon Knoles and Otis A. Pease. Of interest to teachers and students is Marchand's discussion of lawyers favoring a world court, business leaders supportive of international economic stability, and labor unions arguing that the victim of war was the working class - he entitled one chapter, "The Workingmen's Burden." According to Marchand, organizational patterns and "profound ideological changes" were the "hallmarks of the peace movement between 1898-1918." Peace became a "truly protean reform" because the movement against war represented "an extension of . . . domestic attitudes or programs that brought diversity and change into the movement." Like Chatfield's work, a superb bibliographic essay is appended to the text.[16] Lastly, in *Toward a Warless World,* Patterson looks at the keepers of judicial arbitration within the pre-World War I peace movement. He received his direction from Lawrence W. Levine at Berkeley. The strength of Patterson's work is the way in which he dutifully dissects the four types of peace advocates under examination: pacifists, federalists, legalists, and generalists. With a careful eye, he zeroes in on peace workers for not standing behind any one program for international reform. The shift from non-institutional pacifism to institutional pacifism, moreover, is another important contribution. Patterson elaborates on how the political culture in prewar America created elite peacemaking tendencies and how the world war transformed the movement in the direction of radical peace action. Patterson links them to his own period under discussion and drives home his point that "These groups attracted not only peace seekers disenchanted with the timidity of the peace societies and endowed organizations but impelled many more pacifistic liberals and socialists into the cause for the first time. Many of these antiwar newcomers became absolute pacifists and boldly linked peace advocacy with social justice causes."[17]

The particular contributions of these four works, published between 1969 and 1976, was in calling attention to the emergence of the "Modern American

Peace Movement" - in the late 1970s peace historian Charles DeBendetti explored its development in his own book, *The Origins of the Modern American Peace Movement, 1915-1929* (1978). According to these studies, this was a movement which sought to "advance peace as a process in human social relations." Leaders of the movement understood justice as the amelioration of social wrongs and not simply the adjudication of courts; they viewed nationalism in terms of cultural diversity rather than some form of Anglo-Saxon exclusivity; they saw war as a byproduct of militarism, nationalism, and imperialism and not merely as an irrational outburst of mass ignorance; and they sought a reformed and democratized international system by which responsible policymakers would manage peace through applied social justice and world agencies. These studies were most direct in their argument: "for peace to advance in the world, reform must advance at home through the nonviolent extension of justice under order."[18]

Although the weight of evidence in these works, as well as the many other studies published during this period, praises the efforts of peace leaders and their organizations of the past, some historians followed Curti's example of emphasizing the movement's shortcomings - particularly its middle class composition and non-radical ideology - as well. Patterson's *Toward a Warless World* examined carefully the leadership of the pre-World War I movement. What he found was that the elitism of peace advocates and the idealism embodied in their efforts both blunted attempts for meaningful peace while placing a conservative veneer over the entire movement: "The rich and powerful increasingly penetrated the hierarchies of the established peace groups and foundations. In consequence, despite its growth the peace movement never developed meaningful contacts with movements for social and political change." Moreover, he adds, peace workers were "too optimistically deterministic": ". . . in emphasizing inevitable progress, peace leaders tolerated the status quo in international life while still holding out hope for gradual evolution toward a peaceful world order"(pp. 258-59). Michael Lutzker also presents a similar argument in "The Pacifist as Militarist: A Critique of the American Peace Movement, 1898-1914," Societas 5 (Spring 1975). In his examination of leaders like Nicholas M. Butler, Elihu Root, and William H. Taft, Lutzker points out "the consensus that existed between an important segment of the leaders of the peace movement and those generally perceived as having a more military orientation" (pp. 87-104). Additionally, Charles Chatfield's *For Peace and Justice*, correctly notes that "Throughout most of the interwar period their [liberal pacifists] assertions that war is futile and the Americans must accept world responsibility and transnational values were not seriously contested. They were often ignored and their implications were disputed. . . ."(pp. 341-42).

Biographies of noted peace activists, the second category, also added a new dimension to peace historiography. Previously, most accounts were written by the activists themselves. During the charged atmosphere of the 1960s and 1970s, however, younger historians began pouring through the rich archival depositories like the Swarthmore College Peace Collection and Hoover Institution on War, Revolution and Peace. Many were interested in the lives of such individuals in contrast to the numerous works detailing the actions of famous military figures such as Generals Lee, Grant, MacArthur, Eisenhower, and Patton.

In addition to numerous scholarly biographies, including Charles F. Howlett's *Troubled Philosopher: John Dewey and the Struggle for Peace* (1977), Harold Josephson's *James T. Shotwell and the Rise of Internationalism in America* (1975), Michael Wrezin's *Oswald Garrison Villard:Pacifist at War* (1965), and Nick Salvatore's *Eugene V. Debs: Citizen and Socialist* (1982), one particular work remains a model for peace biographies: Jo Ann O. Robinson's *Abraham Went Out: A Biography of A.J. Muste* (1981). This carefully researched work details the public activities of America's most famous pacifist leader in the 20th century.[19]

Robinson's work remains unique in the way in which she interweaves her narrative with a clear focus on "the history of the journey of the soul of A.J.

Muste from a deeply religious Dutch Reformed background to a leading place among pacifists, antiwar spokesmen, and fighters for the civil rights of workers and American minorities." Robinson's interest in Muste's commitment to social change had developed as a graduate student at Johns Hopkins and while teaching at Morgan State University. Unlike many biographies praising their subjects, Robinson explains the "personal development of this complex personality who was given to brooding, mystical experiences and an apparent sense of indignant self-righteousness." Her analysis of Muste's abandonment and then return to pacifism in the 1930s is a must read for those seeking to understand the dilemmas conscientious objectors face when encouraged to employ force against the state. *Abraham Went Out* presents a thorough account of a "hard-nosed, dedicated believer in peace and in the dignity of all humanity." This biography constitutes a complete discussion of the "development of radical pacifism in the U.S. during the twentieth century and one which convincingly places Muste in the forefront of this movement."[20]

Having received its impetus during the Vietnam War, the field of peace history soon encompassed that war, at first with popular accounts like Thomas Powers, *The War at Home: Vietnam and the American People, 1964-1968* (1973), and Nancy Zaroulis and Gerald Sullivan, *Who Spoke Up? American Protest against the War in Vietnam* (1984). These were followed by a growing number of carefully research scholarly works representing the third category.[21]

Of the many works analyzing antiwar protest, Charles DeBenedetti and Charles Chatfield's, *An American Ordeal: The Anti-war Movement of the Vietnam Era* (1990), remains the most comprehensive and inclusive study available. The book was completed by Chatfield after DeBenedetti's death in 1987. De Benedetti had an established reputation in the field and studied American foreign policy under the direction of Norman Grabner at the University of Illinois. As a comprehensive and interpretative history of the antiwar movement, *An American Ordeal* begins with "the rise of a liberal peace movement against atmospheric nuclear testing from 1955 to 1963" to "the emergence of radical pacifists and politically motivated groups who eventually created a diverse coalition" against the war, and, finally, culminating in "how extremist elements came to dominate the movement in the late 1960s" only "to be supplanted by a larger consensus of liberal and pacifist groups in the early 1970s."[22] The work's greatest contribution to Vietnam peace scholarship is the authors' appreciation of the difficulties encountered in trying to analyze the subject. In *An American Ordeal* three motifs characterized the antiwar movement: (1) the belief that modern life was "devolving into institutional insanity"; (2) "critics of the war perceived a growing moral deafness in American life." The Cold War arms race "discouraged democratic participation in the political process and eroded moral judgments" among policymakers; and (3) the antiwar opposition "was grounded in an ethic of personal moral commitment." Most notably, the forces "arrayed against the war were amorphous and 'overwhelmingly local.'"[23]

One of the unique aspects of the Vietnam era is the number of insider accounts available. Despite some rather interesting reads, Fred Halstead's *Out Now! A Participant's Account of the American Movement Against the Vietnam War* (1978) is indispensable. Unlike many personalized accounts which discuss numerous side bars to one's life, *Out Now!* sticks entirely to the war itself.[24]

Halstead pulls no punches. A dedicated socialist, Halstead closely examines the struggles to end the Vietnam War. He disagrees totally with those who insist that radical opposition tactics helped prolong the war. In his opinion, antiwar agitation and mass mobilizations achieved five primary objectives. First, "It changed the political face of the United States and a healthy distrust of the rulers in Washington." Second, "It broke the fever of the anticommunist hysteria and weakened the efficacy of the 'red scares.'" Third, "It challenged and changed the stereotyped image of GIs as obedient pawns of the brass." Fourth, "The abhorrence of any further military ventures abroad has restricted the options available to Washington" - for a period of time that was the case, indeed! Fifth,

278

"The American movement against the Vietnam War broke the pattern of large and successful movements for social reform." Readers interested in radical critique of the war, based upon a personalist perspective, can either agree or disagree with Halstead's interpretation that "The American movement against the Vietnam War knocked a gaping hole in the theory that because of its control over the military, the police, the economy, and the tremendously effective modern media, the ruling class could get away with anything so long as there was some degree of prosperity."[25]

One of the most important byproducts of the 1960s social protest movements was the growing radicalization of female activism. Emboldened by Betty Friedan's monumental work, *The Feminine Mystique* (1962), a wave of young female scholars began connecting international peace and domestic justice as issues important to women. An essential survey to consult is Harriet Hyman Alonso's *Peace as a Women's Issue: A History of the U.S. Movement for World Peace and Women's Rights* (1993). Alonso quickly established herself as a leader in women's peace history after completing her doctorate at SUNY-Stony Brook. Starting in the mid-1980s, Alonso went beyond standard studies on women's peace activism by maintaining that "women's political agendas and their general belief that only a world without war can provide a climate in which women's equality can flourish." Exploring the dynamics of political feminism in the peace crusade became an important focal point in her research. Thus, four major themes characterizing peace as a feminist enterprise during the nineteenth and twentieth centuries are highlighted in her survey: (1) women who saw the relationship between women's rights and peace issues made the connection "between institutional violence and violence against women"; (2) feminist pacifists defined this connection by "condemning militarism and government oppression as well as the social and economic exploitation of women"; (3) the cause of sexual, physical and psychological abuse of women was placed at the doorstep of the male power structure; and (4) Alonzo also "reveals the linkages between white women's work for the abolition of slavery, their identification with the sexual degradation of female slaves and their consciousness of their own oppression." Tying these connections together "was a concern for nonviolent resistance as a means and a measure of determining relationships."[26]

Most notably, the new female peace scholarship of the post-Vietnam period challenged the long-held concept of women as mothers as the basic organizing principle behind their peace activities. The old Victorian notion that women were the guardians of moral standards in society and sought nothing more came under attack as female peace historians began identifying "the motherhood theme as a conscious political tool."[27]

Numerous works reflected the view that "women's political agendas" for full equality were directly linked to a warless world. Among the works promoting this theme is Amy Swerdlow's, *Women Strike for Peace: Traditional Motherhood and Radical Politics in the 1960s* (1993).

Swerdlow's careful study of an organization she helped found is most rewarding. It is a mature work which developed while completing her graduate studies at Rutgers University. The strength of her book is the view that "WSP's militant struggle against militarism in the 1960s helped to give dignity to the denigrated term housewife and to change the image of the good mother from passive to militant, from silent to eloquent, from private to public." The real virtue of this work is exposing "one of the most powerful myths of male militarists - that wars are waged by men to protect women and children." Moreover, "By making a recognized contribution to the achievement of a test ban, the demise of MLF, the withdrawal of U.S. troops from Vietnam, and the end of the draft for Vietnam, WSP also raised its participants' sense of political efficacy and self-esteem as women." Perhaps the book's most telling contribution is describing how her organization made nuclear arms a women's issue. In doing so, "the women who build on traditional female consciousness to enter the political arena do not have to be trapped in that culture or bound forever to stereotypical notions of maternal rights and responsibilities."[28]

The last major category during this period of proliferating peace histories dealt with the spiraling arms race. Peace advocates had never lost focus on the larger issues of the Cold War despite dramatic efforts to halt the war in Vietnam. "Antinuclear activism mushroomed across the country in the 1970s," but its primary objective had been to curb construction of power plants. By 1979 concern over nuclear war expanded and a Nuclear Weapons Freeze Campaign emerged "which grew spectacularly for three years." Led by such diverse groups as the pacifist Atlantic Life Community, traditional peace organizations like the Fellowship of Reconciliation and War Resisters League, and the civil resisters of the Honeywell Project, the peace movement after Vietnam gradually "understood that all issues were interrelated - peace and justice at home, order and revolution abroad, militarism and environment everywhere - but also that political effectiveness required attainable priorities around which to mobilize public support." As activists prepared to address the threat of nuclear annihilation, concerned scholars attempted to catch the spirit of protest in their own writings on the subject.[29]

Previously, the sobering experience of McCarthyism and Cold War hostilities had quieted the historical profession's interest in peace scholarship. One of the ironies of the post World War II period was that anti-revisionist liberals, fearful of a return to a post World War I pattern of isolationist pacifism, resorted to a militant, interventionist nationalism. These war liberals, who previously championed a leftist cause, were now competing with conservatives for leadership in the battle against Communism. The entire theory of containment and of peace through force strengthened the position of the military in American postwar diplomacy. 1950s peace work was not only considered subversive, but meager at best.[30]

Although the scholarship was minimal, the activities of pacifists and their organizations continued in spite of the suspension of civil liberties. It was left to post-Vietnam scholars to uncover and record the various strains of peace activism related to arms control and anti-nuclear protests. Tracing the earliest forms of protest is James Tracy, *Direct Action: Radical Pacifism From the Union Eight to the Chicago Seven* (1996). Nonviolent resisters championed the cause of civil disobedience. Leaders like A.J. Muste, Dave Dellinger, Staughton Lynd, and Bayard Rustin managed to develop an experimental style which revitalized American radicalism and social protest in the 1950s and 1960s shaping later civil rights, antiwar, and antinuclear movements. According to Tracy, who completed his doctorate under Estelle Freedman at Stanford, "the radical pacifist program of direction action, decentralism, and participatory democracy within organizations has continued to deeply inform American protest since the Vietnam era, as is evident in the history of the antinuclear and environmental movements of recent decades." In particular, *Direct Action* demonstrates that the goal of these activists was not simply one of avoiding nuclear annihilation, but also the renewal of society by using one's life as the agent of social change.

Like some of the specialized era studies, Tracy looks more closely at individuals' actions rather than the movements they helped perpetuate. The activists own notion of "personalism" ultimately demanded individual accountability for the benefit of the community.[31]

While certain works probed deeply into social change activism--that is, the issue of nuclear disarmament became tied to morality and this, in turn, heightened protestors commitment to activism--more conventional studies surveyed the historical origins of the fight against weapons of mass destruction. Looking closely at the efforts of Norman Cousins and his politically-correct Committee for a SANE Nuclear Policy is Milton S. Katz's *Ban the Bomb: A History of SANE, the Committee for a SANE Nuclear Policy* (1986). Noted diplomatic historian Robert A. Devine adds his perspective in *Blowing on the Wind: The Nuclear Test*

Ban Debate, 1954-1960 (1978). The most perceptive work published during the post Vietnam era, however, is Paul Boyer's *By the Bomb's Early Light: American Thought and Culture at the Dawn of the Atomic Age* (1985).

Boyer's work represents a contribution to original scholarship. Harvard trained and Merle Curti Professor of History at the University of Wisconsin, Boyer persuasively focuses on "the bomb's effects on American culture and consciousness." Boyer questions the American public's switch from activism to apathy. In an earlier article, which became the basis for this book, he presented a chilling forecast dampening pacifist enthusiasm for the prospects of total disarmament. What led to a general feeling of arms control assurance on the one hand, while, on the other, nuclear weapons research, construction, and deployment proceeded at a rapid pace after 1963? In Boyer's analysis, "the perception of diminished risk," fading "memories of Hiroshima and Nagasaki" along with the downplaying of civil defense, the "neutralizing effect of the 'peaceful atom'" marked by power plant construction in the 1970s, "defense intellectuals" transforming "nuclear strategy into a rarified quasi-scientific discipline," and the "effects of the Vietnam War and rise of the New Left" created a void in the campaign to eliminate nuclear weapons which would only resuscitate itself in the early 1980s. Scanning the historical landscape from the end of the 1963 Nuclear Test Ban Treaty to the signing of the Camp David Accords, Boyer keenly observes, demonstrated that "most Americans had seemed at least superficially oblivious to a mortal danger that many in earlier years had considered the most urgent ever to confront the nation and, indeed, the entire human family."[32]

Collectively, the peace scholarship of the Vietnam period and subsequent years attempted to explain the influence of the peace movement as a whole upon the rest of American society and on the way that national and international events impacted the thoughts and attitudes of peace seekers and their organizations. Some of the important contributions these studies offered were tying the efforts of voluntary peace groups to policymakers in national government, explaining how new peace organizations proved useful in keeping the issue of peace in the public consciousness, developing searching criticisms of American foreign policy with regards to its capitalistic and imperialistic dimensions, and, most importantly, explaining various factors in the culture that worked against the tireless efforts of dedicated antiwar advocates: namely, the relation of consumerism, leisure, profit, and patriotism to the value of peace. New connections were also being made with respect to American social thought and domestic political policies in time of war as well as in peace.

CITIZEN ACTIVISM, INTERDISCIPLINARY AND TRANSNATIONAL TRENDS

Since the late 1980s peace history research has benefited from studies on citizen activism. Sam Marullo's *Ending the Cold War at Home: From Militarism to a More Peaceful World Order* (1994), Paul Wehr, Heidi Burgess, and Guy Burgess, eds., *Justice Without Violence* (1994), and Robert Elias and Jennifer Turpin, eds., *Rethinking Peace* (1994) offer interesting case studies and theoretical analyses premised on establishing a politics of pacifism; such peace consciousness is based on encouraging citizen awareness for respecting individual judgment while at the same time transforming it into a form of collective responsibility. The enhancement of democracy, environmentalism, human rights, and economic security rests upon concerned citizens and their commitment to social change.[33]

More recently, the journal *Peace and Change* has expanded the dimensions of citizen-peace activism in two special issues: Wendy E. Chmielewski and Michael S. Foley, eds., "The Politics of Peace Movements," Vol. 26 (July 2001); and "Non-Governmental Organizations and the Vietnam War" with a special introduction by historian George C. Herring, Vol. 27 (April 2002). The role of Non-Governmental Organizations (NGOs) is especially interesting and adaptable for classroom discussion. While the "Cold War divided the globe," NGOs "attempted to pull it together by breaking down national boundaries through such things as good works, development projects, and efforts to improve communications, understanding, and cooperation among different peoples." As a new field of inquiry in diplomatic and peace history, it raises many interesting issues for consideration. The interest in shifting the direction of their societies has also encourage peace activists to work on many levels, "including traditional paths to political power, through parties, legislative politics, bureaucracies, and other governmental hierarchies" while some "deemed it essential to remain separate from those traditional lines of access to political power and the state" due to their own personal belief that state action is equated with the continuance of violence.[34]

Interesting issues for classroom discussion are how NGOs work without government support and how the proliferation of national groups like Amnesty International and community groups such as Atlantic Life Community have evolved beyond traditional religious peace groups and non-sectarian antiwar organizations. Seeking to avoid state sponsorship, voluntary sector grassroots development organizations are rapidly multiplying throughout the world. Yet, little research has been conducted to determine their successes and failures. As a topic worthy of additional research, scholars would do well to examine the role of NGOs as part of peace history. Perhaps the most important issue to discuss is that "Advocates of decentralized, people-centered development, in governmental and international funding agencies, are turning to them, hoping they can do what forty years of centralized, top-down, capital-centered development has failed to: produce nonviolent, just, and sustainable development."[35]

Today, peace history has also benefited from some excellent interdisciplinary studies. A fine example is David S. Meyer's political analysis, *A Winter of Discontent: The Nuclear Freeze and American Politics* (1990). Sociologists have brought resource mobilization analysis from social movement theory to peace history, notably in Robert Kleidman's comparative study, *Organizing for Peace: Neutrality, the Test Ban and the Freeze* (1993), John Lofland's more theoretical, *Polite Protestors: The Peace Movement of the 1980s* (1993), Sam Marullo and John Lofland's, eds., *Peace Action in the Eighties: Social Science Perspectives* (1990), Steve Breyman's "Were the 1980s Anti-Nuclear Weapons Movements New Social Movements?," *Peace and Change* (July 1997), and Charles Chatfield's *The American Peace Movement: Ideals and Activism* (1992).[36]

Since the Vietnam period one of the more innovative developments in the field has been a focus on international dimensions. It is not that peace movements abroad have been ignored over the years. Rather, given the realization that we live in an increasingly closer world marked by significant developments in communications and transportation, peace historians are now calling for more attention to the transnational perspective of peace activism; they are relating the U.S. movement to peace advocacy abroad and to global markets. In a geopolitical context, researchers are now going beyond traditional diplomatic history. Initially, in his *Twentieth Century Pacifism* (1970), Peter Brock set the precedent by investigating the application of various kinds of pacifism in a transnational framework, and W.H. Van der Linder compiled *The International Peace Movement, 1815-1874* (1988). Vincent C. Kavaloski's "Transnational Citizen Peacemaking as Nonviolent Action," *Peace and Change* (April 1990) examines citizen diplomacy involving Nicaragua and the former Soviet Union. "Much international citizen activity," Kavoloski insists, "constitutes nonviolent resistance, specifically nonviolent social intervention." Like other studies focusing on grass-roots activity, the primary aim "is to undermine 'enemy images'" and thus help to build a global peace culture beyond the often adversarial nation-state system."

Additional studies have explored the interaction of peace movements and diplomacy, especially Solomon Wank, ed., *Doves and Diplomats: Foreign Offices and Peace Movements in Europe and America in the Twentieth Century* (1978), Jackie Smith, Charles Chatfield, and Ron Pagnucco, eds., *Transnational Social Movements and Global Politics: Solidarity beyond the State* (1997), and Charles Chatfield and Peter van den Dungen, eds., *Peace Movements and Political Cultures* (1998).[37]

These particular studies seek to overcome nationalistic biases and inherent cultural differences in the name of world peace. In the late 1980s and early 1990s, as Cold War hostilities ceased to exist, scholars from various parts of the world shared information regarding the roles of their own native peace movements. At first, prompted by fears of a nuclear holocaust, and, later, encouraged by citizen activism, historians gladly talked about the historical underpinnings of their own nation's peace groups to abolish war. The scholarly research that has developed looks at how each nation defines its own security and how loyalty to the nation state can be transcended into respect for the world community.

These studies represent the first step in analyzing the historical roots of global consciousness. Thus, as more and more historians find transnational links in the struggle against war, cultural and political differences will gradually dissipate in favor of humankind. Teachers and students should examine the efforts of the American Peace History Society, Nobel Institute, and International Peace Research Association. In conjunction, these groups have organized annual conferences under the leadership of the Peace History Commission thereby offering fresh scholarship on international aspects of peacemaking.[38]

There are some interesting approaches on the horizon. Recently, the editor of this volume has undertaken an extensive study of case law in American courts as it relates to anti-draft protests, free speech, and conscientious objection. In "Case Law Historiography in American Peace History," *Peace and Change* (January 1997), a discussion offers examples of the utility of employing case law in the classroom as a way of teaching more effectively the legal and moral implications involving antiwar activism in 20th century America. The focus of this research deals with the complexities of reconciling conscience with statutory enforcement. According to Howlett, "no unified and universal theory of antiwar rights and responsibilities exist. The interests of conscientious objectors as well as antiwar activists have received only limited judicial protection." He also suggests how these cases can be written into plays as part of a lesson plan.[39]

Teams of U.S. and Russian historians have also surveyed concepts of peace in western civilization from antiquity to 1945 in *Peace/Mir: An Anthology of Historic Alternative to War*, edited by Charles Chatfield and Ruzanna Ilukhina (1994 in English and Russian). Most impressively, Lawrence Wittner has been wandering the globe in a tireless effort to chronicle the worldwide popular struggle against nuclear weapons. A planned trilogy, the first two volumes have presented the first comprehensive account of international nuclear disarmament activism: *The Struggle Against the Bomb, One World or None: A History of the World Nuclear Disarmament Movement Through 1953* (1993), *Resisting the Bomb, 1954-1970,* (1997), and *Toward Nuclear Abolition, 1971 to the Present* (2003).[40]

Wittner's research, moreover, represents a prodigious effort. He has taken the study of the peace movement to a new transnational level. His research has been conducted in fifteen countries, examining over a hundred peace groups and government agencies, and he has looked at recently declassified files from the U.S. State Department, the Atomic Energy Authority of Great Britain, and the Central Committee of the Communist Party of the Soviet Union. Combined with personal interviews and peace movement periodicals, his work offers "a vivid panorama of the global antinuclear campaign" and provides "startling revelations about the efforts of government officials to repress, contain, and, finally, accommodate to popular protest." In compelling terms, Wittner challenges the conventional explanation "that the Bomb itself has deterred nuclear war." The expressed purpose of his research is "to grapple with the question of why despite the clear necessity of freeing humanity from a the threat of nuclear destruction, that movement has not been more effective." As one reviewer noted: "Lawrence S. Wittner's trilogy is innovative because it is a transnational story--the vast social movement beyond national boundaries that was roused by the threat of nuclear disaster."[41]

CONCLUSION

The evolution of peace history writing has come a long way, especially in the last half of the twentieth century. The ebb and flow of peace history scholarship has generally followed four paths: the writings of pacifists and peace activists from the War of 1812 to the start of World War I; the early synthesis of peace history occurring between the two world wars, marked mainly by Curti's scholarly works; the remarkable proliferation of works from the Vietnam War to the late 1980s; and newly published studies involving international and interdisciplinary trends, capped by non-government initiatives.[42] Much of the present scholarship focuses on social movements and citizen activism. The large body of works is testimony to its viability and current interest as a scholarly endeavor. "Peace activists," as Larry Wittner argues, "have been sentimental and naïve, but no more so, and arguably less so, than supporters of war. Unmoved by fantasies of national glory, martial valor, and other romantic notions of the warmakers, they have often been quite realistic about the causes and consequences of international conflict." Certainly, "as war has grown more total, even genocidal, the basis for assessing what is, in fact, realistic has shifted substantially."[43]

The argument among scholars regarding the effectiveness of peace activism and its place in history will not abate anytime soon.[44] The recent events in the Middle East have certainly served to question the degree of influence peace historians have had on foreign policy and whether peace history should seek greater acceptance and influence within mainstream American history or emphasize a separate, activist ethos. Nevertheless, peace historians are hard at work cataloguing and interpreting "the complex strata of assumptions about values and ideals, individual and social nature, conflict and its resolution, from diverse periods and cultural contexts--from antiquity to the cold war" and after. The result has been "a very large body of literature."[45] The profusion of peace history literature has, in the words of the late historian Charles DeBenedetti, one primary objective: to provide "a cohering, compelling vision of a realizable global order in which different peoples would preserve their various traditional values without relying upon a war system that requires well-armed preparedness, threats, and ultimately mass violence."[46] The challenge continues as it had for the early peace pioneers as well as the scholars who began recording the history of the movement during the early years of the last century.

END NOTES

1. For a curriculum on peace and war issues designed for secondary school teachers consult, William A. Nesbitt, ed., *Teaching about War and Its Control: A Selective Annotated Bibliography for the Social Studies Teacher*. Albany, N.Y.: State Education Department, 1972.

2. See Charles F. Howlett & Glen Zeitzer, *The American Peace Movement: History and Historiography*. Washington, D.C.: American Historical Association, 1986: 1-3; Charles DeBenedetti, "Peace History in the American Manner," *The History Teacher* 18 (November 1984): 75-110; Lawrence S. Wittner, "Peace Movements and Foreign Policy: The Challenge to Diplomatic Historians," *Diplomatic History* XI (Fall 1987): 355-70; Gerloff Homan, "Peace History: A Bibliographical Overview," *Choice* (May 1995): 1408-1419; Charles Chatfield, "Peace Movements," in Neil Smelser and Paul Baltes, eds., *Encyclopeida of the Social and Behavioral Sciences*. Amsterdam: Pergamon, 2002, contains an historiographical underpinning.

3. Jeffrey Kimball, "Alternatives to War in History," *OAH Magazine of History* 8 (Spring 1994): 5-9; Charles Chatfield, "Peace as a Reform Movement," *OAH Magazine of History* 8 (Spring 1994): 10-14.

4. Consult Charles F. Howlett, *The American Peace Movement: References and Resources*. Boston: G.K. Hall & Co., 1991; Howlett, "Peace History: The Field and the Sources," *OAH Magazine of History* 8 (Spring 32; Howlett & Zeitzer, *The American Peace Movement*, 55-64.

5. William F. Galpin, *Pioneering for Peace*. Syracuse: Syracuse University Press, 1933; Devere Allen, *The Fight for Peace*. N.Y.: Macmillan Co., 1930; A.F.C. Beales, *The History of Peace*. London & N.Y.: Dial Press, 1931.

290

6. Quoted in Charles F. Howlett, "Merle Curti and the Significance of Peace Research in American History," *Peace and Change* 25 (October 2000): 431-466. See Curti's works: *The American Peace Crusade, 1815-1860*. Durham, N.C.: Duke University Press, 1929; *Bryan and World Peace*. Northampton, MA.: Smith College Studies, 1931; *Peace or War*. N.Y.: W.W. Norton & Co., 1936; *The Roots of American Loyalty*. N.Y.: Columbia University Press, 1946.

7. Curti, Peace or War, 13-14. Merle Curti capped off his own contributions in the field of peace history in his "Reflections on the Genesis and Growth of Peace History," *Peace and Change* 11 (Spring 1985): 1-15. See also, John Pettegrew, "The Present-Minded Professor: Merle Curti's Work as an Intellectual Historian," *The History Teacher* 32 (November 1998): 67-76. Former student, G. D. Lillibridge, wrote a fond recollection, "So Long, Maestro: A Portrait of Merle Curti," *American Scholar* 66 (Spring 1997): 263-70.

8. These observations were also included in Paul Lewis Todd and Merle Curti's popular textbook, *America's History*. N.Y.: Harcourt, Brace, Jovanovich, 1950. The high school social studies textbook, later renamed, *The Rise of the American Nation*, became one of the most widely-used books in secondary schools throughout the nation from the 1950s to early 1980s. It was also the first high school text to devote sections to the study of peace movements in America. It bucked the traditional pattern of promoting the martial spirit as part of patriotic indoctrination.

9. Arthur A. Ekirch, Jr., *The Civilian and the Military*. N.Y.: Oxford University Press, 1956; H.C. Peterson & Gilbert Fite, *Opponents of War*. Madison: University of Wisconsin Press, 1957; Mulford Q. Sibley and Philip E. Jacob, *Conscription of Conscience*. Ithaca, N.Y.: Cornell University Press, 1952. Recent works detailing the role of conscientious objection include: Peter Brock, editor, *Liberty and Conscience: A Documentary History of the Experiences of Conscientious Objectors in America through the Civil War*. New York: Oxford University Press, 2002; Charles C. Moskos & John W. Chambers II, editors, *The New Conscientious Objection: From Sacred to Secular Resistance*. New York: Oxford University Press, 1993; Theron F. Schlabach & Richard T. Hughes, editors, *Proclaim Peace: Christian Pacifism from Unexpected Quarters*. Urbana: University of Illinois Press, 1997; and Rachael Waltner Goossen, *Women Against the Good War: Conscientious Objection and Gender on the American Home Front, 1941-1947*. Chapel Hill: University of North Carolina Press, 1997.

10. DeBenedetti, "Peace History in the American Manner," 76-77.

11. F. Hilary Conroy, "The Conference on Peace Research in History: A Memoir," *Journal of Peace Research* 4 (1969): 385-88. Minutes of CPRH By-Laws (1971, 1972), Swarthmore College Peace Collection, Document Group 94, Swarthmore College. See also, Charles DeBenedetti & Charles Chatfield, *An American Ordeal: The Antiwar Movement of the Vietnam Era* . Syracuse: Syracuse University Press, 1990, *passim*.

12. Peter Brock, *Pacifism in the United States*. Princeton: Princeton University Press, 1968; Charles DeBenedetti, *The Peace Reform in America*. Bloomington: Indiana University Press, 1980; Charles Chatfield, ed., *Peace Movements in America*. N.Y.: Schocken Books, 1972. A recent historical survey from the friendly pacifist persuasion is James C. Juhnke & Carol M. Hunter, *The Missing Peace: The Search for Nonviolent Alternatives in United States History*. Kitchener, Ontario: Pandora Press, 2001. Consult also the interesting interpretation offered by Mel Small, *Democracy & Diplomacy: The Impact of Domestic Politics on U.S. Foreign Policy, 1789-1994*. Baltimore: The Johns Hopkins University Press, 1996.

13. David S. Patterson, *Toward a Warless World: The Travail of the American Peace Movement, 1887-1914*. Bloomington: Indiana University Press, 1976; Warren F. Keuhl, *Seeking World Order: The United States and International Organization to 1920*. Nashville: TN.: Vanderbilt University Press, 1969; C. Roland Marchand, *The American Peace Movement and Social Reform: 1898-1918*. Princeton: Princeton University Press, 1972; Sondra R. Herman, *Eleven Against War: Studies in American Internationalist Thought, 1898-1921*. Stanford, CA.: Hoover Institution Press, 1969; Charles Chatfield, *For Peace and Justice: Pacifism in America, 1914-1941*. Knoxville: University of Tennessee Press, 1971; Charles DeBenedetti, *The Origins of the Modern American Peace Movement, 1915-1929*. Millwood, NY: KTO Press, 1978; Justus Doenecke, *Not To the Swift: The Old Isolationists in the Cold War Era*. Lewisburg, PA.: Bucknell University Press, 1979; Ernest C. Bolt, *Ballots before Bullets: The War Referendum Approach to Peace in America, 1914-1941*. Charlottesville: University of Virginia Press, 1977; Lawrence S. Wittner, *Rebels Against War: The American Peace Movement, 1933-1983*. Philadelphia: Temple University Press, 1969 rev. 1984; Michael B. Friedland, *Lift Up Your Voice Like a Trumpet: White Clergy and the Civil Rights and Antiwar Movements, 1954-1973*. Chapel Hill: University of North Carolina Press, 1998; Eileen Eagan, *Class, Culture, and the Classroom: The Student Peace Movement of the 1930s*. Philadelphia: Temple University Press, 1981; Van Gosse, *Where the Boys Are: Cuba, Cold War America and the Making of the New Left*. NY: Verso, 1993; Patricia McNeal, *Harder Than War: Catholic Peacemaking in Twentieth Century America*. New Brunswick, NJ: Rutgers University Press, 1992; Valerie Zeiger, *Advocates of Peace in Antebellum America*. Bloomington: Indiana University Press, 1993; Robert David Johnson, *The Peace Progressives and American Foreign Relations*. Cambridge, MA.: Harvard University Press, 1995; John W. Chambers, II, ed., *The Eagle and the Dove: The American Peace Movement and United States Foreign Policy, 1900-1922*. Syracuse; Syracuse University Press, 1991; Staughton Lynd, ed., *Non-Violence in America: A Documentary History*. Indianapolis, IN.: Bobbs-Merrill & Co., 1966. Lynd's anthology was widely used in college classrooms during the Vietnam War.

14. Howlett, *The American Peace Movement: References and Resources*, xl-xli, 207; Wittner, *Rebels Against War*, 54-56; Blanche Cook's review in *American Historical Review* 75 (December 1969), 618-619. One effort to explore links between the labor and peace movements, for example, is found in Charles F. Howlett, *Brookwood Labor College and the Struggle for Peace and Social Justice in America*. Lewiston, NY: Edwin Mellen Press, 1993.

15. Chatfield, *For Peace and Justice*, 3-8, 428-29; Howlett, *The American Peace Movement*, 186; Chatfield, "World War I and the Liberal Pacifist in the United States," *American Historical Review* 61 (December 1970): 1920-37.

16. Marchand, *The American Peace Movement and Social Reform*, 4-9, 381-90.

17. Patterson, *Toward a Warless World*, passim. See also, David S. Patterson, "Citizen Peace Initiatives and American Political Culture, 1865-1920," in Charles Chatfield & Peter van den Dungen, eds., *Peace Movements and Political Cultures*. Knoxville: University of Tennessee Press, 1988, 200.

18. DeBenedetti, *Origins of the Modern American Peace Movement, passim;* DeBenedetti, *The Peace Reform in American History*, 105-107.

19. Jo Ann O. Robinson, *Abraham Went Out: A Biography of A.J. Muste*. Philadelphia: Temple University Press, 1981; Robert Moats Miller, *How Shall They Hear without a Preacher?*

292

The Life of Ernest Fremont Tittle Chapel Hill: University of North Carolina Press, 1977; Charles F. Howlett, *Troubled Philosopher: John Dewey and the Struggle for World Peace.* Port Washington, NY: Kennikat Press, 1977; Albert Marrin, *Nicholas Murray Butler.* Boston: Twayne Publishers, 1976; Harold Josephson, *James T. Shotwell and the Rise of Internationalism in America.* Rutherford, NJ: Fairleigh Dickinson University Press, 1975; Bernard K. Johnpoll, *Pacifist's Progress: Norman Thomas and the Decline of American Socialism.* Chicago: Quadrangle Books, 1970; Nick Salvatore, *Eugene V. Debs: Citizen and Socialist.* Urbana: University of Illinois Press, 1982; Michael Wreszin, *Oswald Garrison Villard: Pacifist at War.* Bloomington: Indiana University Press, 1965; Joseph F. Wall, *Andrew Carnegie.* NY: Oxford University Press, 1970; Stephen J. Whitefield, *Scott Nearing: Apostle of American Radicalism.* NY: Columbia University Press, 1974; Charles Chatfield, Blanche W. Cook, & Sandi Cooper, eds., *The Garland Library of War and Peace.* New York: Garland Publishers, 1971; Charles DeBenedetti, ed., *Peace Heroes in Twentieth Century America.* Bloomington: Indiana University press, 1986. The role of African-American leaders involved in the peace movement is sorely lacking. DeBenedetti's work does include an essay on Martin Luther King, Jr. One interesting article on the matter is Jennifer D. Keene, "W.E.B. Du Bois and the Wounded World: Seeking Meaning in the First World War for African-Americans," *Peace and Change* 26 (April 2001): 135-52. However, much more work needs to be done in this area. Simon Hall's new work does much to shed light on the failure of the peace movement to align itself with the civil rights movement during the Vietnam War. Consult, Simon Hall, *Peace and Freedom: the Civil Rights and Antiwar Movements in the 1960s* .Philadelphia: University of Pennsylvania Press, 2005.

20. Consult review in *Journal of American History* 70 (September 1983): 449-450. A useful narrative account of Muste's life is Nate Hentoff, *Peace Agitator: The Story of A.J. Muste.* New York: McMillan Co., 1963.

21. Thomas Powers, *The War at Home: Vietnam and the American People.* Boston: G.K. Hall & Co., 1973; Nancy Zaroulis and Gerald Sullivan, *Who Spoke Up? American Protest Against the War in Vietnam* Garden City, NY: Doubleday & Co., 1984; Charles DeBenedetti and Charles Chatfield, *An American Ordeal; Mel Small, Johnson, Nixon and the Doves.* New Brunswick, NJ: Rutgers University Press, 1988; Andrew Hunt, *The Turning: Vietnam Veterans Against the War.* NY: New York University Press, 1999; Richard Moser, *The New Winter Soldiers: GI and Veteran Dissent during the Vietnam Era.* New Brunswick, NJ: Rutgers University Press, 1996; Terry H. Anderson, *The Movement and the Sixties: Protest in American from Greensboro to Wounded Knee.* NY: Oxford University Press, 1995; Rhodri Jeffreys-Jones, *Peace Now! American Society and the Ending of the Vietnam War* New Haven, CT: Yale University Press, 1999; Kenneth J. Heineman, *Campus War: The Peace Movement at American State Universities in the Vietnam Era.* NY: New York University Press, 1993; Mel Small and William D. Hoover, eds., *Give Peace a Chance: Exploring the Vietnam Antiwar Movement.* Syracuse: Syracuse University Press, 1992; Marc Jason Gilbert, *The Vietnam War on Campus, More Distant Drums.* Westport, CT: Praeger, 2001; "Vietnam War Forum," special issue, *Peace and Change* 20 (April 1995) - of interest to teachers is an article by Sandra C. Taylor, "Teaching the Vietnam War in the 1990s: A Personal View," 250-63.

22. DeBenedetti & Chatfield, *An American Ordeal,* 1-3, 387-408.

23. Consult review in *Journal of American History* 78 (June 1991): 395-96.

24. Michael Ferber & Staughton Lynd, eds., *The Resistance.* Boston: Beacon Press, 1971; Daniel Berrigan, *To Dwell in Peace.* San Francisco, CA: Harper & Row, 1987; David Dellinger, *From Yale to Jail: Life of a Moral Dissenter.* NY: Pantheon, 1993; Fred Halstead, *Out*

Now!: A Participant's Account of the American Movement Against the Vietnam War NY: Monad press, 1978; Tom Hayden, *Reunion: A Memoir*. NY: Random House, 1998; Sidney Lens, *Unreprentant Radical: An American Activist's Account of Five Turbulent Decades*. Boston: Beacon Press, 1980; Anne Klejment, *The Berrigans: A Bibliography of Published Writings by Daniel, Philip, and Elizabeth McAlister Berrigan*. NY: Garland Publishers, 1979. The Berrigan bibliography needs updating.

25. Halstead, *Out Now!*, 1-2, 728-29.

26. Harriet Hyman Alonso, "One Woman's Journey into the World of Women's Peace History," *Women's Studies Quarterly* XXIII (Fall/Winter 1995): 170-71; This special issue is properly titled, "Rethinking Women's Peace Studies" and contains sections such as "New Directions for Feminist Peace Studies," "Gender and the Culture of Militarism," and "Teaching: Reflections, Resources, and References." Alonso, *Peace as a Women's Issue: A History of the U.S. Movement for World Peace and Women's Rights*. Syracuse: Syracuse University Press, 1993, *passim*.

27. Alonso, *Peace as a Women's Issue*, 6.

28. Amy Swerdlow, *Women Strike for Peace: Traditional Motherhood and Radical Politics in the 1960s*. Chicago: University of Chicago Press, 1993, 242-43.

29. Charles Chatfield with Robert Kleidman, *The American Peace Movement: Ideals and Activism*. NY: Twayne Publishers, 1992, 146-148.

30. Charles F. Howlett's review of Robbie Liberman, *The Strangest Dream* entitled, "Forgotten Fellow Travelers," in *Reviews in American History* 28 (December 2000): 615-624.

31. James Tracy, *Direct Action: Radical Pacifism from the Union Eight to the Chicago Seven*. Chicago: University of Chicago Press, 1996, 152-153. See also, Barbara Epstein, *Politics, Protest, and Cultural Revolution: Nonviolent Direct Action in the 1970s and 1980s*. Berkeley: University of California Press, 1991; R. Allen Smith, "Mass Society and the Bomb," *Peace and Change* 18 (October 1993): 347-72; David Cortright, *Peace Works: The Citizen's Role in Ending the Cold War*. Boulder, CO: Westview Press, 1993; Robert D. Holsworth, *Let Your Life Speak: A Study of Politics, Religion, and Antinuclear Weapons Activism*. Madison: University of Wisconsin Press, 1989.

32. Milton S. Katz, *Ban the Bomb: A History of SANE, the Committee for a SANE Nuclear Policy*. Westport, CT: Praeger, 1986; Robert A. Devine, *Blowing on the Wind: The Nuclear Test Ban Debate, 1954-1960*. NY: Oxford University Press, 1978; Paul Boyer, *By the Bomb's Early Light: American Thought and Culture at the Dawn of the Atomic Age*. NY: Pantheon Books, 1985; Paul Boyer, "From Activism to Apathy: The American People and Nuclear Weapons, 1963-1980," *Journal of American History* 70 (March 1984): 821-844. At the failure of the Nuclear Freeze Referendum, one peace scholar attributed five reasons why peace movements are largely ineffectual: (1) peace movements are reactive and change as situations do; (2) they are "drawn from too narrow a social base to succeed"; (3) they suffer from individual co-optation or group incorporation; (4) they are hurt by harassment by those in power; and (5) they are overcome by "feelings of weakness and a sense of despair in the face of the enormity of the problem of war." Consult, Nigel Young, "Why Peace Movements Fail: An Historical and Social Overview," *Social Alternatives* 4 (March 1984): 9-16.

294

33. Sam Marullo, *Ending the Cold War at Home: From Militarism to a More Peaceful World Order*. NY: Lexington Books, 1994; Paul Wehr, Heidi Burgess, & Guy Burgess, eds., *Justice without Violence*; Robert Elias and Jennifer Turpin, eds., *Rethinking Peace*. Boulder, CO: Lynne Reinner, 1994.

34. Wendy E. Chmielewski and Michael S. Foley, eds., "The Politics of Peace Movements," *Peace and Change* 26 (July 2001): 277-391; "Non-Governmental Organizations and the Vietnam War," special issue, *Peace and Change* 27 (April 2002): 161-300.

35. Editor's introduction to "Non-Governmental Organizations and the Vietnam War," 162-63; Elizabeth Mathiot (Moen), "Attaining Justice Through Development Organizations in India," in *Justice Without Violence*, 233-56. On issues related to human rights consult Paul Shaffer, "A Rape in Beijing: GIs, National Protests, and U.S. Foreign Policy," *Pacific Historical Review* 69 (2000); and "Cracks in the Consensus: Defending the Rights of Japanese-Americans During World War II," *Radical History Review* 72 (1998).

36. David S. Meyer, *A Winter of Discontent: The Nuclear Freeze and American Politics*. NY: Praeger, 1990; Robert Kleidman, *Organizing for Peace: Neutrality, the Test Ban and the Freeze*. Syracuse: Syracuse University Press, 1993; John Lofland, *Polite Protestors: The Peace Movement of the 1980s*. Syracuse: Syracuse University Press, 1993; Sam Marullo and John Lofland, eds., *Peace Action in the Eighties: Social Science Perspectives*. New Brunswick, NJ: Rutgers University Press, 1990; Steve Breyman, "Were the 1980s Anti-Nuclear Weapons Movements New Social Movements?" *Peace and Change* 22 (July 1997): 303-329; Chatfield, *The American Peace Movement, passim*.

37. Peter Brock, *Twentieth Century Pacifism*. NY: Nostrand, Reinhold, 1970; W.H. Van Der Linder, *The International Peace Movement, 1815-1874*. Amsterdam: Tillenl Publications, 1988; Vincent C. Kavaloski, "Transnational Citizen Peacemaking as nonviolent Action," *Peace and Change* 15 (April 1990): 173-194; Solomon Wank, ed., *Doves and Diplomats: Foreign Offices and Peace Movements in Europe and America in the Twentieth Century*. Westport, CT: Greenwood Press, 1978; Jackie Smith, Charles Chatfield, & Ron Pagnucco, eds., *Transnational Social Movements and Global Politics: Solidarity Beyond the State*. Syracuse: Syracuse University Press, 1997; Charles Chatfield and Peter van den Dungen, eds., *Peace Movements and Political Cultures*. Knoxville: University of Tennessee Press, 1998.

38. "Papers of the Peace Commission IPRA/Malta (October 31-November 4, 1994)," in author's possession.

39. Charles F. Howlett, "Case Law Historiography in American Peace History," *Peace and Change* 22 (January 1997): 49-75. Also consult, Stephen M. Kohn, *Jailed for Peace: The History of American Draft Law Violators, 1658-1985*. New York: Praeger Publishers, 1986. The current war on terrorism is raising a number of constitutional issues. The legal treatment of American citizens accused of being active members of Al Qaeda - John Walker Lindh, Yasser Esam Hamdi, and Jose Padilla -- centers "on whether they must be tried promptly or detained indefinitely on the president's mere say-so." How the courts will define "enemy combatant" in this new type of warfare involving those whose loyalties rest with religion rather than state governments will pose a serious challenge to the Geneva Conventions and the U.S. Constitution. For varying viewpoints consult: Richard Gid Powers, "The Evil That Lurks in the Enemy Within"

and Lawrence H. Tribe, "Citizens, Combatants and the Constitution," New York *Times*, Week in Review Section (June 16, 2002): 1, 13-15.

40. Charles Chatfield and Ruzanna Ilukhina, eds., *Peace/Mir: An Anthology of Historic Alternatives to War* . Syracuse: Syracuse University Press, 1994; Lawrence S. Wittner, *The Struggle Against the Bomb, One World or None: A History of the World Nuclear Disarmament Movement Through 1953; Resisting the Bomb: A History of the World Nuclear Disarmament Movement, 1954-1970, Toward Nuclear Abolition: A History of the World Nuclear Disarmament Movement, 1971 to the Present*, 3 vols. Stanford, CA: Stanford University Press, 1993, 1997, and 2003.

41. Wittner, *One World or None*. Vol. 1, ix-xi; Chatfield review in *Journal of American History 86* (March 2000): 1851.

42. Howlett, "Peace History," 26; Wittner, "Peace Movements and Foreign Policy," *passim.*

43. Wittner, "Peace Movements and Foreign Policy," 355.

44. Ralph Summy and Malcolm Saunders, "Why Peace History?," *Peace and Change* 20 (January 1995): 7-38; Charles Chatfield, "Frameworks for the History of Peacemaking"; Lawrence S. Wittner, "Ten Motives and a Misunderstanding"; Sandi Cooper, "The Subversive Power of Peace History"; David S. Patterson, "The Dangers of Balkanization," all responses in *Peace and Change* 20 (January 1995): 44, 58, 61, 79.

45. Chatfield, "Frameworks for the History of Peacemaking," 40. Today, the Peace History Society boasts well over 300 practicing historians, sponsors numerous conferences, and its journal, *Peace and Change*, is widely consulted.

46. DeBenedetti, ed., *Peace Heroes*, 19.

APPENDIX I

NOTED PEACE ADVOCATES IN AMERICAN HISTORY

SEVENTEENTH CENTURY

William Penn   Englishman who established Quaker colony in
                      the New World based on peace and friendship

EIGHTEENTH CENTURY

Anthony Benezet   Advanced Quaker pacifism through literal interpretation
                      of Christianity

Benjamin Rush   Surgeon General of Continental army and author of "A
                      Plan for Peace in the United States"

John Woolman   Famous Quaker pacifist and abolitionist; his journal remains
                      classic in the annals of pacifist thought

NINETEENTH CENTURY

Elihu Burritt   Founder of League of Universal Brotherhood

David Low Dodge   Created New York Peace Society (1815)

William Lloyd   Famous abolitionist and founder of New England Non-
Garrison Resistance Society

William Ladd   Established American Peace Society (1828); wrote
                      "Essay on a Congress of Nations"

Alfred Love   Established Universal Peace Union

Charles Sumner	U.S. Senator (Mass.), opponent of Mexican War, author of "True Grandeur of Nations"
Noah Worcester	Established Massachusetts Peace Society

TWENTIETH CENTURY

Jane Addams	First noted woman pacifist; helped organize Women's International League for Peace and Freedom; shared Nobel Peace Prize in 1931
Devere Allen	Author and editor of Fellowship of Reconciliation's The World Tomorrow
Fannie F. Andrews	Principal organizer of American Peace School League
Emily Greene Balch	Leader, with Addams, of Women's International League for Peace and Freedom and Nobel Prize recipient
Roger N. Baldwin	Founder of National Civil Liberties Union (ACLU)
Daniel Berrigan	Catholic priest opposed to Vietnam War.
Philip Berrigan	Former priest opposed to Vietnam War and proponent of nuclear freeze movement
William Jennings Bryan	Tolstoyan pacifist; anti-imperialist and former secretary of state
Nicholas M. Butler	President of Columbia University; president of Lake Mohonk Arbitration Conferences; president of Carnegie Endowment for International Peace
Andrew Carnegie	Steel magnate who funded Carnegie Endowment for International Peace
Carrie C. Catt	Established Women's Peace party (1915) and National Committee on Cause and Cure of War (1924)

William Sloane Coffin	Social Justice minister and former head of Riverside Church in Manhattan
Julien Cornell	Quaker attorney who defended COs during World War II
David Cortright	Activist educator, past director of SANR and president of Forth Freedom Foundation.
Norman Cousins	Internationalist and leader of SANE; social activist and respected intellectual
Ernest H. Crosby	Tolstoyan pacifist and anti-imperialist in late 1890s and early 1900s.
Dorothy Day	Created Catholic Workers' movement in the 1930s
Eugene Debs	Socialist labor leader who opposed World War I
David Dellinger	Conscientious objector during World War II; radical pacifist opponent of Vietnam War
Dorothy Detzer	Noted leader in Women's International League for Peace and Freedom
John Dewey	Famous philosopher and intellectual spokesman for Outlawry of War crusade
Ralph DiGia	Executive Secretary of War Resisters League
Clark Eichelberger	Director of League of Nations Association
Albert Einstein	Renowned physicist and member of Committee of Atomic Scientists
Harry Emerson Fosdick	Liberal Protestant peace minister; active in Federal Council of Churches
Raymond B. Fosdick	Liberal internationalist; helped form League of Nations Non-Partisan Association
Edward Ginn	Boston publisher; created World Peace Foundation

Richard Gregg   Author of The Power of Nonviolence

Ernest Gruening   Physician, journalist, anti-Vietnam War U.S. Senator

Alice Hamilton   Physician and leader in WWI women's peace crusade

John Haynes Holmes Liberal pacifist minister active in Outlawry of War cause

Hamilton Holt   Editor and founder of League of Nations Non-Partisan Association

Jessie Wallace Hughan   Helped found the War Resisters League (1924)

Homer Jack   Helped organize SANE

David Starr Jordan   President of Stanford University; helped form American, Union Against Militarism during World War I

John Kerry   Leader in the Vietnam Veterans Against the War

Martin Luther King Jr.   Famous nonviolent civil rights leader

Salmon O. Levinson   Chicago lawyer who created Outlawry of War movement, which led to Pact of Paris (1928)

Frederick Libby   Created National Council for Prevention of War in the 1930's

Staughton Lynd   Former history professor and critic of Vietnam War

Brad Lyttle   Member of CNVA and leader in Peace Walks

Peter Maurin   A Christian brother, editor of the Catholic Worker, and leader in the Catholic Worker movement

Charles MacFarland Minister who aided Lynch in forming Church Peace Union

David McReynolds   Leader in War Resisters League; critic of Vietnam War

Edwin D. Mead   Active in pre-WWI practical peace movement

Lucia Ames Mead	Teacher and member of WILPF and World Peace Foundation
Cord Meyer, Jr.	Leader of post-World War II United World Federalists
Charles Clayton	Founding editor of Christian Century and author of Morrison Outlawry of War
A.J. Muste	Most noted pacifist of the 20th century; executive secretary of Fellowship of Reconciliation; leader in war tax resistance
Tracy Mygatt	Helped organize American branch of War Resisters League
Kirby Page	Leading interwar peace leader who helped organize No Foreign War Crusade in the 1930's
Jim Peck	Member of War Resisters League and leader in the direct action movement of the late 1950's
Elihu Root	Legalist who helped form Carnegie Endowment for International Peace; received Nobel Peace Prize in 1913
Bayard Rustin	African American civil rights organizer and pacifist who helped found CORE and member of FOR
John Nevin Sayre	Longtime leader and former executive secretary of the Fellowship of Reconciliation- sponsored peace mission to Nicaragua in 1927-28
Lawrence Scott	Leader and organizer of Committee for Non-violent Action; proponent for Nuclear Freeze
James T. Shotwell	Liberal internationalist and promoter of legal renunciation of war; president of Carnegie Endowment for International Peace
Albert and Alfred Smiley	Quaker brothers who created Lake Mohonk Arbitration Conferences
John M. Swomley, Jr.	Pacifist and leader in Fellowship of Reconciliation
Norman Thomas	Leader of Socialist party, organized Keep America Out of

	War Congress in the late 1930's and Turn Toward Peace in 1961
Trueblood Benjamin	Quaker cosmopolitan peace leader who reinvigorated American Union Against Militarism
Oswald G. Villard	Editor of The Nation; supported American Union Against Militarism
Lillian Wald	Social worker and leading supporter of American Union Against Militarism
George Willoughby	Leader of Committee for Non-violent Action
Howard Zinn	Writer of popular histories of U.S. promoting peace and social justice

APPENDIX II

GLOSSARY OF PEACE TERMINOLOGY

INTERNATIONALIST, Any person who accepts nations as a unit and advocates or works for cooperation within the interstate system. The cooperation may be either political or nonpolitical and may involve governmental and/or nongovernmental agencies. An acknowledgment of each nation's sovereignty and the nation-state system is implicit in internationalist beliefs and actions. Politically inclined internationalists seek to mitigate conflict within the nation-state system, with their strategies and objectives more important historically than their desire for peace.

MILITARISM, The supremacy of or the placing of high priority on military force and military values in the resolution of international or domestic conflicts and in the safeguarding of national well-being. Generally viewed by pacifists as a threat or danger to democracy.

PACIFISM. Either the absolute renunciation of war or the refusal to participate in or the opposition in principle to a specific war or governmental programs on religious, philosophical, humanitarian, or social-justice grounds. The values held in advocating peace as more desirable than war are significantly more important than motives, and the behavior should be predictably consistent.

PACIFIST. One who subscribes to or demonstrates the tenets of pacifism.

PEACE. The absence of war; a condition marked by tranquility and governed order within the international public community.

PEACE ACTIVIST. An individual with clearly stated goals involved in anti-war protest through group action or public activity directed toward policy change. It is generally related to the period since 1960.

PEACE ADVOCATE. Anyone who actively promotes ideas and publicly manifests a concern for eliminating, avoiding, or minimizing the unilateral use of force by nation-states, usually by suggesting alternative proposals that would modify national policy or behavior. Some leadership is implied.

PEACE MOVEMENT. A loose assemblage of groups and individuals, often with dissimilar programs but in accord on seeking to reduce conflict or end war through achieving some change in foreign policy.

PEACE WORKER. Anyone who contributes time and energy in supporting programs, societies, or agencies seeking to modify organized violence between states or Opposing military systems. Such a person need not manifest special convictions or be instrumental in the development of ideas or programs.

SANCTIONS. Derived from the Latin sanctio or sancire, the term originally implied consecration or bligation. The latter meaning has prevailed, with commitment by pacifists to awaken public opinion by applying moral pressures against wrongdoers. Other observers advocate economic or military action to up-hold agreements or treaties or to curb aggressors.

TRANSNATIONALISM. A belief in or a commitment to values and communities of interest that transcend the nation-state system and that are entirely political or nonpolitical.

WAR. Any conflict in which organized military force is employed. Insurrections and armed rebellions may or may not be included, depending upon their nature.

SELECTED READINGS

Allen, Devere. *The Fight for Peace*. 2 vols. New York: Macmillan, 1931. Reprint. New York: Garland Publishing, 1971.

Alonso, Harriet Hyman. *Peace as a Women's Issue: A History of the U.S. Movement for World Peace and Women's Rights*. Syracuse: Syracuse University Press, 1993.

Beacon, Margaret Hope. *One Woman's Passion for Peace and Freedom: The Life of Mildred Scott Olmstead*. Syracuse: Syracuse University Press, 1993.

Bennett, Scott H. *Radical Pacifism: The War Resisters League and Gandhian Nonviolence in America, 1915-1963*. Syracuse: Syracuse University Press, 2003.

Bess, Michael. *Realism, Utopia, and the Mushroom Cloud: Four Activist Intellectuals and the Strategies for Peace, 1945-1989*. Chicago: University of Chicago Press, 1993.

Brock, Peter. *Pacifism in the United States: From the Colonial Era to the First World War*. Princeton: Princeton University Press, 1968.

Brock, Peter. *Twentieth-Century Pacifism*. New York: Van Nostrand Reinhold Co., 1970.

Chambers, John Whiteclay II. *The Eagle and the Dove: The American Peace Movement and United States Foreign Policy, 1900-1922*. Syracuse: Syracuse University Press, 1991.

Chatfield, Charles. *For Peace and Justice: Pacifism in America, 1914-1941*. Knoxville: University of Tennessee Press, 1971.

Chatfield, Charles. Ed. *Peace Movements in America*. New York: Schocken Books, 1973.

Chatfield, Charles, with Robert Kleidman. *The American Peace Movement: Ideals and Activism*. New York; Twayne Publishers, 1992.

308

Crittenden, Ann. *Sanctuary: a Story of American Conscience and Law*. New York: Weidenfeld & Nicholson, 1988.

Curti, Merle E. *Peace or War: the American Struggle, 1636-1936*. New York: W.W. Norton & Co., 1936.

Davis, Allen F. *American Heroine: The Life and Legend of Jane Addams*. New York: Oxford University Press, 1973.

DeBenedetti, Charles. *The Origins of the Modern American Peace Movement, 1915-1929*. Millwood, NY: KTO Press, 1978.

DeBenedetti, Charles. Ed. *Peace Heroes in Twentieth Century America*. Bloomington: Indiana University Press, 1986.

DeBenedetti, Charles. *The Peace Reform in American History*. Bloomington: Indiana University Press, 1980.

DeBenedetti, Charles with Charles Chatfield. *An American Ordeal: The Antiwar Movement of the Vietnam Era*. Syracuse: Syracuse university Press, 1990.

Dellinger, David. *From Yale to Jail: Life of a Moral Dissenter*. New York: Pantheon, 1993.

Doenecke, Justus D. *Storm on the Horizon: The Challenge to American Intervention, 1939-1941*. New York: Rowman & Littlefield, 2000.

Eagan, Eileen. *Class, Culture, and the Classroom: The Student Peace Movement of the 1930s*. Philadelphia: Temple University Press, 1981.

Early, Frances H. *A World Without War: How U.S. Feminists and Pacifists Resisted World War I*. Syracuse; Syracuse University Press, 1997.

Ekirch, Arthur A., Jr. *The Civilian and the Military*. New York: Oxford University Press, 1956.

Epstein, Barbara. *Nonviolent Direct Action in the 1970s and 1980s*. Berkeley: University of California Press, 1991

Ferber, Michael & Staughton Lynd. *The Resistance*. Boston: Beacon Publishers, 1971.

Foley, Michael S. *Confronting the War Machine: Draft Resistance During the Vietnam War*. Chapel Hill: University of North Carolina Press, 2003.

Foster, Carrie A. *The Women and the Warriors: The U.S. Section of the Women's International League for Peace and Freedom, 1915-1946.* Syracuse: Syracuse University Press, 1995.

Frazer, Heather T. & John O'Sullivan. *"We Have Just Begun Not to Fight": An Oral History of Conscientious Objectors in Civilian Public Service During World War II.* New York: Twayne Publishers, 1996.

Friedland, Michael B. *Lift Up Your Voice Like a Trumpet: White Clergy and the Civil Rights and Antiwar Movements, 1954-1973.* Chapel Hill: University of North Carolina Press, 1998.

Gara, Larry. *War Resistance in Historical Perspective.* New York: War Resisters League, 1989.

Garfinkle, Adam. *Telltale Hearts: The Origins and Impact of the Vietnam Antiwar Movement.* New York: St. Martin's Press, 1995.

Giffen, Frederick C. *Six Who Protested: Radical Opposition to the First World War.* Port Washington, NY: Kennikat Press, 1976.

Gilbert, Marc Jason. Ed. *The Vietnam War on Campus: Other Voices, More Distant Drums.* Westport, CT.: Praeger, 2001.

Gosse, Van. *Where the Boys Are: Cuba, Cold War America and the Making of the New Left.* New York: Verso, 1993.

Goosen, Rachael Waltner. *Women Against the Good War: Conscientious Oobjection and Gender on the American Home Front, 1941-1947.* Chapel Hill: University of North Carolina Press, 1997.

Hall, Mitchell. *Because of Their Faith: CALCAV and Religious Opposition to the War in Vietnam.* New York: Columbia university Press, 1990.

Hall, Simon. *Peace and Freedom: The Civil Rights and Antiwar Movements in the 1960s.* Philadelphia: University of Pennsylvania Press, 2005.

Halstead, Fred. *Out Now: A Participant's Account of the American Movement Against the Vietnam War.* New York: Monad Press, 1978.

Heineman, Kenneth J. *Campus Wars: The Peace Movement at American State Universities in the Vietnam Era.* New York: NYU Press, 1993.

Holsworth, Robert D. *Let Your Life Speak: A Study of Politics, Religion, and Antinuclear Weapons Activism.* Madison: University of Wisconsin Press, 1989.

Howlett, Charles F. *The American Peace Movement: References and Resources.* Boston: G.K. Hall & Co., 1991.

Howlett, Charles F. *Troubled Philosopher: John Dewey and the Struggle for World Peace.* Port Washington, NY: Kennikat Press, 1977.

Howlett, Charles F. *Brookwood Labor College and the Struggle for Peace and Justice in America.* Lewiston, NY: Edwin Mellen Press, 1993.

Howlett, Charles F. & Glen Zeitzer. *The American Peace Movement: References and Resources.* Washington, D.C.: The American Historical Association, 1985.

Hull, William I. *The New Peace Movement.* Boston: World Peace Foundation, 1912.

Hunt, Andrew E. *The Turning: A History of Vietnam Veterans Against the War.* New York: New York University Press, 1999.

Isserman, Maurice. *If I Had a Hammer: The Death of the Old Left and the Birth of the New Left.* New York: Basic Books, 1987.

Johnpoll, Bernard K. *Pacifist's Progress: Norman Thomas and the Decline of American Socialism.* Chicago: Quadrangle Books, 1970.

Johnson, Robert David. *The Peace Progressives and American Foreign Relations.* Cambridge, MA.: Harvard University Press, 1995.

Josephson, Harold. *James T. Shotwell and the Rise of Internationalism in America.* Rutherford, N.J.: Fairliegh Dickenson University Press, 1975.

Juhnke, James C. & Carol M. Hunter. *The Missing Peace: The Search for Nonviolent Alternatives in United States History.* Kitchner, Ontario: Pandora Press, 2001.

Katz, Milton. *Ban the Bomb: A History of SANE, the Committee for a Sane nuclear Policy.* Westport, CT.: Praeger, 1986.

Kennedy, Kathleen. *Disloyal Mothers and Scurrilous citizens: Women and Subversion During World War I*. Bloomington: Indiana University Press, 1999.

Kleidman, Robert. *Organizing for Peace: Neutrality, the Test Ban, and the Freeze*. Syracuse; Syracuse University Press, 1993.

Klejment, Anne. *The Berrigans: A Bibliography of Published Works by Daniel, Philip, and Elizabeth McAlister Berrigan*. New York: Garland Publishers, 1979.

Klejment, Anne & Alice Klejment. *Dorothy Day and the Catholic Worker: A Bibliography and Index*. New York: Garland Publishers, 1986.

Lasar, Matthew. *Pacifica Radio: The Rise of an Alternative Network*. Philadelphia: Temple University Press, 2000.

Lieberman, Robbie. *The Strangest Dream: Communism, Anticommunism and the U.S. Peace Movement, 1945-1963*. Syracuse: Syracuse University Press, 2000.

Lewy, Guenter. *Peace & Revolution: The Moral Crisis of American Pacifism*. Grand Rapids, MI.: William B. Eerdmans Publishing Co., 1998.

Lofland, John. *Polite Protestors: the American Peace Movement of the 1980s*. Syracuse: Syracuse University Press, 1993.

Lynd, Staughton. Ed. *Non-Violence in America: A Documentary History*. Indianapolis, IN.: Bobbs-Merrill & Co., 1966.

Marchand, C. Roland. *The American Peace Movement and Social Reform, 1898-1918*. Princeton: Princeton University Press, 1972.

McNeal, Patricia. *Harder Than War: Catholic Peacemaking in Twentieth Century America*. New Brunswick, NJ: Rutgers University Press, 1992.

Moser, Richard. *The New Winter Soldiers: GI and Veteran Dissent During the Vietnam Era*. New Brunswick, NJ: Rutgers University Press, 1996.

Moskos, Charles C. & John Whiteclay Chambers II. Eds. *The New Conscientious Objection: From Sacred to Secular Resistance*. New York: Oxford University Press, 1993.

Patterson, David S. *Toward a Warless World: The Travail of the American Peace Movement, 1887-1914*. Bloomington: Indiana University Press, 1976.

Peterson, H.C. & Gilbert C. Fite. *Opponents of War, 1917-1918*. Seattle: University of Washington Press, 1957.

Roberts, Nancy. *Dorothy Day and the Catholic Worker*. Albany: State university of New York Press, 1984.

Robinson, Jo Ann O. *Abraham Went Out: A Biography of A.J. Muste*. Philadelphia: Temple University Press, 1981.

Schott, Linda. *Reconstructing Women's Thoughts: The Women's International League for Peace and Freedom Before World War II*. Stanford, CA.: Stanford University Press, 1997.

Sibley, Mulford Q. & Philip E. Jacob. *Conscription of Conscience*. Ithaca, NY: Cornell University Press, 1952.

Small, Melvin. *Antiwarriors: The Vietnam War and the Battle for America's Hearts and Minds*. Wilmington, DE.: Scholarly Resources, 2002.

Small, Melvin & William D. Hoover. Eds. *Give Peace a Chance: Exploring the Vietnam Antiwar Movement*. Syracuse: Syracuse university Press, 1992.

Smith, Christian. *Resisting Reagan: the U.S. Central American Peace Movement*. Chicago: University of Chicago Press, 1996.

Smith, E. Timothy. *Opposition beyond the Water's Edge: Liberal Internationalists, Pacifists, and Containment, 1945-1953*. Westport, CT.: Greenwood Press, 1999.

Swerdlow, Amy. *Women Strike for Peace: Traditional Motherhood and Radical Politics in the 1960s*. Chicago: University of Chicago Press, 1993.

Tracy, James. *Direct Action: Radical Pacifism from the Union Eight to the Chicago Seven*. Chicago: University of Chicago Press, 1996.

Wells, Tom. *The War Within: America's Battle over Vietnam*. Berkeley: University of California Press, 1994.

Whitefield, Stephen J. *Scott Nearing: Apostle of American Radicalism*. New York: Columbia University Press, 1974.

Wittner, Lawrence. *Rebels Against War: The American Peace Movement, 1933-1983*. Philadelphia: Temple University Press, 1984.

Wittner, Lawrence S. *The Struggle Against the Bomb: A History of the World Nuclear Disarmament Movement*. 3 Vols. Stanford, CA.: Stanford University Press, 1993-2003.

Zaroulis, Nancy & Gerald Sullivan. *Who Spoke Up?: American Protest Against the War in Vietnam, 1963-1975*. New York: Holt, Rinehart, & Winston, 1984.

Zinn, Howard. *Passionate Declarations: Essays on War and Justice*. New York: Perennial Books, 2003.

INDEX

316

STUDIES IN WORLD PEACE